Joss Whedon, Anarchist?

Also of Interest from McFarland

*Blood Relations: Chosen Families
in* Buffy the Vampire Slayer *and* Angel
Jes Battis, 2005

The Aesthetics of Culture in Buffy the Vampire Slayer
Matthew Pateman, 2006

*The Existential Joss Whedon: Evil and Human Freedom
in* Buffy the Vampire Slayer, Angel, Firefly *and* Serenity
J. Michael Richardson and J. Douglas Rabb, 2007

Faith and Choice in the Works of Joss Whedon
K. Dale Koontz, 2008

The Truth of Buffy: *Essays on Fiction Illuminating Reality*
Edited by Emily Dial-Driver, Sally Emmons-Featherston,
Jim Ford and Carolyn Anne Taylor, 2008

*Buffy Goes Dark: Essays on the Final Two Seasons
of* Buffy the Vampire Slayer *on Television*
Edited by Lynne Y. Edwards , Elizabeth L. Rambo
and James B. South, 2009

Buffy and Angel Conquer the Internet: Essays on Online Fandom
Edited by Mary Kirby-Diaz, 2009

Buffy Meets the Academy: Essays on the Episodes and Scripts as Texts
Edited by Kevin K. Durand, 2009

Sexual Rhetoric in the Works of Joss Whedon: New Essays
Edited by Erin B. Waggoner, 2010

Buffy in the Classroom: Essays on Teaching with the Vampire Slayer
Edited by Jodie A. Kreider and Meghan K. Winchell, 2010

The Literary Angel: *Essays on Influences
and Traditions Reflected in the Joss Whedon Series*
Edited by AmiJo Comeford and Tamy Burnett, 2010

Cult Telefantasy Series: A Critical Analysis of The Prisoner,
Twin Peaks, The X-Files, Buffy the Vampire Slayer, Lost,
Heroes, Doctor Who *and* Star Trek
Sue Short, 2011

Power and Control in the Television Worlds of Joss Whedon
Sherry Ginn, 2012

Buffy and the Heroine's Journey: Vampire Slayer as Feminine Chosen One
Valerie Estelle Frankel, 2012

*Joss Whedon and Religion: Essays on an Angry Atheist's
Explorations of the Sacred*
Edited by Anthony R. Mills, John W. Morehead and J. Ryan Parker, 2013

The Comics of Joss Whedon: Critical Essays
Edited by Valerie Estelle Frankel, 2015

*Joss Whedon as Shakespearean Moralist: Narrative Ethics
of the Bard and the Buffyverse*
J. Douglas Rabb and J. Michael Richardson, 2015

At Home in the Whedonverse: Essays on Domestic Place, Space and Life
Edited by Juliette C. Kitchens, 2017

Joss Whedon and Race: Critical Essays
Edited by Mary Ellen Iatropoulos and Lowery A. Woodall III, 2017

WORLDS OF WHEDON SERIES

*Joss Whedon Versus the Corporation:
Big Business Critiqued in the Films and Television Programs.*
Erin Giannini. 2017

Joss Whedon's Big Damn Movie: Essays on Serenity.
Edited by Frederick Blichert. 2018

*The Whedonverse Catalog: A Complete Guide
to Works in All Media.* Don Macnaughtan. 2018

*Joss Whedon, Anarchist?
A Unified Theory of the Films and Television Series.*
James Rocha and Mona Rocha. 2019

Joss Whedon, Anarchist?
A Unified Theory of the Films and Television Series

JAMES ROCHA *and*
MONA ROCHA

WORLDS OF WHEDON
Series Editor Sherry Ginn

McFarland & Company, Inc., Publishers
Jefferson, North Carolina

ISBN (print) 978-1-4766-7383-7 ♾
ISBN (ebook) 978-1-4766-3745-7

Library of Congress and British Library
cataloguing data are available

© 2019 James Rocha and Mona Rocha. All rights reserved

No part of this book may be reproduced or transmitted in any form or by any means, electronic or mechanical, including photocopying or recording, or by any information storage and retrieval system, without permission in writing from the publisher.

The front cover image is from a 2012 photograph
of Joss Whedon by Gage Skidmore

Printed in the United States of America

*McFarland & Company, Inc., Publishers
Box 611, Jefferson, North Carolina 28640
www.mcfarlandpub.com*

Table of Contents

Preface	1
Introduction: An Anarchist Sing-Along (Freely Provide Your Own Music and Lyrics)	6
One. Striking at the Machine: Structural Violence in *Angel*'s Wolfram & Hart	19
Two. Programmable Slaves: Constrained Freedom in the *Dollhouse*	49
Three. Tips for Organizing Anarchy: Marvel and the Push/Pull of Anarchism	79
Four. The Black Reaching Out: Anarcho-Capitalists vs. Anarcho-Socialists on Board the *Firefly*	107
Five. Anarcha-Feminist Scoobies: *Buffy*'s Slaying Critique	134
Six. *Buffy the Vampire Slayer*: The Show That Hierarchy Has Nightmares About	154
Conclusion: Internal Revolution as Solution	174
Chapter Notes	185
Bibliography	203
Index	213

Preface

High school sucks. Having a real job sucks. Trying to start your own secret, governmental organization that monitors superheroes and super villains is much harder than it looks, and it ultimately sucks. Getting repeatedly denied entry into a league of evil also sucks. And finally, vampires—they most definitely suck.

Joss Whedon's TV shows and movies point to problems that we all deal with, but in ways that are simultaneously engaging and poignant. That's what originally drew us in. We watched neither *Buffy the Vampire Slayer*, *Angel*, nor *Firefly* when they first aired. But as soon as we saw our first *Buffy* episode, we were hooked, and we never looked back. Like most true fans, we have now seen every episode of every Joss Whedon TV show, watching most of them several times over. We have both incorporated Whedon into our classes in Philosophy and Women's Studies and have taught two classes just dedicated to analyzing these wonderful TV shows.

When we speak about our love for the shows, there's surely much to say. The characters, the storylines, the settings, and the villains—we loved them all. But what particularly grabbed us were the problems. Each show presents supernatural villains as metaphors for real-life issues. The early seasons of *Buffy* represent fighting with vampires as on par with dealing with Cordelia. Angel's struggles with a demonic law firm are fairly on-point representations of the struggles of fighting the law (only to learn that the law wins). The crew of Serenity is seeking freedom from the long reach of governmental forces. *Dollhouse* introduces a corporation that could single-handedly ruin the world, which is only slightly exaggerated from real life where a handful of corporations seem to run the world. When we turn to Whedon's Marvel work, we see how the hubris of the heroes can be just as dangerous as what the actual villains do—which surely reminds us of all the seemingly good politicians who eventually betray their purported values.

So we are watching all of these shows and start thinking to ourselves: Whedon's critiques of the various systems around him are reminiscent of anarchist critiques. Anarchists are against hierarchy, especially in the form of the state (where the state is the collection of people who hold power over a country, which includes the government as well as people who hold power over the government, such as business or religious leaders). We can say, as an initial definition, that an anarchist is someone who believes that the state cannot be justified because the anarchist believes that no one should hold the kind of power that allows one to dictate the lives of everyone else in a country. Thus, anarchists provide cogent critiques against power in its various forms, such as political power, economic power, and cultural power.

Whedon too provides numerous and significant critiques against power in general and hierarchy in particular. Does this mean that Joss Whedon is an anarchist? We have no idea. On the one hand, these critiques of power and hierarchy are not limited to anarchists: we receive similar critiques from Marxists, feminists, race theorists, even some progressive liberals, and so on. Nor is it clear that anarchists thought of them first (though we would argue there are clear cases where anarchists indeed thought of them first—yet figuring out who came up with what idea first is a fairly fruitless task). That said, what is unique to anarchists (when they are speaking and acting truly according to their system; many anarchists are, of course, hypocrites) is how consistently they present their critiques against hierarchy everywhere. Marxists and anarchists, for example, are at odds because the former often believe there can be a justified socialist state, where anarchists believe any state is unjustified. What it means to be an anarchist is to believe that people should have freedom over their own lives and that hierarchy interferes with this freedom. Anarchists do not care whether that hierarchy is associated with supposedly positive and just views—hierarchy itself is the problem and cannot be fixed.

Anarchists therefore make a sweeping claim against hierarchy, and Whedon's works, when taken together, likewise present a sweeping claim against hierarchy. Regardless of whether this similarity is purposeful, it is both present and illuminating. Whedon provides us a vision of what's wrong with society in the same way that anarchists provide a theoretical critique of what's wrong with the world. Consequently, Whedon's stories provide the metaphorical background for anarchist analysis. While we will save a specific chapter breakdown for the introduction, it is useful here to show some of the connections between Whedon's works and anarchist theory, which will be further explored in the chapters of this book.

For instance, *Angel* presents a team of heroes, led by Angel himself, going up against an archenemy (we will refer to each archenemy as the "big bad") that takes the form of a law firm. This overarching storyline fits quite snugly within an anarchist perspective since anarchists believe that power is not only held by individuals, but also by institutions and social structures.

Therefore, anarchists will critique the power found in law firms (Wolfram & Hart), corporations (the Rossum Corporation), institutions that are meant to do good but are still hierarchal (S.H.I.E.L.D. and the Watchers Council), states (the Alliance), and so on. Throughout the book, we will provide anarchist critiques of these various evil and supposedly good institutions that populate the Whedonverse. For instance, in Chapter One in particular, we will provide an anarchist critique of Wolfram & Hart, where in other chapters, we will look at various other problems with hierarchal power.

Importantly, our examination of anarchism does not take anarchism as a fearful or scary viewpoint, which might be common in some popular culture and media representations. For instance, *The Purge* film series could be viewed as depicting anarchy as a frightening, chaotic social arrangement since, in those films, laws are suspended one day a year and anarchy represents heightened levels of serious crimes. Anarchists, however, are not interested in promoting violent, crime-ridden societies. Instead, anarchists believe that a society would not need a government or laws if people were more morally responsible and were allowed and encouraged to govern themselves. In the Whedonverse, we often find small examples of societies as groups of individuals who merge for common pursuits of justice. Thus, we will argue that the Scoobies (Buffy's helpers in *Buffy the Vampire Slayer*), Angel Investigations (Angel's PI firm and his partners), the crew of Serenity, and so on all attempt to organize around equality and work together, usually without clear leaders (though there are exceptions), to fight evil and work for what's right. For instance, we will argue, in Chapter Three, that the individual Avengers are not likely to consider themselves to be anarchists, but they characteristically resist hierarchy since they have to treat each other as equals: no Avenger is fit to solely rule and each Avenger demands to be treated as a full and equal member of the team. An anarchist society is meant to be one where people are responsible, autonomous, collaborative, and treated equally.

Hence, anarchism has some general, positive messages about how to organize society. For example, *Buffy the Vampire Slayer*, which we save for Chapters Five and Six, represents the positive anarchist message of Joss Whedon's oeuvre: an anarcha-feminist outlook that argues that we can remove hierarchy and have instead an anarchist society founded on the principle of love. That is, once we learn to be motivated by a general sense of love for our neighbors and our society in general, then we can organize a society with no hierarchy whatsoever. This kind of positive message brings together most of Whedon's works as they are often centered on teams of individuals who not only act out of love for each other, but also act out of love for strangers, thus risking their lives over and over to save the world. Consequently, Whedon's TV shows and movies make anarchist critiques as well as positive anarchist viewpoints come alive. And this book shows how.

Of course, one cannot write a book on anarchism and not recognize that labor is jointly achieved. There are two authors of this book, but countless people have influenced us in positive ways that enabled the creation of this book. We want, therefore, to thank both large groups whose work has been indispensable to our work and particular individuals who have helped us as we have labored over writing this book.

Let's start with the anarchists. Anarchists are rarely acknowledged for their general contributions to the progress of the world. For example, at the turn of the century, anarchists and, later, the labor union Industrial Workers of the World made it possible for us working folks to work eight hour days in a safe working environment, and to have weekends, so we'd all have time to pursue intellectual activities for our own flourishing. These activists' work, long in the past, made it possible for us in the present to develop and indulge our Whedonverse fascination.

Thank you, anarchists!

Next, we must acknowledge the Whedon teams and fans. Joss Whedon does not work alone. In this book, we will reference Joss Whedon as a person, but we want to acknowledge here our recognition and appreciation for the thousands of people who have worked tirelessly to make Joss Whedon's works as awesome as they are. In various ways—some of whom we easily recognize (such as the writers, directors, and actors) and others of whom we may not know by name (such as the crew, whose jobs are absolutely necessary to production)—the greatness of Whedon's project is surely a team effort, and we are incredibly grateful to those teams.

At the same time, examining and analyzing Whedon is likewise a team effort. It should be recognized as uncontroversial that the Whedonverse has the most intellectual fans of any set of fandom out there. In this book, we cite scholars whose works on Whedon influenced us. In particular, we want to point out that we have been aided by listening to and appearing on Paul Smith's podcast, "Conversations with Dead People: A Buffy & Angel Podcast." It must also be noted that there is so much intellectual discussion on Whedon out there, that Whedon scholarship, ours included, is immensely indebted to fan theories, critiques, and analyses of each and every moment of everything that Whedon has made.

Thank you, Joss Whedon, Joss Whedon's teams, and the Whedonverse scholars and fans!

We also want to thank all of our students who studied Whedon, anarchism, or anything else with us. You've all challenged us in a variety of ways, and we are incredibly grateful for it.

Thank you, former and current students!

There are also a number of people who we would like to thank as individuals. We are immensely grateful to our parents and to our families for all of their support as we were working on this book (but also for their support all along the way as we made it to this point). We are sorry to have missed family functions and grateful for your understanding as we worked long hours and talked to you about Buffy and Angel. So thank you, Jim, Deanna, Carmen, Bridget, Greg, Stephanie, Rex, Savannah, Kimi, Derrick, Kyle and Katherine!

Thank you, family!

There's also our scholarly community, especially those folks at Fresno State who have made us feel welcome and supported at our new school. Thank you Carolyn Cusick, Jacki Alvarez, Ruth Aparicio, Laura Gribben, and Kristi Eastin.

Thank you for your friendship and encouragement, Bulldogs!

And we would like to thank Gary Mitchem of McFarland, along with the team working at McFarland for assisting us in so many ways as we all worked to put this book together.

Thank you, McFarland!

Finally, we would like to thank each other. Together, we have watched these TV shows and movies for countless hours, leading to countless discussions, and, ultimately, to all the work we put in together to write this book. Neither of us could have accomplished any of this without the other.

Thank you, Mona; thank you, James!

Introduction:
An Anarchist Sing-Along
(Freely Provide Your
Own Music and Lyrics)

You can't just treat the symptom. Homelessness, sexism, and environmental degradation—they are all symptoms. Instead of treating symptoms, you must cure the disease—the disease that is consuming the human race. Dr. Horrible, whose Ph.D. is in fact in Horribleness, explains this point with a metaphor: "The fish rots from the head as they say. So my thinking is, why not cut off the head?" (Act I). Of course, when the disease is consuming the human race, maybe cutting off the head isn't the best idea. Dr. Horrible himself admits that "it's not a perfect metaphor" (Act I).

We learn in *Dr. Horrible's Sing-Along Blog* (*Dr. Horrible,* as we will refer to it from here on, is a 2008 miniseries produced by Joss Whedon's own production company, Mutant Enemy Productions) that the system, which we all inhabit, is rotten to the core: police brutality, racism,[1] and death from curable diseases are just some of the problems that we see around us every day.[2] *Dr. Horrible* discusses how social problems do not arise accidentally, but are predictable results of the corrupt structures that organize contemporary society.[3] The system is fundamentally broken, which leads to Dr. Horrible to call for "an overhaul of the system. Putting power in *different* hands" (Act I).[4]

Dr. Horrible's utterance illustrates why it is so difficult to fix a broken system: even where many of us see problems inherent in the current system of power, we feel that the only way to change things is to replace one power system with another one.[5] The hope is that the new model will eliminate the difficulties that plagued the old one. However, such a transition will merely swap biases and limitations and rewire power relations so that new rulers oppress new victims.[6] One cannot escape the trappings of power by switching around the top of the hierarchy. While Dr. Horrible correctly identifies the problems, he cannot imagine a solution that does not replicate the difficulties in different forms. That is why, when Dr. Horrible discusses "destroying the status quo because the 'status' is not 'quo,'" his response to this problem is that "the world is a mess and I just need to *rule* it" (Act I). Dr. Horrible provides an anarchist critique of contemporary society—as mired in injustice and social ills that desperately need solving—but his solution would create more tyranny. Or, as he sings in a confused and contradictory fashion,

> All the cash, all the fame
> And social change
> Anarchy that I run! [Act III].

Instead of anarchy somehow run by Dr. Horrible, let's consider anarchism in and of itself. Anarchism is a social arrangement that is, by definition, run by no one. Anarchism is the idea that society without hierarchy—a stateless social arrangement—would solve many of the social injustices we see around us. Anarchism is opposed to statism, which is the view that there should be a state. A state is not exactly the same thing as a government (we will return to this distinction shortly), but is instead the power structure that runs the society. Anarchists are not against postal workers or dog catchers (who are governmental employees), but are against people having the power to dictate what the rest of society should do. Instead, anarchism trusts the people to run their own society where each person is considered a free and equal member of the society and no one is empowered to make moral or political decisions for anyone else, and then the people will take on responsibility and do what is just and right for themselves. While anarchism has been around as a theory for a long time, there has been no significant society that is run in a fully anarchist way. Thus, if we want to delve more deeply into the meaning of anarchism, it is useful to turn to works of fiction. Fortunately, a good way to learn more about anarchism is to watch Joss Whedon's TV shows and films.[7]

Whether it is intentional, Joss Whedon's works display numerous anarchist themes. Thus, one might see Captain Malcolm "Mal" Reynolds as a kind of anarchist in outer space. Buffy and the Scoobies certainly develop into anarcha-feminists. Further, like *Dr. Horrible*, numerous other Whedon TV shows and movies critique society in anarchist fashions. *Angel*'s use of a law firm as the main villain is a perfect metaphor for anarchist critiques of social structures that limit, define, and manipulate us. While the Avengers can't help but to resist an anarchist model (since they are all alpha/macho superheroes who try to take charge), they also simultaneously fall into an anarchist organization (since no one of them can truly rule the others). Joss Whedon's works provide a perfect standpoint from which we can gain richer understandings of both anarchist critiques of contemporary society and anarchist visions of how society ought to work. This book therefore uses the Whedonverse (that is, the combined set of Joss Whedon's works) to better understand anarchism (though at the same time, we are also using anarchism to better understand the Whedonverse).

This attempt to use the Whedonverse to better understand anarchism will be an original undertaking, but other works have provided groundwork that assists our project. For instance, Erin Giannini provides a critique of corporations within Joss Whedon's works in her *Joss Whedon Versus the Corporation: Big Business Critiqued in the Films and Television Programs*.[8] Giannini explores the idea Whedon used his works to show the problems that arise through the unchecked power of corporations, which we will argue is a very anarchist viewpoint. Sherry Ginn, in *Power and Control in the Television Works of Joss Whedon*, argues that Joss Whedon provides a useful analysis of the relation between power and control.[9] Similarly, Linda Jean Jencson argues, in "'Aiming to Misbehave': Role Modeling Political-Economic Conditions and Political Action in the *Serenity*verse," that Joss Whedon is always interested in exploring power throughout his works, particularly focusing on "the right and wrong use of power" and the subsequent resultant inequities.[10] Thus Jencson argues that Whedon's work generally deals with issues such as gender inequity, class inequity, racial issues, colonialism, governmental corruption, various problems brought about by capitalism, and so on. This analysis will be useful in an examination of how anarchists critique the power and control of the state in particular and hierarchy in general while anarchists also seek out ways to provide power and control to the people—two projects that Ginn and Jencson show are prevalent in Whedon's works.

Moreover, Howard Harris, in his "*Buffy the Vampire Slayer* in the Business Ethics Classroom," explains that Whedon's work is didactic in how to deal with such issues, since Whedon's TV shows have a universal moral structure that is applicable throughout the world, which is a moral point that is further supported by Richard Greene and Wayne Yuen's "Morality on Television: The Case of *Buffy the Vampire Slayer*."[11] We will see that anarchists rely on such a moral perspective when they argue that morality is enhanced by and grounded in people being free to make their own decisions without interference from the state. As will become clear in our citations, there are many other sources that will influence our journey of developing an anarchist analysis of Whedon's works, in spite of this being the first explicit use of anarchism to understand the Whedonverse.

It is important to note briefly here that we are using Joss Whedon as a stand-in for all the people whose work go into making the TV shows and movies that make up the Whedonverse. Joss Whedon is just one person, and he is surely guided and aided through all of these endeavors by his teams of writers, directors, actors, producers, and others. Each of these persons surely adds to the finished product, and our concentration on Whedon is for ease and does not diminish our appreciation of all these other folks' invaluable contributions. While that decision is not very anarchist in a sense, as the greatness of these shows and movies should always be recognized as collaborative efforts, it is made here merely as a matter of convenience.

Anarchism involves two specific theses, one negative and one positive: there can be no justified state (negative thesis) and society can be effectively and justly organized without a state (positive thesis). The negative thesis is not only more familiarly associated with the view, but also easier to support. The negative thesis, put more generally, is that hierarchy, in all forms, is wrong. Not all anarchists would agree with that more general, negative claim. Anarcho-capitalists in particular would argue in favor of economic hierarchy while taking a strong stance against political hierarchy. We will discuss the anarcho-capitalist position much more in Chapter Four, where we discuss *Firefly*. For now, to get a clear negative definition that is without much controversy, we can say that anarchism is consistently against political hierarchy.

The state can be understood as the source of political power within a given society. The state is conceptually distinct from (though overlaps with) the government. The government is the persons or groups that perform political activities to organize a given society. We can imagine people who are members of the state without being members of the government—say, moneyed interests that hold significant power, but do not perform governmental work. We can likewise imagine people who work for the government, but are not members of the state because they have no real political power (say, dog catchers). Finally, we can imagine people who both have political power (and are in the state) and also officially work in ways that organize political processes (and are in the government). Major political leaders, including presidents and prime ministers and many others, fall into this last group where they are both in the state and the government.

Anarchism denies that state actors can be justified in holding political power since anarchists deny that small groups of people should be able to dictate what's right and wrong to the vast majority of society. One of the clearest arguments for the view comes from theorist Robert Paul Wolff.[12] Wolff argues that we all have a right and an obligation to act autonomously. Autonomy is an ideal met by an agent who rationally figures out what she values in her life and then successfully acts according to those values. Where an individual determines her own course of action, through her own reasoning over the permissibility of her action and the ways that her action meets her considered goals, she ought to be allowed to freely pursue her action without having to face any coercion, deception, or manipulation from others.

As Wolff notes, "The autonomous man, insofar as he is autonomous, is not subject to the will of another. He may do what another tells him, but not *because* he has been told to do it."[13] The autonomous person does what they determine is right. When the autonomous person does what someone tells them to do, it is only because they independently determine it is also the right thing for them to do. This does not mean the autonomous person is selfish, only that they make their own decisions on how to act, which can sometimes be selfish and other times be selfless—it is up to the autonomous person to decide when they will act selfishly, selflessly, or somewhere in between.

Wolff argues that we all have a moral obligation to act autonomously because we are only acting morally if we make sure our own actions are morally permissible prior to acting. As Wolff says, "The responsible man is not capricious or anarchic, for he does acknowledge himself bound by moral constraints. Instead, he insists that he alone is the judge of those constraints. He may listen to the advice of others, but he makes it his own by determining for himself whether it is good advice."[14] Autonomy means figuring out what's right for yourself prior to acting. In the moral realm, this means that agents make sure that they are doing what is morally right for themselves—they cannot simply trust others to choose what's morally permissible for them since others might get it wrong.

Let's consider some quick examples. In a prudential case, if you tell us that we would enjoy bobsledding and we don't think through whether we would, then we are not autonomous when we bobsled. Of course, in this example, not much is at stake if we end up not having a good time bobsledding (more could be at stake in a larger prudential case, such as if you told us we'd enjoy dropping out of school and joining the circus). In a moral case, however, more is usually at stake. If you tell us that it is morally okay to steal from the homeless because they won't expect to be robbed and won't notice, then our not thinking this action through and proceeding as you recommend makes us morally bad people. Failing to be autonomous in a prudential case means that we're risking or even forgoing some of our happiness (and how much happiness is at stake alters how much it matters that we're not thinking things through). In a moral case, failing to be autonomous makes us risk or forgo our moral duty, which could lead to us being morally bad people. In this way, agents are not only within their rights to act autonomously, but ought to act autonomously to make sure that they are acting morally.

Yet Wolff notes that the state requires that its authority—its right to command—be followed just because it is the state.[15] The state is, by definition, the seat of power in a society. Power means that the state can make certain things happen. Authority is the kind of power that is justified. For example, the state has the power to wage war if it can make the country go to war rightly or wrongly. The state only has authority to wage war if it is a just war that the people democratically support. For a state to count as legitimate, its authority must be recognized by the people under its power. The people must not question the state's authority. The people must not be acting only because they fear the state's power. Instead, the people must do as the state tells them to do simply because the state tells them to do it and they accept that the state is in the right—the people must respect the state's authority. Even if the legitimate state has authority and people generally respect that authority, the state will always back up its authority with coercion: it will make acting against it illegal, threatening to fine and/or jail anyone who defies its laws.[16] Even if the state is legitimate, it will not assume that the people will respect its authority. It will instead use coercive laws to assert its power, just in case some of the people do not respect its authority or some day stop respecting its authority.

Wolff argues that the state and autonomy are inconsistent: "The defining mark of the state is authority, the right to rule. The primary obligation of man is autonomy, the refusal to be ruled."[17] This point is not a substantial observation that requires years of studying the state's historical activities, but a conceptual analysis of states and autonomy. Where there is a separation between powerful state actors and the subjects that they have power over (and there is always such a separation in states, ranging from tyranny to representative democracy, since this just means some people have the power to pass and enforce laws and others at most have indirect powers to vote), the state will pass laws that not all of the governed accept. The state commands that *all* the people follow those laws simply because the state fashioned them. Further, those laws will be backed by coercive threats: if the governed fail to follow these laws, then they can be fined, jailed, and sometimes even put to death.

Wolff's analysis just tells us what a state does: it passes laws that it demands be followed in recognition of the state's authority. Laws are not autonomously chosen by all of the governed since laws are not unanimously chosen (if laws were unanimously chosen by all the people, you would have direct democracy and that would be anarchism since nobody would have state-power and everyone would rule together). Some subset of the governed is coerced out of their autonomy. Since we all should have the right to act autonomously, the state necessarily interferes with our rights. Or, to put it a bit more strongly, since we have a moral obligation to act autonomously, the state interferes with our ability to be moral agents. The state stands in the way of moral agency.

This point is not merely conceptual since the various systems of society have winners and losers, rich and poor, oppressors and oppressed. As Dr. Horrible sings:

> Listen close to everybody's heart,
> And hear that breaking sound:
> Hopes and dreams are shattering apart,
> And crashing to the ground [Act II].

Though we live within an illusion that everyone can be a winner, society is operated in ways that ensure that some people will be in power, and other people will suffer from shattered dreams, as Dr. Horrible points out. Some people make the laws, while others cannot autonomously agree to those laws insofar as the laws worsen the conditions under which they live. Anarchism's negative thesis is that hierarchy inevitably means that the organization of society makes some people—those who are in power, such as the people who make up the state—better off, and other people—those who lack power—worse off.

Dr. Horrible embraces anarchism's critique of hierarchy. Dr. Horrible sees that homelessness does not occur accidentally, but is a product of the social structures that organize our society. Dr. Horrible understands that real villains are not monsters or evil horses, but are structural violence, odious influences on our minds, and institutional bigotry.[18] Yet what neither Dr. Horrible nor Captain Hammer realizes is that the solution to these problems is not yet another re-organization of power into different hands. We see this lack of understanding as Captain Hammer sings:

> I'm poverty's new sheriff.
> And I'm bashing in the slums.
> A hero doesn't care if you're a
> Bunch of scary, alcoholic bums [Act III].

In this refrain, it is clear that Captain Hammer just does not understand the depth of problems like poverty insofar as he thinks a hero can just as easily fight poverty as he might fight a super villain. Contrary to Hammer's singing, you cannot bash in the slums.

To respond to this conundrum, anarchism turns to its positive thesis. The positive thesis holds that the solution to society's deepest and most fundamental problems lies in trusting people's morality. Insofar as the negative thesis claims that hierarchy causes the problem, the positive thesis claims that the absence of hierarchy will cultivate a solution. A good person to look to for a better understanding of the positive thesis is Henry David Thoreau, who can safely be classified as an American anarchist.

Henry David Thoreau (1817–1862) was an American writer, philosopher, abolitionist, and anarchist. He is well known for his book *Walden*, which advocates simple living and a focus on personal natural growth. His essay "On the Duty of Civil Disobedience" argues for disobedience to an unjust state and sets up his anarchist views. Thoreau begins "On the Duty of Civil Disobedience" by saying:

> I heartily accept the motto, "That government is best which governs least"; and I should like to see it acted up to more rapidly and systematically. Carried out, it finally amounts to this, which also I believe—"That government is best which governs not at all"; and when men are prepared for it, that will be the kind of government which they will have.[19]

For Thoreau, government is not only troublesome in itself, but the removal of government will ultimately lead to positive results—once we are all prepared for that stage. The idea is that the government is not only coercive, but that it is also corrupting. Put another way, if we blindly follow the laws that we are told to follow—which could be immoral—we become sloppy moral thinkers. And once we become sloppy moral thinkers, we put ourselves in danger of becoming negligent agents who do the wrong thing because we just don't think about it enough.

Anarchists believe that hierarchical systems lead to less moral deliberation and lowered abilities for moral thinking. Thoreau explains the corruption problem this way:

> Must the citizen ever for a moment, or in the least degree, resign his conscience to the legislator? Why has every man a conscience then? I think that we should be men first, and subjects afterward. It is not desirable to cultivate a respect for the law, so much as for the right.[20]

When we are members of a hierarchical society, we are not equal members of our community. In our current systems, we allow others to make many of our moral decisions, do much of our moral thinking, and limit our full moral development. While the voter has some say over who legislates, the legislators determine what should be law. The citizens, at that point, are expected to treat the law as if it represents the ultimate say on what is right and wrong. But, as Thoreau here points out, each citizen has their own conscience to determine what is truly right, so it is worrisome to allow legislators to override the citizens' own determinations—or, worse, to preclude them from ever making those determinations (since what is the point when you cannot change the laws yourself?).

Since the citizens' determinations are of no use, and they are expected to follow the law regardless of what their own consciences say, the citizens' moral faculties are in danger of going under-used, under-developed, and under-appreciated. As Thoreau notes, "In most cases there is no free exercise whatever of the judgment or of the moral sense; but they put themselves on a level with wood and earth and stones; and wooden men can perhaps be manufactured that will serve the purpose as well."[21] Dr. Horrible sings a similar point:

> Amazing how sheep'll show up for the slaughter,
> No one condemning,

> You lined up like lemmings,
> You led to the water [Act III].

In a true community, where we take full responsibility for our actions and decisions, anarchists believe we will more fully develop our moral skills, become more connected to each other, and advance a society where there are greater feelings of belonging, charity, and care. To make a telling contrast, Thoreau says, "It is truly enough said that a corporation has no conscience; but a corporation of conscientious men is a corporation *with* a conscience."[22] Thus, while a corporation cannot have a conscience (the Rossum Corporation, in *Dollhouse*, certainly does not have one), the grouping together of multiple persons who follow their own consciences, instead of parroting that of their leaders, will lead to a worthy "corporation" of moral agents.

Robert Paul Wolff likewise agrees that anarchism, and anarchism alone, can solve the autonomy problem: "anarchism is the only political doctrine consistent with the virtue of autonomy."[23] For Wolff, anarchism involves unanimous direct democracy: each person votes directly for the laws, and they only follow laws that they all agree to.[24] In this way, each citizen ensures that they can morally endorse the laws that they become committed to following. They do not give up their moral responsibility to representatives, but work with everyone else to develop the best understanding of what morality requires in their anarchist society. Through a system of direct democracy, as Wolff notes, "men would learn—what is now manifestly not true—that their votes made a difference in the world, an immediate, visible difference. There is nothing which brings on a sense of responsibility so fast as that awareness."[25]

Is the anarchist right about these positive, fairly utopian views? It is really difficult to know given how rarely anarchism has been tried out. However, it does seem that the anarchist critique of hierarchy makes a lot of good points, even if we cannot be sure what humans would be like if they could separate away from hierarchy. Still, we can at least agree with the anarchist that it is a good idea to distance ourselves from hierarchy as much as possible, at which point we may see whether humans would begin to morally improve. Of course, that's a hard social experiment to run. It would be grand to set up a full anarchist community and let it run for a few generations without outside interference. However, one is unlikely to get Institutional Review Board approval for such an experiment.

So our best method for thinking about these very difficult anarchist questions is to turn to the works of brilliant minds that attempt to imagine morally rich, alternative universes. Therefore, we are turning to the collected works of Joss Whedon in attempts to both obtain anarchist critiques of contemporary society and to imagine positive anarchist visions of how things should be run instead. In pursuing this analytical journey through Whedon's works, we will not follow the chronological order in which the shows appeared. Instead, we will pursue an order that will best illuminate anarchist themes. Thus, we will begin with anarchism's negative thesis, which will highlight the critiques and failures of contemporary society. We will use critiques based on Whedon's works, specifically *Angel* and *Dollhouse*, to argue that the shows exhibit the negative thesis of anarchism by exposing what is wrong with contemporary society. From there, we will transition toward the positive anarchist thesis, through discussing issues such as which anarchist views are represented by Whedon's *Firefly* and *Buffy*. Let's examine the chapter breakdown to further explain the framework of this book.

Starting with critiques, in Chapter One, we will examine an anarchist assessment of structural violence found in the final season of *Angel* (a TV show that was a spin-off from *Buffy*, ran from 1999 to 2004 on the WB network, and was produced by Mutant Enemy Productions, along with Greenwolf Corp [season 1], David Greenwalt Productions [seasons 2–3], Kuzui Enterprises, Sandollar Television, and 20th Century–Fox Television). Structural violence occurs when the structures or institutions of society make certain groups worse off, especially through the use of active or threatened violence. As we see in Dr. Horrible's critiques, poverty in general and homelessness in particular are instances of structural violence. There are structures in society (such as the economic system as a whole and also specific laws that regulate and limit the ability of the impoverished to make significant economic upgrades) that help protect the privileged position of the rich and provide obstacles to limit the advancements of the poor.

In the Whedonverse, one institution that engages in the promotion and protection of structural violence is Wolfram & Hart, the law firm that serves as the main villain in *Angel*. Wolfram & Hart's job, of course, is to use the law to protect villains from being caught and punished, yet, in an ingenious twist, in the fifth and final season of *Angel*, Wolfram & Hart decides to give Angel and friends the Los Angeles branch of their law firm as a reward for stopping world peace. Of course, as anarchists would explain, the law firm is not evil just because it happens to have evil people running it. The point of structural violence is that the structures and institutions themselves facilitate and often are agents of evil, even if no one within the institution intends to use it for nefarious purposes. Angel and friends are therefore doomed to fail because Wolfram & Hart will continue to bring about evil in society no matter who is at the helm.

Once we acknowledge the power of structural violence, we transition to Chapter Two, where we are in a position to fully appreciate the mentally invasive nature of hierarchy by scrutinizing *Dollhouse* (a TV show that ran from 2009 to 2010, aired on the Fox Network, and was produced by Mutant Enemy Productions and 20th Century–Fox Television). In *Dollhouse*, the

Rossum Corporation wipes the minds of alleged volunteers and makes use of their hollow bodies as vessels for various purposes to which, we will argue, they did not autonomously agree. In a certain way, many of us in real life are similarly hollow vessels that corporations use for purposes we do not autonomously choose and cannot autonomously embrace. Just as consent and autonomy are problematized and undermined in *Dollhouse*, in the real world, consent and autonomy are sometimes illusory and too often taken for granted within heavily hierarchical systems that are pervaded with structural violence. Echo and friends stand in for all of us when Rossum exploits their difficult circumstances (in trouble with the law, dealing with post-traumatic stress, grieving over the death of loved ones, escaping sexual violence, and so on) to manipulate them into agreements that allow the corporation to take advantage of them.

Having examined the problems that provide a basis for anarchism, in Chapter Three, we will analyze Whedon's TV shows and movies from the Marvel Universe to see why society is simultaneously driven toward and away from anarchism. The Avengers provide a particularly pointed case of how anarchist society is not a path toward mediocrity, but is instead the only reasonable solution for developing a society where individuals can excel as equals. Anarchists believe that it is only through anarchist society that individuals can become the best version of themselves. One way to understand why anarchists would believe such a claim is to examine the *Avengers* films (*The Avengers* [2012] and *Avengers: Age of Ultron* [2015] are produced by Marvel Studios). Each Avenger is clearly a truly special individual who, in their independent films, seeks to follow their own paths toward justice and helping others, yet no Avenger would really be able to follow orders or accept a chain of command where someone else's judgment is substituted for their own. In the *Avengers* films, when any of the Avengers attempt to define or force a hierarchy onto the others, the system breaks down. The Avengers are only able to succeed when they work collaboratively without hierarchy. Thus, through the lens of the Avengers, we see that to save the world, we require an anarchist society where each person builds upon and follows their own autonomy and works collaboratively for the common good.

Marvel Agents of S.H.I.E.L.D. (a TV show that runs from 2013 to the present, is produced by ABC Studios, Marvel Television and Mutant Enemy Productions, and airs on the ABC network) is the one Whedon show that represents a political hierarchy, but the failures of the S.H.I.E.L.D. organization itself indicate how we are inclined to fear anarchism yet still need it. In particular, it is telling that S.H.I.E.L.D. turns out to be Hydra in disguise. Therefore, this show twist flips the idea from the *Avengers* films: if unique individuals seeking to do good are forced to work within hierarchy, an evil foundation may build up and undermine their good works. This result, which also shows the other side of the trend seen in *Angel*, is in fact quite common as good people who join together to serve a good cause (say, a charity organization, an activist group, or a labor union) often find that their work eventually becomes subverted through the same sort of problems that typically plague hierarchy, such as leadership becoming greedy, over-bearing, and losing sight of the mission.

There are certainly positive anarchist visions on what to do in response to these various problems that plague hierarchal societies, yet there is quite a bit of strong disagreement among anarchists over what the best course is for developing a new society. The strongest disagreement is between anarcho-capitalists and the various kinds of anarcho-socialists. Anarcho-capitalists believe that anarchism entails removing the state and then permitting whatever social arrangement thereafter emerges, based on everyone having the freedom to do what they please with their own property rights. Thus, anarcho-capitalists are against political hierarchy, but they believe that hierarchy is justified if it results from economic decisions, such as if one invests his or her money wisely and then comes to control the work-lives of twenty employees. Anarcho-socialists oppose economic, political, and any other kind of hierarchy wherever possible. They believe that people should be able to achieve autonomy both in their political and work lives.

Firefly represents both of these versions of anarchism in the various characters aboard Serenity. In Chapter Four, so as to better understand these various positive theses of anarchism, we will seek to determine which kind of anarchism best represents the main message of *Firefly* (a 2002 TV show that was produced by Mutant Enemy Productions and 20th Century–Fox Television and ran on the Fox network) and *Serenity* (a 2005 film produced by Universal Pictures and Barry Mendel Productions). On the surface, it seems that *Firefly* is an anarcho-capitalist show, since two of the main characters, Jayne and Captain Mal, often behave like anarcho-capitalists. They are interested not only in avoiding the state (The Alliance), but also in enriching themselves, and they accept the value of non-political hierarchy: Mal is in charge because he owns the ship, yet we will argue that the rest of the crew is much more anarcho-socialist: they stand against hierarchy in all of its forms and represent a group that is focused on community more than on becoming economically enriched. Further, Mal is on a voyage of self-discovery that is leading him much more toward an anarcho-socialist viewpoint. Thus, for the positive thesis, *Firefly* points toward a general, anarcho-socialist view.

To get more specific, we then return to the roots of the Whedonverse: *Buffy, the Vampire Slayer* (a TV show that aired from 1997 to 2001 on the WB network and 2001 to 2003 on the UPN and was produced by Mutant Enemy Productions, Sandollar Television, Kuzui Enterprises, and 20th Century–Fox Television). We argue in chapters Five and Six that *Buffy* presents an anarcha-feminist picture of how a group ought to organize around values of community, equality, and feminism. The Scoobies grow over the period of the series, and, by the end, there's a sense of equality among them, and they develop certain anarchist tendencies. They make decisions as a group, they seek consensus, and they look out for each other and for other members of the Sunnydale community, regardless of whether the people they are saving are friends, associates, or strangers. Buffy and the Scoobies develop a sense of community that leads them to act out of love for others, even at the point of repeatedly risking their own lives to do so.

In the conclusion, we examine the journey that went from an Angel team that could not find an adequate solution to structural violence (instead, Angel's team goes out in a futile fight simply for the purpose of striking a minimal blow that would hopefully annoy the greater forces of evil) to a Buffy team that found a solution that largely realized the values of anarcha-feminism through the elevation of all of the potentials to being vampire slayers. Of course, in summarizing what we learn about anarchism from watching the various Joss Whedon TV shows and movies, we must recognize that the negative thesis is much more firmly grounded and substantiated than the positive one. Thus, we conclude by considering one last movie. That is, we end by examining *Cabin in the Woods* (a 2012 film produced by Mutant Enemy Productions), where the ultimate solution at first appears to be bleak and hopeless.

However, through a careful analysis of *Cabin in the Woods*, we find the solution to the broken system that we've been attempting to fix all along: the answer lies in standing up to hierarchy, and switching out the value of blind obedience to hierarchy with the value of respecting moral autonomy. And, ultimately, the answer is about using love to form stronger relationships that will strengthen social binds, just as the schoolchildren in Japan do to defeat the facility. Therefore, while this book starts in bleak critiques of seemingly undefeatable evil that pervades our very social structures, we end with the hope of an anarchist society based in the love of humanity.

ONE

Striking at the Machine

Structural Violence in Angel's *Wolfram & Hart*

Worse Than Devils in the City of Angels

When Angel gets his chance, he jumps at the opportunity to take a ride (on an elevator heading straight down, of course) to the source of evil: Wolfram & Hart's Home Office ("Reprise" 2.15). Holland Manners (who is deceased by this point—but death does not get you out of a contract with Wolfram & Hart), the former head of Special Projects, warns Angel that it will be a one-way trip. At the end of their descent to evil, the elevator doors open to reveal that the source of evil is in fact on Earth—or, at least, in Los Angeles.

Joss Whedon has pointed out that "there are a lot of demons in L.A."[1] But this scene unveils an evil rampant throughout L.A. that is much more frightening than demons.[2] Through this pivotal scene, Whedon reveals two key insights. First, the worst evil in *Angel* will not come from devious super villains or hideous monsters, but will instead be rooted in real life issues.[3] Second, evil is structural: social structures and institutions facilitate evil—an excellent example of such an institution being the Wolfram & Hart law firm.[4]

For the first point, we must take note of what Angel sees when the source of evil is unveiled: as the elevator doors open, Angel lays eyes on a homeless person, an exasperated mother fighting with her children, and a couple fighting ("Reprise" 2.15). Evil is not a simple villain that can be vanquished, but a society where people ignore the suffering of others, or are mean to each other, either through yelling at loved ones or denying kindness to each other. Evil is not always as remarkable as hideous monsters would be—although there are plenty of those in the Whedonverse and unfortunately in real life (child molesters, rapists, serial killers, etc.). Instead, evil is often commonplace and mundane, which makes it even more insidious. After all, as Holland puts it, "if there wasn't evil in every single one of them out there, why, they wouldn't be people. They'd all be angels" ("Reprise" 2.15). And, of course, even Angel isn't an angel.

This revelation connects to the second insight: evil in the real world relies upon and sometimes derives from cultural, economic, and political institutions. This point is exemplified by the main big bad for the run of the *Angel* series being, quite ingeniously, a law firm. Wolfram & Hart is a legal institution that assists with, facilitates, and often enables the evil activities of its clients. Holland tries to tell Angel in the elevator that it is not Wolfram & Hart's job to create evil, but merely to facilitate it. Evil lies within ordinary people walking around Earth, but Wolfram & Hart brings that evil out of them and allows it to grow to its full potential. That is why Holland points out that they "have no intention to do anything so prosaic as 'winning'" ("Reprise" 2.15). Wolfram & Hart's goal is just to ensure that the world, fueled by evil animus, just keeps on going. On this view, evil is made up of mean people, some of whom are cruel and many of whom are just insufficiently nice, whose activities are facilitated and governed by various evil institutions, such as corporations (Rossum from *Dollhouse*), governments (Alliance from *Firefly*), organizations purporting to do good (the Watchers Council from *Buffy*, the facility from *Cabin in the Woods*, and, as we will see in Chapter Two, even S.H.I.E.L.D. from *Marvel's Agents of S.H.I.E.L.D.*), and organizations that are openly evil (Evil League of Evil from *Dr. Horrible*). These organizations assist with, protect, and promote a social structure that breeds, enables, and ensures the continued operation of evil in the world.

The anarchist critique of contemporary society similarly involves analyzing evil as complex and rooted in institutions in ways that make it nearly impossible to remedy society's deepest ailments. Anarchists believe that the state, which is the power structure that runs the country, is often the most worrisome source of evil in society. While anarchists recognize that sometimes people are morally reprehensible, they are more concerned with the various state apparatuses that enable and reinforce the evil of individuals. Anarchists argue that state systems tend toward self-reinforcement: the state is a central source of power within a society and it wants to protect and maintain its hold on power. The state both creates and protects the conditions that solidify and advance the state's interests. But these interests often coincide with the motivations and actions of bad people.

States operate through a set of social structures (the law, the economy, the culture, etc.). These social structures are best understood through the individual institutions that constitute them: the law is made up of law firms, courts, governmental and nongovernmental legal entities, etc., just as the economy is made up of corporations, businesses, better business bureaus, unions, etc. The institutions ensure their social structures operate as they are meant to do, and the social structures combine to make sure that the state's power is maintained as it is meant to be. Although this structure is abstract, the state sits atop a hierarchy of power that includes many of the institutions and organizations that constitute the society.

Insofar as individuals have their own interests, such as interests in their own liberty and welfare, state power and individual interest inevitably come into conflict. While it may seem that the individuals could simply replace heads of states, such as presidents, prime ministers, or dictators, doing so leaves the social structures and institutions intact. Thus, we all inhabit hierarchal systems that are rooted in complex power relations that regulate almost all aspects of our lives. For example, we are all familiar with these ideas: you have to obey the law, you have to pay taxes, you have to work, you have to follow cultural norms or else you are thought of as weird, etc. Through the social structures and institutions, the state limits our liberty and detracts from our welfare. For the anarchist, heads of states or institutional directors are never truly the problem: the real trouble lies in the structures and institutions that enable and protect the power relations that make our everyday lives problematic.

It is not just monsters that cause violence. Additionally, the state can organize society so that violence is built into the very systems that arrange our everyday activities. Anarchists believe that one of our biggest problems is that the state forms a hierarchal society that creates and enables the conditions of structural violence. Peace scholar Johan Galtung originally defined "structural violence" as the harm or violence that "is built into the structure and shows up as unequal power and consequently as unequal life chances."[5] Structural violence can be understood as an organization of social structures and/or institutions such that some individuals are significantly made worse off than they would be without that organization, especially where threats of violence maintain or enable those structures. As an easy example, consider a monarchy where the privilege of nobility and royalty are enshrined into how the society is run and the peasants of the society are unable to challenge that privilege without being violently suppressed. Such a monarchy is built upon structural violence even if the peasants never revolt: their suffering is real and they know that they will face violence if they tried to do something about it (consider the similar position of the mudders on *Firefly*).

While monarchies and other tyrannies are clear cases of structural violence, hierarchal and unequal democratic societies can also include structural violence in more subtle forms. Galtung noted that structural violence results in "resources [that] are unevenly distributed, as when income distributions are heavily skewed, literacy/education unevenly distributed, medical services existent in some districts, and for some groups only, and so on. Above all *the power to decide over the distribution of resources* is unevenly distributed."[6] The real problems of society are not blood-sucking monsters, but the arrangement of society where some people are stuck being hungry, sick, or poor. Consider how much we fear monsters that eat children, but how little we fear a social system that allows children to die early deaths from preventable diseases because they lack sufficient nutrition and/or health insurance. While we normally do not think of as these sorts of issues to be results of violence, they derive from a particular way that the state has arranged society so that some people cannot afford enough food, medicine, or much else. Further, if the marginalized try to seize these basic necessities to protect themselves or their children, then the system will use actual, physical violence to prevent them from taking what they desperately need.[7] As such, structural violence harms those who are least well off because the people who have power are ensuring that they stay the most well off. Structural violence perpetuates cycles of marginalization and inequity.

When considering *Angel*, Wolfram & Hart is a law firm (and so an institution) that makes up a small part of the legal structure of society, and its legal practice involves protecting individual violent people and monsters from exposure in ways that directly harm their clients' victims. As they note in one of their commercials ("Harm's Way" 5.9), Wolfram & Hart represents evil corporations such as Yoyodyne (from Thomas Pynchon's novels), Weyland Yutani (from the *Alien* movies), and Newscorp (Rupert Murdoch's real-life media corporation). Anyone attempting to circumvent Wolfram & Hart's legal activities will be met with harsh responses that are nonetheless permissible under the law. Wolfram & Hart thus fits snugly within Galtung's understanding of structural violence: they rely upon a currently existing legal structure that allows them to engage in violence without fear of legal retribution. Wolfram & Hart's legal work is therefore representative of certain kinds of actual legal practices: lawyers, whether they work for corrupt corporations, powerful drug dealers, gang bosses, or criminal governments, find ways to shield evil and violent activity through the law. Wolfram & Hart use the law (just like some real-life lawyers) to enable evil agents and organizations to structure society so that evil goes unpunished.

Given Wolfram & Hart's role in enabling structural violence, *Angel*'s fifth and final season is quite fascinating. Just prior to the final season, Angel and team are handed the Los Angeles branch of Wolfram & Hart as a reward for preventing world peace. The show's bad guys just give their multi-billion-dollar law firm to Angel as a gift—challenging him to try to do good with it. Over the course of the season, Angel and friends realize the futility of using an evil organization for the purpose of righteousness. Wolfram & Hart is a mere cog in larger systems of structural violence, and so one cannot simply undermine Wolfram & Hart's evil by replacing its leadership with morally preferable bosses, as we will discuss shortly. Through *Angel*'s final season, we gain an advanced understanding of why anarchists believe that structural violence becomes intractably entrenched within state systems. Hence, we begin our tour of anarchist theory with a critique of structural violence.

A Business Proposition: Biting Eve's Apple

When Angel and crew take over Wolfram & Hart's Los Angeles branch—which just happens to be built on a site blessed in the blood of a serial killer—they do so in the hopes that they will be able to use the firm's vast resources in their fight for good, yet their conduit to the Senior Partners, Eve, illuminates the difficulty of their challenge when she tells them that they are in charge "of the Los Angeles offices of a multi-dimensional *corporation*. Now, I'm stressing that last word because that's what we are. We're a business, and we have a bottom line" ("Conviction" 5.1). Eve explains that almost all of their clients are evil—but evil pays well. If they give up all of their clients, they would have to shut down the firm—thus undermining any ability to do good with it. Eve further elucidates: "See, in order to keep this business running, you have to keep this business running. And that means keeping your clients—most of them, anyway—happy" ("Conviction" 5.1). Doing good with the law firm necessitates doing what it takes to keep the law firm running, i.e., doing bad.

Team Angel's fundamental mistake is their belief that they can simply turn around the L.A. branch of Wolfram & Hart, which has been an institutional agent of evil for much of history (from its founding in 1791 until it is destroyed by the Beast in 2003 in "Habeas Corpses" [4.8]). They act as if they can take an entire law firm whose compass points to evil and simply turn the compass around (of course a real compass would reset as you turn it and continue to point to north, or to evil in this case). As Wesley Wyndam-Price says when they are deciding to take the deal, "As much as it pains me to admit it, there's probably a great deal we could accomplish with the resources available here" ("Home" 4.22). Their dangerous assumption is that the law firm can be used in a new fashion that runs against the larger social structures that it has operated within for over two hundred years.

Angel's takeover of the L.A. branch of Wolfram & Hart raises two questions that are discussed throughout the *Angel* scholarship. The first question is whether Angel and friends can turn Wolfram & Hart into a force for good. The second question is whether Wolfram & Hart would endanger the morality of Angel and friends. The responses in the literature have been pessimistic on both counts. For instance, Erin Giannini explains that "it is only when they offer the firm and all its resources to Team Angel that Wolfram & Hart does the most damage to the characters. By placing them in a position where profit margins trump everything, they successful [sic] keep the heroes from changing the system."[8] Further, Chelsea Quinn Yarbro explains that Wolfram & Hart is unlikely to be changed by our heroes, and that rather they themselves are more likely to be damaged through their attempt to change things either through or even within the law firm.[9] As U. Melissa Anyiwo puts it, the folks at Angel Investigations end up limited/defeated by the bottom line at Wolfram & Hart, and do so "at the expense of their souls."[10] Anyiwo reasons that "each action they take to 'help the helpless' increasingly drives them further into the debt of the very evil they are trying to defeat."[11] Further, Jacqueline Lichtenberg argues that Angel is no hero, but rather reacts to the circumstances he finds himself in; he does not make his own rules, but is manipulated by outside factors. As such, his association with Wolfram & Hart likely would lead to compromising his values and to losing his sense of self.[12] Finally, Stacey Abbott argues that the attempt to take over Wolfram & Hart results in a hybridity in Angel—a split between Angel trying to do what's right and Angel becoming consumed by the darkness of Wolfram & Hart.[13] The consensus in the literature then is that Wolfram & Hart is much more likely to change Angel and friends than vice versa.[14]

The deeper question then is why is it that it is more likely that the institution would make the individuals morally worse as opposed to the individuals making the institution morally better? Why don't good people improve bad institutions? If *Angel* is realistic in this regard, answering this deeper question about the show will reveal important insights about real life power relations. As we indicated at the start of this chapter, anarchists would answer this question by reference to institutional power and structural violence. Thus, we must now go deeper into that analysis, which will enable us to better understand a key anarchist critique of institutional power, which is exhibited in the final season of *Angel*.

As we already saw, institutions must be understood within the social structures within which they operate. We will use the phrase "social structure" to mean the larger systems that include some identifiable segment of society. So, for the United States, the political social structure is republican democracy, the economic social structure is capitalism, the religious social structure is largely Christian but it attempts to be inclusive of most other faiths as well, and so on. We will say that each social structure includes a number of institutions that are the less abstract operators of the social structure. The U.S. political social structure is comprised of the White House, Congress, state governments, lobbying firms, Political Action Committees, etc. The economic social structure would be made up of corporations, small businesses, unions, etc. The cultural social structure would be made up of various cultural institutions, such as media companies, sports franchises, music producers, etc. Finally, institutions include a variety of individuals who either run them, work for them, or serve as owners, members, or associates.

Any given institution will likely operate within various social structures. Wolfram & Hart, as an institution, is a law firm. Most directly, that means it is part of the legal social structure. The law, though, is a significant part of the political social structure, and so Wolfram & Hart must also be understood as part of the political system as well. And to keep running, the law firm must make money, and so, as Eve pointed out, it is also a business, and therefore part of the economic social structure—that is, it must act as a capitalist institution. And as Lorne (whose actual name is Krevlornswath of the Deathwok Clan) heads the entertainment division, they are also a part of the cultural social structure. In other words, institutions usually must be multi-faceted.

Running Wolfram & Hart thereby requires meeting the various conditions that are placed on the firm as a small part of much larger legal, political, economic, and other social structures. As a part of the legal social structure, the law firm must not only follow the law—or at least do its best to appear to be doing so—but it also must represent its clients as faithfully and earnestly as it can. As part of the economic social structure, the law firm must make money. Since evil pays well, it may turn out that it is much more profitable to represent evil clients than to represent tenants being wrongfully evicted by slumlords, for example. And so on.

Individuals too must act within, and even are somewhat defined by, the systems that they inhabit.[15] To a certain extent, this point is trivial and unavoidable. Angel is a vampire with a soul.[16] Angel's identity traits necessarily set up conditions, limits, and values that partially define both Angel and his various available options in life. For example, as a vampire, Angel certainly has biological standards that he must meet (we are assuming that "vampire biology" makes sense): Angel cannot walk in the sun, must drink blood, etc. These biological facts obviously constrain Angel's life changes in unavoidable ways: Angel certainly should not give up his detective agency to choose a job directing traffic in the middle of the day or to serve as a daytime lifeguard at the beach. There are also social traits associated with Angel that he can never fully avoid: in part because he must fear turning back into Angelus, but also because others see him as a vampire and he has certain tastes and values that derive from his long history as Angelus. Thus, Angel should not pick up a job as a social worker for the Romani people.[17] Angel's vampire relations, vampire history, and vampire tastes are all undeniably part of who he is.

At the same time, Angel is a warrior for goodness, a private investigator, and, eventually, the head of a law firm branch. Each of these roles also comes along with various social standards and commitments. What it means to take on any job, such as private investigator, has to be at least partially defined in specific ways so that there is a general social sense of what it means to perform that job. After all, if you go to hire a private investigator and what they mean by "private investigator" is something random like they suck your blood for money, then that will only lead to bizarre confusion and a possible increase in anemia disorders. Similarly, you cannot be a warrior for goodness if you are seeking to commit genocide. And, as we will see, managing partners of law firms have associated standards and responsibilities as well.

Individuals take up roles that help lay out what they do, what they don't do, and what types of persons they are. In an important way, these roles help make life simpler: we can surmise that Angel is more trustworthy as a vampire with a soul and a champion for righteousness, and surmise that he is much less trustworthy as a P.I. or as head of a law firm. Notice this usage of these roles allows for a kind of reasonable stereotyping. While it is wrong to stereotype on the basis of race, gender, sexuality, etc., it makes a lot more sense to stereotype a P.I. as someone who can help track down a lost person or stereotype a vampire as someone who you don't want to be alone with in a dark alley. These stereotypes are reasonable because they are based on roles that almost always have certain traits associated with them. And they are not bigoted stereotypes because they do not involve tying someone down to their race, gender, or sexuality.

Stereotypes, however, can be wrong. We tend not to trust vampires, lawyers, or private investigators, but surely our stereotypes against these roles can sometimes deceive us. Angel is a good vampire, and you are probably fine with being alone with him in a dark alley (unless he has turned into Angelus, of course). And some private investigators may have no idea how to track down a lost person (maybe it is their first day). Thus, we must be careful when we stereotype even in these reasonable situations since there are always exceptions to stereotypes. At the same time, many people tend to fall into line with the stereotypes of their roles since doing so will likely be required to succeed at the role. The private investigator who doesn't know how to track down people better learn in a hurry if they want to make money at the job (or at least advertise that they aren't that kind of private investigator and forfeit that bit of income). Hence, it is mostly reasonable to stereotype based on these roles since most people try to live up to them, and they are not formed through bigotry.

Importantly, individuals make sense of the various roles they play in life through the institutions that those roles fit in. Angel takes up a role as boss of a law firm, which is necessarily defined through the law firm institution: you cannot be boss of a law firm without a law firm. Angel's job running a law firm in part defines his actions and how people view him, but what it means to run a law firm depends on what it means for a law firm to operate, so Angel's role as law firm boss depends on what a law firm is and does. That is a trivial point since "law firm boss" clearly refers to the law firm. Similarly, Angel's membership in the community of vampires places him, whether he likes it or not, in vampire culture. We make sense of much of what Angel does by virtue of what vampires like him tend to do or have to do. Even his soul defines him in contrast with the rest of vampire culture: to certain extents he fits vampire culture (he stays out of the sun), while in other ways, Angel, due to his soul, is defined as opposing and being excluded from vampire culture. Other vampires are surprised that Angel has remorse and a sense of duty but such attributes are not at all surprising for humans. It is only because he is a *vampire* with a soul that we are surprised that he has basic *human* decency. Thus, even Angel's differences are reflections of him being a vampire: only a vampire with a soul is surprisingly a morally good person.

Prior to the issue of whether the institution will morally change the individual, we must recognize that the institution necessarily changes the individual in many ways. Taking up roles within institutions entails at least minor changes insofar as you are now enacting those roles. You cannot take a job as a philosophy professor at a university and then insist that you will not be teaching philosophy. Such an insistence just means that you are not really performing the job. Insofar as you have the job, you have to execute the tasks that make up the job. There's no wiggle room here: institutional roles are characterized by the activities that people who take up those roles have to do, so it is trivial that institutions change the individuals who take up roles since the individuals have to change to fulfill their new roles.

Therefore, when Angel becomes boss of the Wolfram & Hart L.A. branch, he is necessarily changed at least in the respects that essentially define what it means to be boss of that branch. That is why Charles Gunn and Winifred "Fred" Burkle at first bristle at the oddity of them taking over an evil law firm:

> GUNN: You want to give us your evil law firm? We ain't lawyers.
> FRED: Or evil... Currently.
> LILAH MORGAN: What we're offering you is a turnkey, state-of-the-art, multitasking operation. What you do with it, well ... that's up to you ["Home" 4.22].

Taking over the law firm requires that Angel and friends take up roles that they are not sufficiently trained for, so it is constitutive of the type of work that a law firm does that at least some of its employees be lawyers. You can work at a law firm and not be a lawyer (law firms have plenty of employees that are not lawyers). You can even possibly run a law firm and not be a lawyer. But whatever role you take up in a law firm, you will necessarily have some dealings with the law since it is a law firm. Even if they aren't lawyers, Angel and team will have to work in legal settings if they are to run a law firm.

Perhaps more importantly, they would have to take up roles that would challenge them morally since it is an *evil* law firm. Fred makes an important point when she notes that they are not evil. She then adds, after a brief pause, "currently." That "currently" could refer to past deeds, but it could also foreshadow future trouble. We have seen that it is trivial that institutions change individuals who take up institutional roles at least in some respects. It is also plausible that evil institutions will endanger the moral character of the people who take up roles in those institutions.

Given a tension between an evil institution and a good individual taking up a role there, the institution is not likely to change because the institution fits within a larger social structure. And we know the institution fits well within the social structure because it continues to operate: institutions that do not fit within the relevant social structures die out. If a law firm does not win cases in court because it doesn't really fit within the legal system in the right ways, it will eventually go bankrupt. An institution that has been operating a long time, as Wolfram & Hart has, has proven to fit well in the relevant social structures. Accordingly, it is unlikely to change easily since significant change will endanger its existence. The individual, however, has to change to fit into the institutional role, so there's a greater likelihood that the individual takes up the institution's moral character (especially while acting in the institutional role) than vice versa. None of this is to say that the institution will always win out. But momentum is on the institution's side: the institution has already established itself within its social structure while the individual is taking up new changes to fit in because they joined the institution. It is not guaranteed that the institution will win out, but it is more likely. Consequently, when good guy Angel joins evil Wolfram & Hart, the latter is likely to continue its proven path while Angel is going to have to make some changes just to take on the new job.

That's why when the firm's representative Lilah tells Angel that this offer is an opportunity, he corrects her: "an opportunity to be part of the problem" ("Home" 4.22). In fact, he corrects her again when she attempts to explain the true value of this opportunity:

> LILAH: People don't need an unyielding champion. They need a man who knows the value of compromise and how to beat the system from inside the belly of the beast.
> ANGEL: The beast's belly? Doesn't that usually mean you've been eaten?
> LILAH: Maybe ["Home" 4.22].

Angel, at least in this early moment, sees through Lilah's argument for pragmatism due to her unintentionally revealing metaphor. The pragmatist urges compromise, but compromise involves capitulating to evil. Once they agree to take over the law firm, Angel and friends will indeed find themselves in the belly of the beast. And this is the point: once you take up a role in the institution, you find yourself trying to adjust to the way the institution works. It often is the case that your attempts to change the institution from within look a lot like someone trying to change a monster that has just eaten them: you can at best give the monster an upset stomach, but you aren't likely to stop it from being a monster while you are being digested.

We will therefore be arguing that it is more likely that the institution changes the individuals, morally speaking. In part that is because the institution already fits within its relevant social structures and so there is significant pressure for it to stay the course. These problems are magnified when the social structure involves structural violence. For example, if Wolfram & Hart's comfortable position is maintained through a violent social structure, then it will be nearly impossible for Angel and friends to reverse Wolfram & Hart's evil, countermand their violence, and maintain that comfortable position within a violent social structure. In other words, if Wolfram & Hart's evil is rewarded by the violent social structure, then Angel's team cannot reverse that evil without a huge reaction from the rest of the social structure. Which is why, as we will see next, Team Angel ends up promoting, quite unintentionally, structural violence.

The Gray CEO of Hell, Incorporated

There are initially some positive signs once Angel takes over Wolfram & Hart's L.A. branch. In "The Cautionary Tale of Numero Cinco," Gunn tries to explain to Angel that they are making significant strides through Wolfram & Hart: "You just bankrupted a company that dumps raw demon waste into Santa Monica bay, banished a clan of pyro warlocks into a hell dimension, and started a foster care program for kids whose parents have been killed by vampires" (5.6). When Angel fails to respond positively to this assessment, Gunn notes that "we've done more good here in a month than Angel investigations did in a year" ("The Cautionary Tale of Numero Cinco" 5.6). While Gunn is able to note the quantifiably positive benefits, Angel continues to be dismayed.

There are two potential explanations for Angel's dismay. First, the legal and bureaucratic fight is displacing the heroic narrative. Sarah Upstone argues that Angel wants to return to his original reason for being: his P.I. business and helping those who are marginalized.[18] Gunn also explains it in this way: "Look, I know legal weasels and business deals aren't as heroic to you as rescuing young honeys from tumescent trolls, but I love what we do" ("The Cautionary Tale of Numero Cinco" 5.6). Angel admits that he feels "disconnected" from this new, overly bureaucratic job. As Angel tries to convince their mail guy, Number 5, to still believe "in being a hero," he is surely also trying to convince himself ("The Cautionary Tale of Numero Cinco" 5.6). Wesley also tells Angel that it feels like the work has lost meaning ("The Cautionary Tale of Numero Cinco" 5.6). In a cynical reading of Angel's self-doubt, what troubles him is that running the law firm is not heroic in the macho sense of running around and cutting off demon heads. Angel is somewhat emasculated due to his administrative CEO job, especially when that is contrasted with his numerous years of fighting with fists and fangs.[19] Surely this reading is a part of the story: the transition from heroic champion to passive law firm CEO frustrates Angel.

There is a second explanation for Angel's dismay: even if they are quantifiably more successful according to Gunn, they are at the same time reinforcing structural violence and coming to realize that they cannot defeat institutional evil from within (nor were they previously successful from the outside). They are reinforcing structural violence because their positive gains occur alongside various activities that keep Wolfram & Hart in power. The latter is absolutely necessary because they are acting through Wolfram & Hart: they cannot use the law firm without keeping it running, yet insofar as Wolfram & Hart—an institution of structural violence—stays in power, structural violence is being reinforced. Thus, the institution is changing them, as opposed to them changing it, in part because there is nothing they can realistically do to stop Wolfram & Hart from being evil given the role it plays in the greater society's structural violence. We will see that they cannot defeat the institution's evil from within because that evil is what keeps the institution running, and Angel and friends must keep it running if they are to use it. They are stuck in the middle of a circle of evil that they are hopeless to stop: using an evil institution to do good still protects the institution's evil and just leads to more evil.

Consistently killing monsters of the week at least provided Angel Investigations a (false) feeling of progress. While Gunn might be right that they are more effective while working through Wolfram & Hart, this work exposes that the problems they are taking on exist within society's core structures and, therefore, there is nothing that they can do to truly eradicate structural violence (unless of course they truly change the entire society). Angel and team are coming to directly experience structural violence close up, which exposes that their previous approach of killing one monster per week was misled due to their ignorance of evil's structural framework and which also indicates how depressing and helpless the real world's problems really are.[20] We will see that structural violence causes and relies upon ignorance about these real world problems, while the truth about those problems remains quite depressing.

Structural violence involves an organization of social structures and/or institutions that make some group of individuals worse off, especially where threats of violence enable and/or maintain that social organization. In the previous section, we saw that individuals are defined by and restricted to norms, standards, and roles that exist within the institutions that they are parts of (either as members, employees, leaders, etc.). We also saw that institutions exist within social structures that delineate the roles and limits of those institutions. Structural violence occurs when the institutions and/or structures create oppressive conditions that unfairly and unjustly allow for some individuals to become empowered at the cost of other individuals' suffering. It is fairly trivial and not necessarily bad that individuals are partially defined by their roles in institutions and that institutions are largely defined by their roles in social structures. That is just how a society is organized. The organization, though, becomes problematic when these social structures involve an unjustifiable and oppressive hierarchy that is backed by violence. When the institutions divide us and harm many of us in unfair ways and violence ensures we cannot rectify these wrongs, we have structural violence in our society.

We should remember that one of the first things that Angel sees when he gets to the source of evil (Earth/Los Angeles) is a homeless person. Homelessness exists within a certain social organization of society. While there is no institution of homelessness, there are institutions that regulate who can take out loans for homes (banks), who can earn salaries (businesses), what laws harm or protect homeless people (legislative bodies), and the specific harms that befall particular homeless people when they break those laws (police departments). Therefore, the political, legal, and economic structures intersect in ways that both enable people to lack homes and make their existence immensely difficult, so social structures and institutions create the conditions where some people are homeless and suffer while other people can more easily avoid the problems of homelessness. And if the homeless attempt to merely seize the basic necessities of life, the police will protect property instead of helping the homeless to find what they desperately need. Thus, homelessness is one instance of structural violence.

William Godwin (1756–1836), one of the earliest modern anarchists, provided early explanations for this kind of social inequity along with how social structures and institutions shape individuals' moral characters. Godwin was an English writer, philosopher, and anarchist whose *Enquiry Concerning Political Justice* is an anarchist critique of the state. He was married to an early feminist, Mary Wollstonecraft, with whom he had a daughter, Mary Shelly, who wrote *Frankenstein*. In his *An Enquiry Concerning Political Justice*, Godwin argued that political institutions could have both coercive and beneficial effects on individuals.[21] Godwin believed that "it is sufficiently obvious that a despotic government is calculated to render men pliant, and a free one resolute and independent."[22] In other words, the government and similar social structures play key roles in the moral development of the people. Godwin understood that social structures, especially the government, had significant influence over individuals' moral thoughts.

Just as he saw most governmental systems as having negative influence, he also envisioned the possibility of developing a system of positive influence: "A system of government, that should lend no sanction to ideas of fanaticism and hypocrisy, would presently accustom its subjects to think justly upon topics of moral worth and importance."[23] In other words, a positive government would be one that steps aside and allows the individuals to think about moral topics on their own. A negative government is one that attempts to shape the individuals' moral thoughts in a specific direction, usually a self-serving one that promotes the government's own interests.

In his arguments for institutions' strong influences, Godwin linked social inequality with structural violence. He argued, "The opinions of individuals, and of consequence their desires, for desire is nothing but opinion maturing for action, will always be in a great degree regulated by the opinions of the community."[24] It is simply natural for humans to think like other people with whom they have much in common. Hence, we tend to be similar to others in our own communities. Moreover, Godwin pointed out that those people who hold power have significant influence on our thinking: "The rich are in all such countries directly or indirectly the legislators of the state; and of consequence are perpetually reducing oppression into a system."[25] The rich are the influential members of the state who lead most of the powerful institutions that make up the structures of society. For Godwin, the rich, due to these positions of power, carve out systems that maintain their privilege and continue the oppression of the marginalized, thus influencing how society works. Thus, in the above quotation, Godwin points out that the rich are taking oppression and reducing it into a system that further privileges them. Our communities influence who we are and the rich have the largest influence over community standards. The predictable result is that social opinions favor values that honor the rich. As Godwin put it, "the manners prevailing in many countries are accurately calculated to impress a conviction, that integrity, virtue, understanding and industry are nothing, and that opulence is everything."[26] Consequently, we learn to value people who are rich, as opposed to valuing people who labor with great effort and intellectual skills (including many such skills that we devalue and do not think of intellectually) to make our lives better (such as custodial staff, sanitation workers, farmers, nurses, teachers, etc.).

The people who run Wolfram & Hart consequently enjoy social honors and esteem because it is assumed that their status implies that they are worthy of such praise. They are evil lawyers, but cultural institutions, such as movies, TV, and literature, make it seem like lawyers are not only necessary for society to run well but also are good people. Notice that even though we make fun of lawyers, we continue to respect them enough to consistently elect them into political offices (for example, 25 out of 45 United States presidents were lawyers). The fact that we make fun of lawyers is part of our tacit acknowledgment that many of them perform evil deeds in their jobs, yet we also highly respect lawyers, often without even questioning what they may have done in their jobs. And part of the reason for this high respect is that we so often see them act honorably in fiction, such as in TV shows like the various *Law & Order* series, *JAG*, *The Good Wife*, *Ally McBeal*, etc. Even on TV shows where lawyers have questionable morals, such as *The Practice*, *Boston Legal*, *Suits*, *Goliath*, etc., we consistently see them using those seemingly questionable morals to fight for cases where they are ultimately in the moral right. In other words, cultural institutions are used to support the moral status of the rich and powerful who benefit from structural violence.

Further, the system replicates itself: institutions do not only limit the ability of the masses to fight back, they also limit the ability of the rich and powerful individuals to make significant changes. Henry David Thoreau, whom we discussed in the last chapter, insightfully said, "the rich man ... is always sold to the institution which makes him rich."[27] The rich person owes their wealth to the institutions that enabled them to become rich, and they likewise must support institutions that protect and lend value, including moral value, to wealth. To put the point at the general level: the rich cannot be rich without institutions of capitalism, and the rich, if they wish to stay that way, must then support institutions of capitalism to maintain the power and high esteem that is afforded to wealth. As Godwin pointed out, "the inequality of conditions usually maintained by political institution, is calculated greatly to enhance the imagined excellence of wealth."[28]

The lawyers at Wolfram & Hart find it easier to gather esteem because they are rich lawyers, and they, in turn, use that esteem to enhance the misconception that all rich people are upstanding, law-abiding citizens. Wolfram & Hart became rich by hiding the evil crimes of moneyed persons and demons. To maintain that wealthy business, they must continue hiding those crimes. The institutions of oppression become interlocked with the oppression that they create. Put another way, Wolfram & Hart became successful by enhancing social oppression. Were they to suddenly stop enhancing oppression, they would lose many of the benefits that allowed them to both survive and thrive as an institution that existed within structural violence. Therefore, keeping an institution of oppression operating inherently involves continuing oppression.

That is why Angel and friends run into trouble as soon as they take over. The money and power that secures the firm derives from the performance of legal trickery that protects and promotes evil. Without that money and power, they can do no good with the firm. Thus, it is nearly impossible to change the moral standing of the institution without losing the pragmatic power of the institution. Turning the law firm into a force for good entails turning the law firm into an inefficient and dying institution. That is because the institution exists in a social structure that rewards a morally corrupt drive for profit, which entails that a morally positive institution that doesn't put profit first will struggle to compete. Individuals cannot change the institution without risking the complete loss of the institution.

This point is initially hard to understand because the system hides that there is an underlying arrangement that keeps everything in place just so. The capitalist social structure presents itself as natural and not worthy of further scrutiny. The rich are thought to simply be rich due to their hard work and upstanding values. Moreover, many of the institutions in question (law firms, public relations firms, advertising firms, and certain parts of academia) obscure, perhaps inadvertently, the operations of these structures so that they appear natural. This obfuscation purposefully gives the illusion that this is just how things always have been and always will be. Law firms, like Wolfram & Hart, and public relations firms hide many of the illicit operations that make some people so rich. Academics make these systems appear to be incomprehensible through unnecessary jargon and over-theorizing. After so much legal maneuvering, manipulative marketing, and academic obfuscation, social inequity and social injustice come across as murky, overly complex, and somehow the fault of the oppressed themselves. And the structures that cause the problems are safely maintained. Because of this type of willful muddling of the truth, and in spite of their initial doubts, Angel and team think they can in fact do good through Wolfram & Hart. This point suggests that misconceptions, to the point of widespread confusion and ignorance, are easily devised and spread in systems maintained by structural violence, which is a point that also is argued by a contemporary anarchist, David Graeber.

Graeber, in his *The Utopia of Rules: On Technology, Stupidity, and the Secret Joys of Bureaucracy*, argues that structural violence tends to breed stupidity. He defines "structural violence" as "forms of pervasive social inequality that are ultimately backed up by the threat of physical harm."[29] For Graeber, the fact that social inequality is ultimately violent is easy to see, though we often miss this crucial fact. The social inequality is rooted in

> institutions involved in the allocation of resources within a system of property rights regulated and guaranteed by governments in a system that ultimately rests on the threat of force. "Force" in turn is just a euphemistic way to refer to violence: that is, the ability to call up people dressed in uniforms, willing to threaten to hit others over the head with wooden sticks.[30]

For Graeber, one version of structural violence involves institutions that regulate the economic social structure, through the political social structure along with threats of force from the police. The way of arranging property in a given society is a method for determining, quite literally, who has what and who does not. Where property is distributed so that some (the homeless) have none, and that distribution is protected through coercive institutions (such as the police department), then the society is steeped in structural violence.

The reason that structural violence breeds stupidity is that its very nature is elusive for two reasons. First, the violence is merely implicit and eventually gets taken for granted as it fades into the social background. Second, the suffering itself soon disappears into the social background in a similar fashion: most of the people who are not suffering take the suffering of others for granted, and so their suffering almost appears ordinary and their own fault. The final result is, as we will see, that an understanding of structural violence reveals how deeply entrenched it is and how futile it is to try to fight it.

Graeber argues that structural violence usually operates so that the violence becomes nearly invisible even to the very people studying it:

> This is what makes it possible, for example, for graduate students to be able to spend days in the stacks of university libraries poring over Foucault-inspired theoretical tracts about the declining importance of coercion as a factor in modern life without ever reflecting on that fact that, had they insisted on their right to enter the stacks without showing a properly stamped and validated ID, armed men would have been summoned to physically remove them, using whatever force might be required.[31]

Everyday activities within a system of structural violence are routinely backed by threats of physical harm to anyone who attempts to disrupt the structure, even with the smallest measure. The threat is in fact so routine that we simply do not think about it. We bring and show our IDs in the "appropriate" places, let people search our homes, cars, offices, computers, and bodies in the "appropriate" contexts, and generally do as we are told when we are told it is "appropriate" to do so. We inhabit an everyday hierarchy that is backed by a structurally violent system that keeps us from challenging our places within that hierarchy, yet the actions that we are told are "appropriate" have become so routine and unquestioned that we do not see the violence, which, in turn, silently lurks in the background.

The very violence that regulates and protects the system resides so deeply in the background that we take it for granted. Our very understanding of our own hierarchal system becomes deficient in that we do not see the underlying violence that allows the system to operate. To be clear, we become ignorant about how our own system is a system of violence, even though that fact would become obvious if one simply attempted to buck the system—at which point the violence would quickly surface. To see this point, Graeber recommends that you "try driving down the street ... in a car without license plates."[32] Of course, it is best not to try out Graeber's test. He tells us what the obvious result would be: "Uniformed officers armed with sticks, guns, and/or tasers will appear on the scene almost immediately, and if you simply refuse to comply with their instructions, violent force will, most definitely, be applied."[33] Graeber's point makes sense of why an established firm like Wolfram & Hart can so easily be on the side of the law while Angel Investigations struggles to work with police detective Kate Lockley: the law protects a system of social structures that happen to allow for the continued operation of violence by anyone who follows the rules that maintain that system, which works out a lot better for Wolfram & Hart than for Angel Investigations.[34]

That is why it seems like the appropriate response to the ailments of the system is to fight vampires, demons, and monsters. These boogeymen represent the observable violence that easily frightens us, appears to surround us, and that we at least believe we know how to fight. Crime, violence in the streets, and boogeymen, as Dr. Horrible notes, are symptoms, "and the disease rages on, consumes the human race" ("Act 1"). The disease, of course, is the structural violence that creates the systems of inequality, which in turn lead to increased crime and boogeymen. It is only when Angel and team take over Wolfram & Hart that they truly realize how much they have simply been treating the symptoms.

Secondly, in addition to making the violence disappear into the background, structural violence does the same disappearing act on suffering. If we do not see how real the violence is that enforces the social inequality and oppression, then we cannot fully appreciate why the victims of structural violence have a hard time overcoming their oppression. Structural violence presents complex, largely hidden troubles in a way that makes it appear as if there is nothing too awry. Given this hidden complexity, it is especially hard for privileged outsiders to appreciate structural violence's oppression.

Adding to the difficulty caused by the incomprehensibility of structural violence is that it is psychologically difficult to spend one's privileged life feeling bad for the distant suffering of others. Graeber notes, "The poor, however, are so consistently miserable that otherwise sympathetic observers are simply overwhelmed, and are forced, without realizing it, to blot out their existence entirely."[35] It is easier to forget the poor exist, or even blame them for their own problems, than it is to attempt to understand and then feel sorrow for their complex situation, which is born through structural violence.

A similar difficulty of comprehension will befall the victims of structural violence. They will struggle to pinpoint who is to blame for their plight since the blame is diffused through complex structures where no one person or set of persons is intentionally trying to make them specifically suffer. While, as we have seen, the beneficiaries of structural violence will find little time to think about the poor (and thus will have little sympathy for them), the victims, as Graeber points out, will find themselves quite concerned with the wishes and feelings of the system's beneficiaries without being able to pinpoint which specific beneficiaries are the actual oppressors.[36] The victims are unable to pinpoint the direct source of their oppression and so they must vaguely respond to the oppressors in general with the hope that helping their oppressors in general will somehow get the oppression to stop.

As an example of this phenomenon, Graeber argues (based on his understanding of feminist critiques of structural violence) that women—the victims of the structurally violent system of patriarchy—have to figure out the minds of men, while men can joke that they cannot understand women.[37] In other words, patriarchy involves, among many other things, a vague, complex, and confusing system of men oppressing women. Women have to figure out how to navigate this system while men can passively benefit from it. As the beneficiaries of patriarchy, men do not need to work out a deep understanding to operate within the confines of patriarchy. The way patriarchy works, men can thrive regardless of whether they understand what is going on, yet women must find their own ways to operate within a patriarchal system that oppresses them, that is fairly incomprehensible, and that is not operated by any single man or small group of men. And so women cannot say, "This man is to blame for patriarchy," or even "This small group of men are to blame for patriarchy," because sexist oppression is much more complicated than that. But unlike men, women cannot simply ignore the sexist ways in which patriarchy operates since it is *hurting* them. Even if women do not think of the social structure as patriarchy or even as sexist, they still have to figure out how to respond to sexist institutions and structures that are actively oppressing them. And, as Janine Harrison notes, Wolfram & Hart is permeated by "a masculine management style" which causes its female lawyers, such as Lilah, to adopt the same style in order to survive within the firm.[38]

Just as it is difficult for the beneficiaries and the victims to figure out structural violence, it is likewise difficult to figure out for our fictional champions of justice. Prior to the fifth season, Angel Investigations was merely treating the symptoms, but their plight to do so left them feeling fairly certain about their righteousness. As they take up positions at Wolfram & Hart, they realize that their roles in the fight are much more difficult to pinpoint, often leaving them in morally gray areas. They are consistently trapped within these moral gray areas because they cannot really figure out how to navigate around the issues of structural violence, which is much more complex than pummeling a different monster each weak.

Consider their attempt to deal with warlock and cult leader Lucien Drake. Wesley and Gunn point out that it would not be good for business to take the entire cult out, since the cult has key alliances and connections. Instead, they should merely take out Drake as leader, which will redirect the other cultists' energies by causing infighting that will allow for increased billing for their law firm. Angel responds with understandable concern:

> ANGEL: So are we doing this because it's right ... or because it's cost-effective?
> GUNN: Uh, well, a little of both actually.
> WESLEY: Yes, oddly, once again we find ourselves in a bit of a gray—
> ANGEL: Don't...
> WESLEY: —area.
> ANGEL: ... say that! Can we just get through one damn day without saying that? ["Soul Purpose" 5.10].

Wolfram & Hart, the institution, is changing Angel and his friends, not the other way around. Angel is becoming increasingly frustrated with the fact that his work at Wolfram & Hart involves discovering corporate-type responses to evil, which must balance the values of being cost effective, profitable, and ensuring that their largely evil clientele remains sufficiently pleased to keep paying their bills, yet as a law firm that wishes to stay in business, these values are necessities. The law firm fits within social structures that require corporate values. If they wish to run a law firm, Angel and team must weigh corporate values alongside their chosen value of doing what's right.

K. Stoddard Hayes and Stacey Abbot discuss this moral ambiguity as they note that Angel's heroism entails doing bad things for good ends.[39] Angel and his Wolfram & Hart branch are constantly in gray areas given their attempt to balance moral and corporate values. Of course, this moral gray area is a direct response to them taking up institutional roles. As we saw, it is trivial that taking up institutional roles requires that individuals change. If you are not working for an institution, you have no reason to care about the institution's budget problems. But now that Angel and team run a branch of Wolfram & Hart, they have to care about its budget. While that change is a trivial part of taking up a role, it necessitates a moral change: as soon as they start weighing budget issues against moral issues, they end up having to deal with moral gray areas as an inevitable result. The moral ambiguity is a necessity of their new institutional roles. Hence, the institution is changing the individuals not merely in trivial ways but also by worsening their moral characters.

Of course, balancing values is simply part of the pragmatic cost of doing business in the real world. The real world is made up of social structures that require certain costs for "doing business." At the same time, when agents take pragmatic measures that compromise their moral codes to get involved in a certain immoral type of business, then the cost of doing business involves their own moral corruption. It is through working at Wolfram & Hart that Angel and his team come to realize that their pragmatic cost of doing business involves further entrenching themselves into the very structures that they wish to challenge and defeat. They are more effective numbers wise, as Gunn points out, at fighting individual instances of violence, but their effectiveness masks that they are also becoming enmeshed in the structures that facilitate and promote violence and evil. They eventually come to realize that they cannot defeat structural violence by working for, or even running, an institution that plays a key role in managing the violent structure. As we will see next, they especially cannot make meaningful change to society's violent structure through a law firm in particular.

No More Employee Sacrifices

It is of particular interest that Wolfram & Hart is a law firm.[40] As we have seen, a law firm tends to involve all of the main social structures: the law, politics, economics, and culture. The law in fact is the structure that is meant to organize and bind society. All the other social structures fall under its purview in that they are all supposed to adhere to the law. At the same time, the law is beholden to other social structures—thus showing their interconnectedness—as we see by the fact that politicians create and change the law, the legal system operates through money thus binding it to the power of the economic system, and the cultural system helps promote the law and lawyers as valuable and good. A law firm is a central locus for understanding the inner workings of society in that it presents a power that is placed over the other social structures, while simultaneously having to respond to the power of those same social structures.

William Godwin provided an acute, anarchist analysis of the law that helps explain how this central role within the interconnected social structures leads the law to being key for understanding power relations that enable structural violence. The problem with the law, for Godwin, is that it pretends to do something that cannot be done. The law purports to provide a fixed standard by which we can judge the conduct of humans, but, as Godwin argued, "every case is a rule to itself."[41] In other words, every instance of human interaction is so unique and so filled with distinct particulars that apply only to that case that there can be no unified standard written in advance that will apply to every human interaction. The politicians who write the laws and the lawyers and judges who adjudicate them are constantly attempting to put finite limits on future human activity that will be infinitely diverse.[42]

Godwin explained that the law thus misleads us all into wrongful thinking about human activity: "Law tends no less than creeds, catechisms and tests, to fix the human mind in a stagnant condition, and to substitute a principle of permanence, in the room of that unceasing perfectibility which is the only salubrious element of mind."[43] Godwin's point is that the whole idea of the law suggests that certain people (legislators) can develop a set of permanent, rigid rules that would guide the rightful conduct of humans who are attempting to morally improve themselves based on their own moral consciences. The law then substitutes some distant legislator's judgment for the judgment of the moral agent who attempts to navigate her own, unique and complex personal circumstances. The law, then, is attempting to do the impossible: decide what will be right for every given individual without really knowing what their circumstances will involve and how their own moral judgment could and should guide them in those circumstances.

Godwin, being a good anarchist, concludes that there should be no such thing as law. Of course, that leads to him drawing the natural inference: "If there ought to be no such thing as law, the profession of a lawyer is no doubt entitled to our disapprobation."[44] The law attempts to provide a firm standard for human behavior that cannot make sense given the immense diversity of human behavior. Lawyers are tasked with applying this rigid standard to the entirely unique situations that more often than not will not fit it. For this reason, Godwin spoke of the "quibbles of lawyers and the arts by which they refine and distort the sense of the law."[45] His point reflects the impossibility of the legal profession: lawyers are to act as if the law yields right answers to complex moral situations where it is impossible for there to be any such right answer predicted in advance.

Accordingly, Godwin reasoned that "the very education that enables the lawyer, when he is employed for the prosecutor, to find our offences the lawgiver never meant, enables him, when he is employed for the defendant, to find out subterfuges that reduce the law to a nullity."[46] Lawyers adapt so much to their legal institutions—the prosecutor to the District Attorney's Office and the defense attorney to their defense law firm or the Public Defender's Office—that they completely change their views on the law depending on the role they are in at that moment. This point both emphasizes the importance of institutional roles and challenges the way in which we think of the law as static and unchangeable. The misleading narrative that the law is one, universal, and good then obfuscates the fact that legal work is constantly changing, involves unlimited debate over what the law requires, and constantly occurs within moral gray areas.

Complex legal obfuscation is the very task that Wolfram & Hart excels at, under their old or even new management. When Charles Gunn undergoes an operation to gain magical legal knowledge and skills (along with a touch of Gilbert & Sullivan to improve his voice and diction), his first case involves saving Corbin Fries, who is on trial for smuggling young Asian girls for prostitution ("Conviction" 5.1). Gunn uses his new legal abilities to find a concealed loophole that earned his guilty client a trial delay. Eve notes that Gunn has saved the day without having to use violence ("Conviction" 5.1), yet Lorne corrects her, "Of course, saving the day meant getting the scumbag who was ready to sacrifice his own son off on a technicality and then returning said son to said scumbag" ("Conviction" 5.1). Gunn's best response is that at least now the scumbag will have to tone down his criminal activities until the trial ("Conviction" 5.1).

Godwin would argue that this scene represents the limitations of lawyers. Gunn's job is to represent his client, which implies shaping and fitting the seemingly rigid law into a form that satisfies his client's needs. Insofar as his client is evil, Gunn "wins" by allowing his client to get away with his crimes (at least for the time being). The law does not so much respond to what's right and just, but to who can hire the best legal team that can most warp their rhetorical spin to make the law meet their goals, regardless of the morality of those goals.

Godwin notes that the lawyer's morally troubling position, which requires being "perpetually conversant in quibbles, false colours, and sophistry," is entirely dependent on the workings of the system: "A lawyer can scarcely fail to be a dishonest man. This is less a subject for censure than for regret."[47] We can barely blame the lawyer, Godwin is arguing, for being dishonest since that is essential to the role they take up as lawyers. The legal social structure is based on forcing rigidity onto fluid human behavior. Since that standard is destined to fail, the law instead becomes about finding ways to bend the supposed rigidity to meet the needs and wishes of one's clients, yet insofar as the law is necessarily beholden to the economic social structure, the rich clients will be able to pay the best. Therefore, the law becomes another method for the rich to increase their power over those who lack the means to bend the law to their ends. As Godwin noted, "In reality, whatever were the original source of law, it soon became cherished as a cloke [cloak] for oppression."[48]

Since the law, by its very nature, is backed by the coercive force of the state, the law is a paradigm case of structural violence. The law just is a fundamental structure of society that increases and then cements the distance between the rich and the poor, the oppressors and the oppressed, the powerful and the powerless. And the police state just is a fundamental social structure that coercively enforces both the law and the resultant inequity and oppression that results from the law's operations. The law is fundamental to structural violence.[49]

Having said all that, it may become even clearer why Angel and team cannot simply take over Wolfram & Hart and make positive changes. After Gunn's ingenious though troublesome defense of Fries, Fred wonders what they have truly gotten themselves into, but Angel tries to comfort her:

> ANGEL: We're gonna change things. We came to Wolfram & Hart because it's a powerful weapon, and we'll figure out how to wield it.

> WESLEY: Or kill ourselves with it.
> FRED (sarcastically): Yay, team ["Conviction" 5.1]

The problem is that they cannot yield the law firm as a powerful weapon if Wolfram & Hart's very power lies in how it enables structural violence. They cannot change things through one legal institution if the legal social structure remains a force for entrenching structural violence. In fact, their very act of trying to change things will consistently be undermined by the inability of the law to be used in that fashion given the larger social roles that the law already plays. The law cannot simply be bent toward good since the problem that Godwin points to is the very fact that the law bends. An attempt to bend the law toward good ignores that someone else will certainly bend it back toward evil. The whole purpose of the adversarial legal system is that the law constantly bends back and forth, depending on the role the lawyer is playing and the needs of the client who is paying them.

William Goldwin describes the problem that Angel and his team necessarily run into when he describes the possibility of a "perfectly honest lawyer":

> This man is no doubt highly respectable so far as relates to himself, but it may be questioned whether he be not a more pernicious member of society than the dishonest lawyer. The hopes of mankind in relation to their future progress, depend upon their observing the genuine effects of erroneous institutions. But this man is employed in softening and masking these effects. His conduct has a direct tendency to postpone the reign of sound policy, and to render mankind tranquil in the midst of imperfection and ignorance.[50]

Clearly, we could replace "man" in the above for "vampire" and we would see an accurate description of why Angel's plan to use Wolfram & Hart as a weapon for good will fail. For Godwin, any attempt to be a morally good lawyer will reduce to a worrisome reinforcement of the highly problematic legal system. Angel and his team, in taking over Wolfram & Hart, are implicitly (even if unintentionally) supporting the work that law firms do to enable and entrench structural violence. The idea that people can see Angel as the head of a law firm and think that law firms can be used for good is itself a subversive idea: it subverts any attempt to build a better system. Angel and his team, as they come to understand this problem, must instead find a way to alter the system—they should not let themselves become incorporated within it. Or, at least, Angel realizes this fact after Cordelia points it out to him.

A Futile Resolution: Hurting the Machine

Far from simply critiquing social ills, anarchists believe in potential solutions. Such solutions are certainly not easy, but instead require an uphill battle to totally restructure society. *Angel* does not provide such complete, anarchist solutions, but it does suggest a start down the road of fighting back. Though it is ultimately a rather futile start, it illuminates the depth of structural violence's entrenchment in contemporary institutions and social structures.

We have seen that the social structures and institutions that constitute structural violence are unlikely to be co-opted for good. One cannot simply extricate the evil out of the institution since Wolfram & Hart exists within a larger set of social structures that further embed evil within society's core foundations. Wolfram & Hart operates within legal, political, and economic systems that demand certain values and activities for Wolfram & Hart to continue its operations. Changing the leadership of Wolfram & Hart does not change those larger legal, political, and economic systems. Wolfram & Hart cannot truly change while those systems remain the same.

The anarchist response to this problem is to restructure all of society, but the start of such a task lies at the individual level. As we saw, William Godwin believed that institutions could influence people for both good and bad. That leaves room for hope: "Our virtues and vices may be traced to the incidents which make the history of our lives, and if these incidents could be divested of every improper tendency, vice would be extirpated from the world."[51] In other words, we simply have to follow the paths where we develop virtues as opposed to the paths that lead to vices. Such a task is made quite difficult—seemingly impossible—by the fact that numerous institutions tend to push us toward the vices. Godwin, though, urges us to continue on: "the man who is anxious for the benefit of his species, will willingly devote a portion of his activity to an enquiry into the mode of effecting this extirpation in whole or in part."[52] That is the path that Angel and his friends pursue: risking their lives to challenge the institutions that make up structural violence.[53]

Once Angel realizes that he will be unable to fully manage a positive change through Wolfram & Hart, he is left at a crossroads. As CEO of the Los Angeles branch of Wolfram & Hart, his efforts are at best mixed as he reinforces an institution of evil in particular and structural violence in general, even as he accomplishes moderate amounts of good. As a hero/champion, Angel is much more comfortable fighting for a lost cause that is thoroughly righteous. Even without a path to fully succeed, Angel eventually chooses the latter path thanks to Cordelia.[54]

When Cordelia first awakens from her coma, she is entirely dismayed at seeing Angel and the rest running Wolfram & Hart. Angel, at the time, was still attempting to rationalize the decision to take over the branch:

>ANGEL: With these resources, there's nothing we can't do, no one we can't save.
>CORDELIA: Except maybe yourself ["You're Welcome" 5.12].

Angel claims things are working out at Wolfram & Hart, but he is likely feigning belief. He claims there is nothing they can't do and no one they can't save, but clearly his point is dubious. They certainly have the resources to win the typical monster-of-the-week battles. They can save the day, one case at a time, more easily than they could at Angel Investigations, yet Cordelia's point hits quite hard: they may be more effective at saving the day and winning battles, but the cost is their own morality. The problem is that their effectiveness derives from working through an institution that is entrenched within—and is further entrenching—larger structures of evil.

Later in "You're Welcome," Angel tries again to tell Cordelia that she does not understand why he took over Wolfram & Hart's L.A. branch (referencing the assistance he was able to give to Cordelia herself and the ability to give his son, Connor, a new life). Before he makes his specific points, though, Cordelia cuts him off to explain her interpretation: "They threw a whole bunch of money at you, plied you with all these expensive toys and penthouses with spectacular views, and—really spectacular" ("You're Welcome" 5.12). Even when Angel explains that it was for Connor (and that he also asked Wolfram & Hart to erase everyone's memories of Connor), Cordelia is not forgiving: "So, not only did you strike a deal with your worst enemy to give up your son, you let them rape the memories of your friends who trust you?" ("You're Welcome" 5.12). Cordelia's choice of words here is quite drastic, but also telling. Angel cannot justify taking over Wolfram & Hart, and his choice to do so involves him in some truly despicable acts. Earlier in the episode, one of the first images that Cordelia sees when she enters the Wolfram & Hart lobby is one of their lawyers capturing and returning Archduke Sebassis' slave (the lawyer notes, "I assume the Archduke's gonna beat him and all that," "You're Welcome" 5.12). The returned slave is a fitting entry to the layers of evil that Angel and the rest have wrapped themselves in. There is no possible justification for Angel's choice, even if Team Angel was able to also use the law firm to do some good. Furthermore, it is as if, through his embrace of Wolfram & Hart, Angel is risking the loss of his soul once again.

Cordelia convinces Angel to return to whom he once was: "I can tell you who you were. A guy who always fought his hardest for what was right, even when he couldn't remember why. Even when he was miserable, which was, let's face it, a not small portion of the time. He did right. And that gave him something" ("You're Welcome" 5.12). As Whedon scholar Jes Battis has noted, Cordelia acts as a truth teller and possesses "incisive honesty."[55] Further, Jennifer Soy argues that Cordelia is the voice of reason or mediator in *Angel*.[56] Thus, just as Godwin recommends, Cordelia is urging Angel to return to being "the man who is anxious for the benefit of his species," so that he can "devote a portion of his activity" to fighting for a changed society.[57]

Angel eventually gets it, and he plans to fight what he knows will be a futile final battle against evil: "We're in a machine. That machine's gonna be here long after our bodies are dust" ("Power Play" 5.21). Angel's words here mirror the words of Henry David Thoreau who recommended: "Let your life be a counter-friction to stop the machine."[58] Angel, however, has no illusion that he can stop the machine; he has chosen to simply hurt the machine as opposed to continuing to work within it: "We are weak. The powerful control everything, except our will to choose. Heroes don't accept the way the world is. The senior partners may be eternal, but we can make their existence painful" ("Power Play" 5.21). Thus, in admitting that "the powerful control everything," Angel acknowledges that the social structures of society limit a hero's ability to make drastic changes through fighting monsters-of-the-week or even through running a single institution, like the L.A. branch of Wolfram & Hart. At the same time, he also is arguing that there is room for a solution: even the weak still have the will to choose. Even if they cannot easily or by themselves change the whole system, they need not accept how it is, and they can strike a blow against it.[59]

Angel and friends therefore plan to fight against the evil structure that they have no ability to take down, with the sole intention of hurting that structure, even if just for a moment: "We can't bring down the senior partners, but for one bright, shining moment, we can show them that they don't own us" ("Power Play" 5.21). As we discussed earlier, we cannot help but to be defined by the institutions that we work for or through. Insofar as Angel and friends worked through Wolfram & Hart, they could not avoid the influence that institution consequently had on who they were and what they did. Their only chance to avoid that institution "owning" them, using Angel's word, is for them to leave it and attempt to strike a blow against it.

Their plan is to kill all of the members of the Circle of the Black Thorn, who are Wolfram & Hart's Senior Partners' representatives on Earth.[60] Tellingly, the members of the Black Thorn represent many of the leaders of the social structures of society. What's interesting about this plan is that it is certain not to cause any significant change: they are dealing a blow to the *individuals* that run things, but the institutions and structures that lead to structural violence will remain. Just as there was no significant improvement in the world when good people took over Wolfram & Hart's L.A. branch, there would be nothing but mere annoyance with the leaders of the social structures being killed. The system would just have to replace the leaders, which obviously can be easily accomplished. Angel and team's violence is ultimately futile and will simply annoy the system without any chance of breaking it. Violence can never be the solution to structural violence since the structures and institutions of structural violence survive intact. Only a meaningful reworking of the system could work.

Angel and his team, of course, realize this point, but they still choose to simply fight the good fight because it is all they can think of to do to at least annoy the forces of evil, even at the cost of their own lives. Angel explains as much to Lindsey McDonald when he asks him to join them. Lindsey mimics the idea back to Angel after having not really paid attention:

> LINDSEY: Well, you get a little speechy, all right? And I breeze out. I got the Cliff Notes: honor and humanity. Absolute good. I heard it. So here's the plot twist: I'm in ["Not Fade Away" 5.22].

They are doing it for—and this is the Cliff Notes version—honor, humanity, and absolute good. It does not matter to them that they are unlikely to completely change the world and defeat evil. It does not matter that they might all get squashed like bugs. What matters is being 100 percent on the side of honor, humanity, and absolute goodness.

And they do indeed kill the members of the Black Thorn, with many of the heroes surviving. Of course, the end of the series occurs when they have rejoined the field of battle after their initial, limited success, now facing the Senior Partners' response. The final words of the TV series are:

> SPIKE: In terms of a plan?
> ANGEL: We fight.
> SPIKE: Be more specific.
> ANGEL: Well, personally, I kind of want to slay the dragon.... Let's go to work ["Not Fade Away" 5.22].

Their final words before their final battle involves an agreement to just keep fighting the forces of evil until it is all over. Their final fight is futile, even if the ending of the show is quite memorable. Nevertheless, at the end, this fight is their (to use Angel's final word) "work." Their work is no longer to support Wolfram & Hart's role within structural violence, but simply to keep fighting the forces of evil, regardless of whether that fight will change anything.

All That Matters

William Godwin, along with pacifist anarchists, would not agree with Angel's solution of fighting. Godwin denied the appropriateness of violence in general, and of martyrdom in particular. Though he could imagine rare instances where each might be called for, Godwin felt that it was almost always better to use reason, persuasion, and argumentation than to resort to violence or martyrdom. Of the latter, Godwin said, "I had rather convince men by my arguments, than seduce them by my example."[61] The problem, Godwin argued, with martyrdom is that Angel and the rest, by risking their lives to simply hurt Wolfram & Hart, are losing out on the "opportunities for usefulness" in their "future years."[62]

Likewise, Godwin was much more worried about the use of violence, which he felt simply mimics the governmental and other institutions that establish structural violence. He again appealed for the use of reason instead:

> Force has already appeared to be an odious weapon; and, if the use of it be to be regretted in the hands of government, it does not change its nature though wielded by a band of patriots. If the cause we plead be the cause of truth, there is no doubt that by our reasonings, if sufficiently zealous and constant, the same purpose may be effected in a milder and more liberal way.[63]

Godwin would thus implore Angel and his band of collaborators to employ reasoning and argumentation to convince others to the side of justice. After all, evil's source is not primarily in Wolfram & Hart, but lies within the hearts and minds of ordinary humans—especially ones who have been infected by the corrupting influence of a society steeped in structural violence.

While Godwin would not agree with Team Angel's methods in this final scene as they involve a violent form of martyrdom, he would agree with the idea that it is important to form some kind of resistance no matter how entrenched the problem lies within social structures and institutions. Godwin urged that "every man is bound to resist every unjust proceeding on the part of the community."[64] The judge of whether there is such an injustice resides in "the private judgment of the individual."[65] And so Godwin would have definitely expected Angel and his team to do something, no matter how futile the situation may seem.

Godwin's hopeful expectation matches the epiphany that finally brings Angel out of the slump that results from his discovery that Earth is the source of evil in "Reprise" (2.15). In "Epiphany," Angel is talking to Kate, who has attempted to kill herself after she was fired from the LAPD:

> ANGEL: If there's no great glorious end to all this, if ... nothing we do matters ... then all that matters is what we do. Because that's all there is. What we do now, today.... I fought for so long. For redemption, for a reward ... finally, just to beat the other guy, but.... I never got it.
> KATE: And now you do?
> ANGEL: Not all of it. All I want to do is help. I want to help because.... I don't think people should suffer as they do. Because if there is no bigger meaning, then the smallest act of kindness is the greatest thing in the world ["Epiphany" 2.16].

All the way back in Season 2, Angel was figuring it out. While "Reprise" left him feeling dismal about the prospect of stopping evil, he later determined that he did not need to defeat evil. It was sufficient that he did whatever he could for the sake of goodness. It was not about fighting for redemption, rewards, or defeating his enemies. The bigger meaning Angel finds lies in doing good just because it is good.

Angel's revelation is ultimately anarchist. In agreement with Godwin's points, Henry David Thoreau argued that "a people, as well as an individual, must do justice, cost what it may."[66] Anarchists believe that people ought to have freedom, but they also believe that anarchism is founded on people doing the right thing just because it is the right thing. Anarchism has to work this way. The initial challenge of starting up a new society without hierarchy requires quite an uphill battle since it involves dismantling the very structures that shape and organize existing society. Anarchism is not about doing violence and it is not about merely replacing leadership. Instead, it is about a moral awakening that brings people to the realization that society needs to change to combat social injustice and structural violence. Of course, such change is only possible where people act for justice, cost what it may, and pursue small acts of kindness because doing so is the greatest thing in the world.

In order to maintain anarchism, it will be necessary that people continue perfecting their moral senses of justice and their commitment to helping each other. The anarchist society is ultimately founded on solidarity and mutual aid. To see such a picture of anarchism, we will continue examining other works of Joss Whedon, with *Buffy* in particular providing us the most positive and complete depiction of how anarchists recommend we organize communities.

But before we get to that positive message, we still have some further negative social critiques to discuss. In this chapter, we saw how social institutions and structures perpetuate structural violence in ways that cause coercive influence on the members of society. In the next chapter, we will use *Dollhouse* to further that argument. In particular, we will argue that these same social institutions undermine the autonomy and consent of the members of the society. We will learn that autonomy and consent are more easily attained and protected within an anarchist system.

Two

Programmable Slaves
Constrained Freedom in the Dollhouse

The Freedom of Dolls

How free are you? You certainly feel free: you chose your career, the company where you work, the stores where you shop, the house where you live, etc. But Dolls (or Actives, as they are called in the Dollhouse) out on engagements certainly feel just as free. At the end of each engagement, however, they return to the Dollhouse where their apparent freedom turns out to actually be constrained by the seemingly contradictory nature of their time as voluntary slaves. As one woman on the street astutely points out, "There's only one reason someone would volunteer to be a slave: is if they is one already" ("Man on the Street" 1.6).

Of course, *Dollhouse* is just science fiction—a fairy tale. Or is it? *Dollhouse* depicts, through a science fiction lens, the ways in which all of our lives are constrained and limited under the various forces of hierarchy that make up our world in capitalist and statist systems (where "statist" simply refers to any system with a state—that is a central power structure that runs the society). We seem to voluntarily make our own choices, but we constantly choose in ways that benefit the powerful while limiting ourselves. We fall into a career where our job involves making excess profits for bosses and owners that we often despise. When we shop, we buy products that marketing agents have manipulated us into thinking that we must have. We even pay large sums of money to buy homes in areas that are polluted in ways that can hasten our deaths. We think we voluntarily choose to do all of these self-harming actions, but we inhabit systems that manipulate us into enslaving ourselves for others' profits. The only way you volunteer to be a slave is if you are one already.

In the last chapter, we used *Angel* to examine how violence and evil can exist within various social structures and institutions. In this chapter, we use

Dollhouse to examine the various limitations that are imperceptibly placed on individuals' freedom throughout such a society. In other words, *Angel* exhibits structural violence under hierarchy while *Dollhouse* exhibits how structural violence inhibits our freedom. In particular, hierarchy leads to a world where we are all Dolls: serving our corporate and state masters through our labor, our purchases, and our everyday lives.

Dollhouse shows us how many of the ideals that we take for granted are mere illusions. Each Doll began with what seemed to be a consensual agreement. Consent, though, is a substantial moral agreement that can only exist when certain standards are met (the agreement must be free, adequately informed, and competently made). As we see in *Dollhouse,* none of the Dolls are really in a position to consent in this substantial sense. Similarly, in real life, we constantly act under constraints that limit our ability to give meaningful consent. Thus, *Dollhouse* exhibits the limitations of consent while simultaneously calling attention to the significance of needing consent for important life decisions where a person's quality of life and moral standing are at stake.

Freedom, on the other hand, is a vague concept that lacks moral significance without further clarification. Echo, even as a Doll, is usually free while on an engagement, at least to the extent that she makes choices, she pursues those choices, and she is often programmed to like the choices that she is acting upon, yet she is only *free to follow her programming*. A Doll's freedom is necessarily shallow as it depends upon programming that others implanted into her. We all yearn for freedom, but shallow freedom is not what it is cracked up to be.

Autonomy is a morally more substantial ideal that entails that the individual is freely able to act according to standards that they set for themselves. You can say that autonomy is more three-dimensional than freedom. You can say someone is free to pursue a goal without having to judge where that goal came from or who judges whether you have met the goal. To be autonomous, you must freely choose your own goals, freely pursue them, and be free to judge for yourself if you meet your goals. The Dolls cannot have autonomy, by definition, because they act according to programmed standards set by Topher Brink and others like him. The rest of us assume that we have not only freedom, but also autonomy: we set our own standards to live by, then we attempt to live by them, and then we are the ultimate judges of whether we are happy at the end of it all. We judge our lives as happy (things have gone well) when we achieve autonomy by acting according to the standards we set. If you say you want to prioritize family and friendship over work, then you are autonomous and your life goes well if you spend more time on family and friendship than you do on work.

Of course, many of us find ourselves prioritizing the wrong things: our apparent autonomy is compromised by a hierarchal society that pushes us to work too hard, to spend too much money on taxes, to mindlessly keep up with the Kardashians, etc. We end up with little time left for ourselves, our families, and our friends (even though we think these values are more important). Autonomy is problematic for us just as it is for the Dolls: we think we make our own life plans, but social constraints limit the available options, and we find ourselves struggling to live according to standards we would choose were we free to do so.[1] In other words, social constructs and constraints act on us all just as Topher acts on the Dolls.

Anarchists have long noted how these cherished ideals are mere illusions in our hierarchal society. Noam Chomsky, who identifies as an anarchist,[2] has argued that the capitalist and statist systems manipulate and control us in a myriad of ways, such as through state propaganda and corporate public relations. Chomsky explains anarchism by saying, "As far as I can see, it's just the point of view that says that people have the right to be free, and if there are constraints on that freedom then you've got to justify them."[3] As we will see, anarchism is primarily about providing meaningful freedom, which includes the ability to give consent and achieve autonomy. *Dollhouse* and Chomsky's works show how the social systems around us inhibit our ability to give consent or achieve autonomy. Thus, meaningful freedom is largely lost in our contemporary statist and capitalist societies.

Although Echo routinely experiences the constraints on her consent and autonomy under the Dollhouse's hierarchy, she is also repeatedly drawn away from her various social constraints and toward an authentic self that is capable of achieving autonomy. As we see in "Epitaph One" and "Epitaph Two: Return," *Dollhouse* is ultimately Echo's tale of self-discovery that leads her toward autonomy. As we will see, *Dollhouse* is a story of how hierarchy restricts us from being ourselves, but it also suggests the possibility of an anarchist response to this problem.

Blurring the Dotted Line: Consent's Limitations in the Dollhouse

Dollhouse begins with a conversation, around a small conference room table (the kind of table where one might expect to sign an important contract—the table includes tea cups, a teapot, a pen, and paper, which appears to be the contract) between Adelle DeWitt, who runs the Los Angeles Dollhouse, and Caroline Farrell, who will become the Doll, Echo. Here is part of their conversation:

> ADELLE: Are you volunteering...?
> CAROLINE: I don't have a choice, do I? How did it get this far?

ADELLE: Caroline, actions have consequences.
...
CAROLINE: I don't deserve this. I was just trying to make a difference, trying to take my place in the world, you know, like she always said, and now I'm.... I know.... I know. Actions have consequences.
ADELLE: What if they didn't? ["Ghost" 1.1]

Consent is a routine, but morally significant part of all of our lives. Consent is a special type of agreement that alters the moral relations between individuals.[4] When two people make a consensual agreement, they gain new moral obligations and rights. If I consent to wash your car on Tuesday in exchange for payment today, then you have a right to have your car washed on Tuesday, just as I have an obligation to wash it. Both the right and the obligation are created by the consensual act. If Caroline consents to become a Doll for Adelle, then she gives Adelle the right to use Caroline's body for five years and, in exchange, Caroline has mistakes from her past erased and receives whatever money her body earns in that five years. Of course, without Caroline's consent, Adelle cannot have any moral rights to control Caroline's body.

Since consent is so morally important—it creates new moral rights and obligations after all—not just any agreement can count as consensual. *Dollhouse* exhibits how there can be illusions of consent when agreements do not seem to be substantial enough to make moral transformations. Only free, adequately informed, and competent agreements can count as consensual,[5] yet is Caroline free to not agree? As numerous scholars note, Adelle manipulates Caroline's agreement, which would challenge the freedom required to consent.[6] In fact, Caroline would agree with these Whedon scholars: she exclaims that she doesn't have a choice. She is sardonic when she suggests, in that same conversation, that Adelle is "just looking out for [Caroline]" ("Ghost" 1.1).[7] Adelle is pressuring and coercing her into agreeing, and so Caroline's agreement is not free. Nor is it clear that she is adequately informed since we have yet to see Adelle explain the deal to her. Perhaps Caroline is competent, though she will certainly have her competency compromised once she becomes a Doll: she will lack any competency to judge any future violations of the agreement, which certainly problematizes her current ability to consent.

Even if Adelle's manipulations endanger consent, she is still offering Caroline an intriguing deal. As Valerie Estelle Frankel notes, Adelle is offering Caroline the ultimate fantasy of escaping responsibility and of "retreating to the simplicity of childhood."[8] In an interview, Whedon himself notes that this arrangement—becoming a doll—is both "a nightmare and a fantasy. The nightmare is, I have no will. And the fantasy is, I have no responsibility or memory of what I've done."[9] In other words, Adelle is asking Caroline to relinquish her freedom for five years so that Caroline can later have freedom that is unrestrained by the guilty conscience for what she has done in the past. This point is noteworthy because consent is by its very nature a trade-off of freedoms. Even when I consent to wash your car on Tuesday, I have thereby limited my Tuesday freedom in exchange for the freedom that your cash will buy me. While our first look suggests that Caroline's agreement is not consensual, we will further analyze their deal later (when we examine the consent of all the Dolls) to confirm this initial view. Before that, it will be useful to explore why consent is morally important.

Consent is an important part of pulling our societies together. Consent entails a social type of freedom. We all have certain freedoms of our own as individuals without having to consent to anything, yet humans are limited creatures, and we can accomplish very little by ourselves. Instead, we must gain assistance from others, which is secured through their consent. Thus, we limit ourselves as individuals through our consent so that we can gain help from others through their consent. Consent typically then involves a voluntary exchange of freedom: you give up some of your individual freedom to another person to gain some more social freedom through that person's assistance. Consent then is a necessary and positive part of life: we become closer as a society and find assistance for the pursuit of our more complex goals through various iterations of consenting with other people. When consent works well, society becomes more interconnected and individuals become freer in meaningful and positive ways.

There is room for difficulty, however. We often think that we have achieved consent when we have not met the necessary standards. While it is good and necessary that we give up certain kinds of freedom in exchange for other kinds of freedom, there are large parts of life where people are attempting to trick you out of your freedom without giving up much or any of their freedom in exchange. For example, the Dollhouse is asking people to give up five years of their lives in exchange for payment at the end of the five years. The Dollhouse asks them to give up their total freedom for those five years—as scholar Sherry Ginn notes, their bodies will lie entirely under Dollhouse control[10]—in exchange for whatever freedom is offered through large sums of money when they leave. The question is whether you can consent to giving up *all your freedom* for five years in exchange merely for money.

Of course, we are all used to giving up freedom of time and control over our bodies in exchange for whatever freedom money buys—that is just what it means to take a job—yet we also are all familiar with exchanges where we give up freedom of time and control over our bodies in exchange for money, but where we know the money is not worth it. Consider any job where you realize after you start that you were lied to, tricked, or where you just realize that there is no way the demands of the job are worth the salary. And quite often in those situations, it just isn't feasible to just quit (because you don't have another job lined up, you have responsibilities that must be met, you signed a contract that limits your freedom to leave without new problems, etc.). That is why we can all identify with the Dolls, none of whose agreements appear to be consensual.

Returning to *Dollhouse*, the lack of consent from the Dolls exhibits how we all take deals that appear to be consensual but that fail to meet the requirements that allow consent to be morally transformative. As another scholar, Tami Anderson, notes, Adelle tangles bait "in front of desperate people."[11] We see this problem in each Doll's supposedly consensual agreement.[12] Let's return to Caroline/Echo's case, which we have already seen is fraught with problems. Caroline was previously a political activist who suspected, correctly, that the Rossum Corporation was engaged in animal abuse ("Echoes" 1.7). Of course, as Caroline and her boyfriend Leo learn, Rossum is not just experimenting on animals, but on humans as well, as Rossum is developing the Dollhouse ("Echoes" 1.7). After Leo is killed trying to flee Rossum, Caroline becomes intent on destroying Rossum—reaching the extreme of setting bombs in the building. Thus, it is because Caroline is guilty of a serious crime that Rossum can place her in a position where she necessarily prefers becoming a Doll rather than facing prison. As Sharon Sutherland and Sarah Swan explain, "the Dollhouse uses its power, and Caroline's desire to escape legal, emotional, and moral responsibility for what has occurred, to motivate her to enter into the transaction."[13]

Adelle is thus engineering Caroline's agreement and, thereby, ensuring that it doesn't count as consent since a manipulated agreement does not create a moral transformation where Adelle would have the *right* to control Caroline's body. Caroline does not feel free to turn down the Dollhouse's offer and the freedom to turn down the offer is an essential requirement for consent.[14] Consent means you are, by your agreement, purposely creating a new moral obligation for yourself. Consent has to be understood as a very intentional act: you are morally obligated after you consent because you purposely meant to create the new moral obligation through consent. Caroline's agreement may be a strategic one for her situation, and there may also be good, pragmatic reasons for her to stick to her word, yet if Caroline does not feel free to turn down the offer, then she is not attempting to purposely create a moral obligation for herself. And without that freedom, she does not consent.

As Sutherland and Swan point out, Echo (who is in some sense Caroline's later self, though we will later discuss how she also is not really Caroline) "recognizes that such a bargain is unconscionable and cannot be morally binding."[15] Sutherland and Swan argue that this position is correct because "one simply cannot alienate one's personhood, contract or no contract."[16] In other words, no matter how pragmatically good the deal was, it was not a deal that anyone could accept since it involved enslavement, even if a temporary one. Since one cannot become morally obligated to accept that they are someone's slaves, Caroline cannot consent to the deal in question.[17] Still, Caroline is trying to get the best agreement she can, so it is a deal she is willing to accept, given her difficult situation, but that is not enough to make it consent. We can say that Caroline has made a pragmatic agreement, and she may have prudential reasons to keep it, but she has not consented since Adelle manipulated her, left her unfree to refuse, and is asking for something (temporary enslavement) that Caroline simply cannot consent to give.

We learn that Alpha's deal is similar to Caroline's: in Alpha's original life as Carl William Craft, he agrees to become a Doll to avoid prison time for kidnapping and attempted murder, so his deal similarly lacks sufficient freedom to amount to consent. Sierra (originally Priya Tsetsang) makes no agreement, and is kidnapped into the Dollhouse against her will so that Nolan Kinnard can repeatedly rape her ("Belonging" 2.4). Sierra clearly does not consent.[18] Most Dolls appear briefly on the show and do not have backstories as, unfortunately, *Dollhouse* only lasted for two seasons. Among the major characters, we do not learn how Whiskey (whose original identity is unknown) becomes a Doll, so we cannot examine her agreement. That leaves two other major characters whose stories we do know: Victor and November. We will argue that competency is compromised in both of their cases, and so neither consents.[19]

Victor and November both join the Dollhouse in exchange for the removal of severely painful memories. Victor, who was originally Anthony Ceccoli, suffered from posttraumatic stress disorder from the war in Afghanistan, and the Dollhouse cures him of his PTSD in exchange for his five years of usage ("Stop-Loss" 2.9). November, originally Madeline Costley, chose to join the Dollhouse in exchange for the removal of her grief after her baby daughter died ("Needs" 1.8). Competency is another significant requirement for consent as people who are not competent to make an agreement, due to being intoxicated, too young, or incapacitated, cannot purposely take on new moral obligations.[20] After all, if you cannot think straight or make clearheaded decisions, then you cannot be intentionally taking on new moral obligations.

While we usually think of something like drugs as undermining the competency required for consent, it is important to see how highly charged emotional states can likewise undermine consent. Topher explains Victor's situation as Victor's contract is ending: "Afghanistan war vet, severe PTSD, which we cured. This one actually makes me feel good about myself" ("Stop-Loss" 2.9). Victor is meant to be one of the rare positive stories from the Dollhouse, and then, as Boyd Langton checks him out, he concludes, "Congratulations, Mr. Ceccoli, you're a free man" ("Stop-Loss" 2.9). Thus, in the exchange, Victor receives a cure for his PTSD, a large sum of money, and whatever freedom that money can buy. All he had to give up was the five-year use of his body, though without being burdened with any memory of that usage.

Of course, the deal is not as good as it sounds. As Anderson notes, when "any of the people we came to know as Dolls, chose to sit out their own stories for a while, they left behind their unique and exclusive physical selves, abandoned to the mercies of the Dollhouse, denied access to their original stories, and blocked from developing new ones."[21] While the trade may seem like a good deal at first, further reflection reveals the horrors lying underneath the exchange. After all, like most Dolls—and as the astute audience realizes as soon as we hear about the show—Victor's body is being prostituted while he is in the employ of the Dollhouse, which is described by Whedon as "kind of a combination human trafficking/whorehouse/corporate fulfillment center."[22] As such, Victor is repeatedly given out to Adelle, who runs the L.A. Dollhouse, for her sexual enjoyment.[23] Right before he is given his freedom, Adelle explains to him, "You're not real. You're a Doll. One whose contract is up, and I was just getting in one last go round before they release your body into the wild" ("Stop-Loss" 2.9). Adelle treats Victor as just a programmable body, and as Sutherland and Swann put it, as an object for the "purposes of her own pleasure."[24] While he may not remember being made to have sex unwillingly, it is fairly well accepted now (and always should have been) that non-consensual sex is not made acceptable because the victim does not remember what happened.[25]

Of course, Victor agreed to give over the use of his body, and it was reasonable for him to assume that it would be used sexually, most likely in ways that he couldn't even imagine in advance. It is precisely because this agreement may have appeared to be a good deal (he did agree after all) that it seems like it could count as consensual, yet at the same time, given how invasive the uses of his body will be, it must be asked what would make someone agree to such a deal. We can only imagine that Victor's PTSD was so horrible that he would do anything to receive a cure. This kind of emotional state of mind—where someone would do anything—questions whether the agreement is made competently. Victor is not intentionally taking on new moral obligations to have his body used in whatever sexual way that Adelle and certainly many others can imagine. He is desperately attempting to escape his PTSD. Since consent is meant to capture an agent's rational decision to take on new moral obligations, it should be calmly made. It should not be made under the emotional pressure that results from someone being desperate to escape the psychological pain of PTSD. As academics Renee St. Louis and Miriam Riggs note, pain as the source for choice can be quite problematic.[26] Since Victor would do anything to get away from his

PTSD, his agreement to enter the Dollhouse should not count as consensual.

Someone might object that there may be good reasons to count desperate, emotional agreements as consensual. We can easily imagine cases where someone is overly emotional, desperate, and must buy something to help them out of their situation: a car to get to work, medicine for a disease, a home to live in, etc. While that's certainly a good reason to count such an agreement as valid, it is not the case that all valid agreements need to count as consensual. We might have reasons to have a system that counts desperate agreements as valid: you are desperate for a car, you should be able to buy the car, and now you will be expected to pay for the car. The reason you must pay for the car is because the system of car buying happens to work that way. The moral obligation to pay does not derive from consent because the person who bought the car was not able to rationally decide what to do without facing significant emotional pressure. The desperate person cannot consent in serious matters because they are not given the opportunity to calmly reason about and weigh out their options, yet a given system may enforce valid, nonconsensual agreements to make the system work: if people can get out of paying for cars because they desperately need them, then the car buying system breaks down. We can say it counts as a valid agreement, based on the system in which it occurs, but the desperate person did not consent since they felt pressured into the agreement.

Note well: an anarchist system attempts to avoid these kinds of pressured situations. If property is distributed based on need, as opposed to being controlled and distributed based solely on wealth, then someone desperate for a car would get a car. The point of an anarchist system is to ensure that people are not routinely pressured into agreements based on the system producing and then exploiting pressure. That is not to say that there would not be desperation or other strong emotions in an anarchist system. It is to say that the anarchist system attempts to be responsive to people's needs, as opposed to being primarily responsive to their money or lack thereof. Thus, when someone agrees under anarchism, there is more reason to believe that their agreement is consensual.

Of course, it also matters how much is at stake. It is easier to consent to lend someone a pen than it is to consent to becoming a sex slave for five years. Consent involves the purposeful creation of new moral obligations. As Sutherland and Swan note, the contract that the Dolls are asked to sign is meant to make them *feel* that they have a moral obligation to the Dollhouse (though Sutherland and Swan doubt there is any real moral obligation here).[27] The standards that must be met for an agreement to be consensual must be roughly as strong as the resulting moral obligation is meant to be. If you ask me for a pen, my consent obligates me to provide the pen, which is not a big deal and so my pen consent is easy to come by, yet Victor is agreeing to give up his body, which will be used in potentially unspeakable manners and put at enough risk that he may not survive the five years. Since so much is at stake, an overly emotional or desperate agreement cannot be consensual. One can wonder whether any calm, perfectly reasonable person could agree to become a Doll for five years, and that may explain why none of the Dolls on the show appear to agree in a completely free and competent manner.

That brings us to November, whose situation is quite similar to Victor's. November becomes a Doll in exchange for giving up the misery she experienced when she lost her baby. Obviously, she would have been in a great amount of emotional pain. Like with Victor, November is surely desperate to rid herself of the grief and misery that she experiences. Like Victor, November would surely do anything to get away from the suffering, so we should likewise proclaim that November couldn't really consent to becoming a Doll. After being released from her contract, November testifies to the Senate, "Three years of my life are gone—stolen by the Dollhouse. They preyed on me when I was at my weakest and forced me to…. And forced me to do things, things I never would have believed, until Senator Perrin showed me evidence. I almost wish I hadn't seen it, but then I wouldn't be here" ("The Public Eye" 2.5). November is right on all of these points: she lost three years of her life, the Dollhouse preyed on her when she was at her weakest, and it probably would have been better if she had not learned the things she was forced to do while working as a Doll. Unfortunately, the Dolls can have their memories removed, but they cannot be guaranteed that they will not find out what happened, that they will not wonder what happened, and that they will not regret their pressured agreements.

All the Dolls, then, lack consent in their agreements with the Dollhouse. They all only agree under tremendous pressure, whether because the Dollhouse has some threat to hold over them or because they are going through emotionally trying times. Of course, as we stated at the beginning, *Dollhouse* is science fiction. These issues still matter, however, because we all face pressure and must make difficult decisions about key matters throughout our lives. And these decisions are pressured, manipulated, and managed by substantial powers that exhibit control over our lives, all of which *Dollhouse* depicts in a science fiction way.

Before showing how these issues play out in real life, it is worth pointing to the most purely science fiction problem with the Doll agreement. When someone agrees to become a Doll, Topher downloads their personality and puts it in storage. During the five-year job, Topher then implants the Doll with the various personalities that are needed for each of their individual engagements. At the end of the five years, Topher then uploads the original personality.[28] Of course, at that point, the uploaded, original personality is simply another implant. While acting as Dolls, the Actives operate under computer programs that fit the engagement they are fulfilling. But when they complete their five years, the return of "their" personality is just another computer program. Their brain was entirely wiped at the beginning of their time being a Doll, and the only truly human personality—the one that they had from birth until their Doll agreement—is destroyed forever. They will, from then on, only have computer personalities, and will never again be fully human (where what it means to be human, at least in part, surely includes not having a computer program running your mind), so, in a significant way, the human person *dies* when they start work at the Dollhouse. An identical simulation will replace them at the end of the five years, but that simulation is at best a computer program version of their original mind. The agreement to become a Doll is essentially an agreement to kill off your human self and to live the rest of your life as a computer program. Obviously, the Dollhouse is not informing the Dolls of this irrevocable and lethal aspect of their agreements, and so the Doll agreement is never adequately informed. And clearly, being adequately informed is a key consent requirement.[29] Of course, this problem is a product of science fiction and likely does not correspond to similar consent issues in real life, so we will not be discussing it as we examine parallels between consent in the Dollhouse and in real life.

The Dolls' agreements are neither free, adequately informed, nor competent. As we will see, we face similar limitations (though with less science fiction involved) in our actual lives. To see the real-world issues that are highlighted by *Dollhouse*, it will be useful to study the works of Noam Chomsky (1928–). Chomsky is an American linguist, philosopher, activist, and anarchist. He is professor emeritus at the Massachusetts Institute of Technology and laureate professor at the University of Arizona.

To emphasize how our consent is undermined in contemporary, capitalist society, anarchist Noam Chomsky entitles one of his most famous books, written with Edward S. Herman, *Manufacturing Consent: The Political Economy of the Mass Media*. The phrase "manufacturing consent" is clearly contradictory, which emphasizes that what we take to be instances of consent in our normal, everyday lives are in fact mere agreements manufactured in large part by the mass media. In particular, Herman and Chomsky argue that "the media serve, and propagandize on behalf of, the powerful societal interests that control and finance them."[30] In other words, they argue that the media are neither neutral nor unbiased presenters of information, but are instead arms of propaganda that present information in a way that serves the interests of the powerful people who run society, such as the governmental leaders of the state and the capitalist leaders of powerful corporations.

As Herman and Chomsky explain, "The mass media serve as a system for communicating messages and symbols to the general populace. It is their function to amuse, entertain, and inform, and to inculcate individuals with the values, beliefs, and codes of behavior that will integrate them into the institutional structures of the larger society."[31] We saw in the previous chapter on *Angel* that we all unavoidably inhabit and act within various social structures and institutions. Here we see that the media provide everyone with the mental tools (values, beliefs, etc.) that in turn lead to individuals supporting those institutions. We live in a society where we are often unsurprised when corporations do horrible things—the Rossum Corporation's abusive animal experimentation is hardly fictional. On the other hand, when the United States Supreme Court grants corporations rights, such as through the *Citizens United* or *Hobby Lobby* decisions, the people do not take to the streets, protesting in either anger or even selfishly as their personal rights are diminished by the granting of competing rights to corporations. What explains this apparent tension? According to Herman and Chomsky, the media present a complex picture that, while allowing for some corporate malfeasance, reassures the public that corporate and state interests should be valued and endorsed. They do this in part by feeding into our "overwhelming wish to think well of ourselves, our institutions, and our leaders. We see ourselves as basically good and decent in personal life, so it must be that our institutions function in accordance with the same benevolent intent."[32] But Herman and Chomsky argue that this inference is unwarranted: the corporations act according to profit motives, and what's profitable does not depend on what's morally acceptable. And, of course, the allegedly "free" media play this propaganda role not because they are forced to, but because the media are corporate: "In essence, the private media are major corporations selling a product (readers and audiences) to other businesses (advertisers)."[33] The media are primarily interested in serving corporate interests because both the media companies and their primary clientele are themselves corporations.

The media's influence on us can lead us to make agreements that we assume are consensual, but that are in fact manipulated and/or pressured. While Herman and Chomsky are quite interested in propaganda on behalf of the state, such as to support unjust wars, the media's manufacture of consent is quite pervasive in everyday life. Theorist Christopher Souza notes this comparison between *Dollhouse*'s undue influence and what we face in real life when he notes that "we too follow certain social norms and practices without consciously thinking about them."[34] Every time we buy a candy bar, choose a restaurant, or purchase clothing, our agreements have already been influenced by a variety of powerful marketing techniques. As previously stated, where not much is at stake, consent standards are easily met. Nonetheless, large purchases in life can be quite meaningful since we all have limited funds to live by. In those cases, marketing can be quite problematic. It is not controversial to point out that marketing will often try to use fear, sexuality, and even desperation to enhance our desire for certain products. At a certain point, there will be enough money on the line that making the purchase will have a significant impact on the buyer's life, while there will also be enough pressure that the person will not feel entirely free to turn down making the purchase.

Let's consider an example. Imagine an advertising campaign for cars that makes viewers feel that their children's safety is at risk in less expensive cars. Imagine that the salesperson plays on this fear once the potential buyer shows up to consider buying the allegedly safer car. While we are clearly not fully replicating the Dolls' agreements, we can easily imagine real life scenarios that exhibit related concerns: high emotions, pressure, and a lot at stake. *Dollhouse* makes us concerned for the Dolls—we the audience do not really think they are consenting. The more typical case, such as someone feeling pressured into buying an expensive car through a fear-based marketing campaign, does not typically concern us as much. But this discrepancy is because the media have normalized the more typical car case. *Dollhouse* can help us problematize that media-based normalization. As Tami Anderson reminds us, "*Dollhouse* is a warning to all of us that at any time it can be so easy to give up control of our own identities."[35] Of course, it is not just our identities at stake, but also our agreements to act in various ways where these agreements have been pressured and manipulated by expert marketers and advertisers (who are standing in for Adelle in her manipulation of the Dolls).

Dollhouse shows us that consent is much more difficult to obtain than is usually assumed. Consent requires that both parties are genuinely free to turn the offer down, are adequately informed, and are competent to make a significant agreement. The Doll agreement is perhaps so horrific that no one could reasonably consent to it. This possibility is alluded to through the fact that none of the Dolls on the show whose stories are explored count as providing meaningful consent. Echo and Alpha feel like they have no choice because the other option is prison. Victor and November feel like they have no other choice because they are desperate to escape their pain. Further, none of them really understand that the Dollhouse ends their human lives and only offers computer programs in return.

Through Herman and Chomsky, we have seen that consent is similarly manufactured in real life. The media present information in a way that supports the development of a value system that serves the interests of the powerful. Just as the Dolls are pressured into joining the Dollhouse, we all experience various pressures when signing contracts or making large purchases.[36] We also saw that consent was a key path toward freedom as we need to make consensual deals to obtain necessary assistance for our larger life projects. In the next section, we turn to those larger life projects and the attempt to develop them autonomously. *Dollhouse* similarly shows us that autonomy can often be illusory: we think that we are developing our own selves, but we are instead subject to a variety of constraints that keep us under significant external influence, just like the Dolls.

Survival Fantasies and Assigned Autonomy

As a Doll goes on an engagement, they are often programmed to believe they are living their dream. For example, in "The Target" (1.2), an outdoorsman rents out Echo, who is programmed to be an avid outdoorswoman herself. Until the client turns out to be a killer who wishes to hunt Echo, Echo is programmed to have the time of her life while hiking, mountain climbing, etc. Even when the Dolls are sexually active, Topher programs them to be thrilled by the sexual activity in question, whatever it may be. The Dolls are often on engagements that allow them to have a fun time, insofar as they are programmed to have the values that perfectly match whatever it is they will be doing.

In a fairly peculiar way, the Dolls have something on the rest of us: their deepest and strongest values consistently match the very activities that they perform on a regular basis. We all have various hopes and dreams. In many cases, we are likely to think of our life plans as fantasies more than as realistic goals, such as when people say their life plan is to win the lottery or play in the Super Bowl. Most of us spend the majority of our lives either sleeping or at work, and very few people think of their jobs as fulfilling their life desires. For most people, their deepest life values and their actions do not match, which suggests that they will find autonomy hard to come by.

Philosophers provide so many distinct meanings for "autonomy" that it quickly becomes overwhelming.[37] It is more useful to concentrate on a basic, core meaning that fits across most autonomy accounts. Autonomy is an ideal met by an agent who rationally figures out, in some sense, her own life values, and then she finds ways to live up to those values. No one can create values out of nothing, and so autonomy does not require that.[38] Instead, autonomy simply involves rationally reflecting on your own life, what you want to do with your life, and then living accordingly.

As noted earlier, the reason we care about autonomy is that it is more meaningful than mere freedom. Freedom involves the ability to act. Even when suffering through solitary confinement in prison, you are literally *free* to bang your head on the wall. We are free to do anything that we are able to do. We are not free to fly using only our bodies, but we are free to jump off a cliff. Being free then is not necessarily good. Whether freedom is good or bad depends on whether the action is good or bad. But determining the value of the action raises the question: who decides which actions are good?

For autonomy, the answer is that you decide for yourself. Thus, autonomy is a meaningful type of freedom where you are free to act in the way that you believe is best for yourself, after having put some rational thought into it.

Autonomy then has two parts. The first part is determining according to which values you wish to live your life. These values will have to derive from the values that are all around you since you have to discover them before you can adopt them, so you get values from your parents and family, your friends and acquaintances, the media (as we saw previously), and various other sources. It is up to you though which values you want to treat as the most important ones for you. And you can then organize your life around those values. The second part, once you have those values figured out, is to act accordingly. The autonomous person knows what she values in life and she goes out and achieves her values through her actions.

The Dolls then accomplish the second part of autonomy (they act according to their values) without coming anywhere near the first part (they don't at all shape or endorse their values to begin with). In real life, both parts can be challenging; in terms of having limited autonomy—and as Rhonda Wilcox notes—we are all Dolls to a certain extent.[39] As we indicated previously, it can be very difficult for most people to achieve autonomy while at work since your job is largely a place where you do what you are told without any sense that your values match your company's values.[40] Of course, many people autonomously choose to work at jobs that they do not love because those jobs pay them enough money, which can be used to assist them with the activities that they truly love. At least, that's an available way to make sense of spending too much time at a job that you hate.

Anarchism offers a more direct path: allow laborers to determine and direct their own jobs. As Chomsky says, "I think that the economic institutions ought to be run democratically—by their participants, and by the communities in which they live."[41] At the very least, in such a society the workers would be able to determine for themselves the best way for the work to be done. There would be much more opportunity for autonomy if the workers could autonomously determine how they did their jobs. The freedom to shape and choose one's work lies at the core of anarchism, and, in turn, the lack of freedom at work under capitalism highlights the difficulty (though not impossibility) of finding autonomy under capitalism. Chomsky explains that freedom under capitalism is a bit of a joke: "if capital is privately controlled, then people are going to have to rent themselves in order to survive. Now you can say, 'they rent themselves freely, it's a free contract'—but that's a joke. If your choice is, 'do what I tell you or starve,' that's not a choice—it's in fact what was commonly referred to as wage slavery."[42] Chomsky's description of the joke of freedom under capitalism of course sounds a lot like what the Dolls are experiencing: they are free, but only after they have rented themselves out to Rossum. Like the Dolls, we struggle under capitalism to find autonomy because we must take jobs to survive, and many of us must take jobs that do not match the values we set for our lives. Sometimes this point is moral such as when we take a job where we feel we must engage in immoral activities. Often though the point is simply prudential: suppose we autonomously set our life values around developing our intellectual capacities, but then our job requires eight to ten hours a day of mindless data entry. We would not be living autonomously because most of our time awake is spent doing things that do not match our values.

Under anarchism, laborers are free to produce in the way that they feel is best since there is no hierarchy to tell people what to do. Under capitalism, laborers are put into a position where they must work as others (the capitalists) order them to, which inhibits their autonomy. It can be argued that the latter system is going to be more efficient and more productive. If people figure out how they should work on their own, they may not produce as much stuff, prioritizing their family lives, leisure time, friends, or personal hobbies. If you can order people to produce with the threat that they will not acquire the money they need to survive, you will most likely get more stuff out of their labor. Even though it is clear that a hierarchal system, with coerced production, will be more efficient at producing stuff, Chomsky questions whether we ought to prioritize having more stuff: "maybe it's a good thing that there wouldn't be the same drive to produce. People have to be driven to have certain wants in our system—why? Why not leave them alone so they can just be happy, do other things?"[43] In other words, capitalism is a better system for producing stuff, including a lot of stuff that no one needs, but Chomsky is open to the possibility that we should prioritize a system where the people can be autonomous and choose how they wish to work, even if that means we live in a society that has less stuff. Anarchism would produce less stuff but more autonomy, and Chomsky thinks that maybe that's a good thing.

That transitions us to where our values come from. Chomsky argues that our prioritizing of more stuff over the autonomy of laborers may be something that we should question. Where, then, does the value for stuff come from? To be autonomous, your values should be your own. That means that you realize where your values came from and are happy to endorse and pursue them. You rationally determine what's important to you and those determinations set your autonomous values. Of course, that is not always easy to do since so many of our values derive from sources outside of our control, such as the media. And those values may not be ones we would autonomously endorse were we to have the time to rationally reflect over them. However, who has the time?

We all obtain values from external sources, and we often do not reflect over whether we should endorse those values. In that respect, we are once again like the Dolls: the Dolls' programming is representative of how we at times imperceptibly receive our own values from external sources without even realizing it and often without ever questioning these values. When looking at consent, we saw that Edward Herman and Noam Chomsky argued that the mass media pressure us to agree to things that we would not independently agree to. Similarly, Chomsky argues that our very values come from the media in ways that may inhibit our autonomy. In his book *Necessary Illusions: Thought Control in Democratic Societies*, Chomsky advances the ideas he developed with Herman in *Manufacturing Consent*. Chomsky states that his book is interested in, "thought control, as conducted through the agency of the national media and related elements of the elite intellectual culture."[44] Chomsky argues that the media and intellectual culture work together to produce values within the populace—in particular, they produce values that support the power structure in command. Thus, we receive values that conflict with our autonomy insofar as they align with the interests of the powerful as opposed to our own interests.

As an example, Chomsky argues that the media promote a "culture of narcissism," where people are convinced that selfishness is good, and that they need not be overly concerned with helping others.[45] Chomsky states that this narcissism is promoted to young people in particular: "every person may know, in private, that the assumptions are not true for them, but at a time of life when one is insecure about personal identity and social place, it is all too tempting to adapt to what the propaganda system asserts to be the norm."[46] The culture of narcissism promotes people only looking out for themselves and their paychecks. And that in turn allows these narcissists to ignore how their jobs may lead them to do bad deeds that hurt others. And that is how the powerful want it since they want to be able to have people perform immoral tasks at work, such as landlords who put collecting the rent over giving breaks to struggling tenants to make ends meet or health insurance workers who attempt to save money by turning down expensive but medically necessary services. Of course, the landlord may not own the building and may live next door to the person who is struggling, and perhaps they would prefer to autonomously help their neighbor if they had not bought into the culture of narcissism. And the health insurance worker perhaps would prefer to help patients in need if they too were not being a narcissist. The narcissism undermines workers' autonomy so that they do what's best for their bosses while feeling like they are merely prioritizing their own paychecks.

The best example of this kind of narcissism is Topher Brink, the scientist who programs and operates the Dolls. Topher's seeming amorality is on display through much of the early episodes of *Dollhouse*. In fact, Andrew Zimmerman Jones argues that Topher is the only character to never show any empathy toward the Dolls in the first season.[47] Consider this exchange between Topher and Boyd after one of Echo's sexual engagements:

TOPHER: We gave two people a perfect weekend together. We're great humanitarians.
BOYD: Who would spend their lives in jail if anyone ever found this place.
TOPHER: We're also misunderstood, which great humanitarians often are. Look at Echo: not a care in the world; she's living the dream.
BOYD: Whose dream? ["Ghost" 1.1].

Echo's lack of autonomy is at center stage in this exchange. Nonetheless, Topher is not at all concerned since her actions meet the values that he programmed into her. As long as Echo *thinks* things are good, then they are good, and Topher decides what she is to think. Boyd is clearly more concerned about Echo supposedly living the dream since it is clearly not a dream she chose. While their exchange references Echo's lack of autonomy, it is important that Topher is allowing his evil vocation to shade his moral thinking: Topher simply rationalizes that what he is doing because Echo is programmed to like what she does. Topher has bought into the culture of narcissism, which allows him to ignore what he is doing to Echo and the other Dolls.

Further, Topher rationalizes this point to such an extent that he is only half-joking when he considers himself a humanitarian. Topher's rationalizations allow him to adopt a narcissistic attitude that lets him avoid serious thoughts about morality, especially while on the job. From the corporate perspective, this mindset is ideal: many good people perform bad deeds while at work.[48] As Adelle explains about Topher, "The cold reality is that everyone here was chosen because their morals have been compromised in some way. Everyone, except you. You, Topher, were chosen because you had no morals. You have always thought of people as playthings" ("Belonging" 2.4). Topher's narcissism has blinded him to his actual moral duty, which is exactly why the powerful wish for people to become more narcissistic: Topher is just doing his job and earning his paycheck—what his employers do with his labor is not his concern.

Of course, many people have jobs, such as the makers of weapons of mass destruction or people who contribute to environmental destruction through their jobs, that require us to do bad things that we normally would not do. The way we get through the job is often by ignoring the negative results of our labor. Perhaps we minimize what we contribute: no single person causes global warming through their job. Perhaps we tell ourselves—sometimes quite truthfully—that we must do our jobs to keep feeding our families. And once we decide we have to keep our jobs, we tend to invest our work time in doing them well. As Adelle explains to Boyd, "You work for Rossum, and that means your options tend to slim to three: carry out Rossum's work without question, the Attic, or death. The moment you stepped into this house, you, in effect, gave us your life, and you must decide if that life is to be put to good use or laid to waste" ("The Attic" 2.10). Unfortunately, that is how too many people feel about their jobs. Often the best way out is to embrace narcissism through rationalization: if you have to do harmful work, it will be easier to digest if you can rationalize it as somehow a humanitarian necessity.

This narcissism is enhanced in the Dollhouse because, as Tami Anderson argues, the higher up employees, such as Adelle and Topher, are blinded from even seeing the Dolls as humans.[49] Seeing the Dolls as humans would make the work much more difficult to perform since it would make Adelle and Topher immediately aware of the morally problematic nature of what they are doing. Ignoring the humanity of the Dolls allows them to excel in the workplace. It also, though, makes morality more difficult to embrace since they do not see the Dolls as having needs for which Adelle and Topher should be morally responsible. Thus, their narcissism and their dehumanizing of the Dolls allows Adelle and Topher to be more effective at their jobs while also being less effective at being moral agents.

Chomsky's point—that the powers that be wish to provide us narcissistic values—is exemplified in Topher, whose lack of morality makes him easily perform evil tasks at work. Thus, the media's manipulation of our values undermines our ability to achieve autonomy, especially when our jobs ask us to do immoral tasks that we normally would not do on our own. That does not mean that autonomy is impossible within a hierarchal society, such as a capitalist one. It does mean that it is harder to come by under hierarchy than it would be under anarchism. While anarchism encourages everyone to flourish according to their own autonomous value systems (at the cost of efficiency and productivity), capitalism hinders autonomy to make more compliant and harder working employees. Even in the latter case, you can always fight to overcome the hindrances to your autonomy that the system puts before you. But the system that you inhabit can either make autonomy easier to come by, as anarchism does, or more difficult to achieve, as capitalism and statism do.

Whedon scholars argue that Topher does grow as a moral person, and maybe as an autonomous agent, as *Dollhouse* develops.[50] While the Dolls, insofar as they are programmed, cannot achieve autonomy as Dolls, other characters on the show, such as Topher, can provide a more hopeful picture as he advances toward achieving a more virtuous character. While there are many moments where Topher's nascent morality starts to mature, two key moments occur when he helps Sierra kill her rapist and after his regretful development of technology that would allow Rossum to program people, presumably without consent, at a distance. Both moments involve Topher being involved in something gravely immoral, which triggers his moral awakening in ways that reveal who he autonomously really is.

As mentioned, Nolan Kinnard, a scientist who assisted with developing the Dollhouse technology, had Priya (Sierra) kidnapped and placed into the Dollhouse where he could repeatedly rape her. And it is entirely appropriate to consider each sexual encounter by Nolan to be a rape even if Sierra is programmed to like them. After all, she did not even make the original agreement, but was instead forced into the Dollhouse for Kinnard's malevolent purposes. Nolan is a serial rapist and kidnapper.

Topher had been told that Priya had joined the Dollhouse because she was being saved from paranoid schizophrenia. Topher later comes to the realization, sparked by Echo, that Priya was in fact kidnapped and forced into the Dollhouse. This realization forces Topher to see that things are much worse at the Dollhouse than he had (unreasonably) assumed. Of course, Topher does not receive a complete awakening from this revelation as his initial response is to send the problem up the hierarchy as if that would solve things. Instead of solving things, the hierarchy returns with orders to hand over Sierra/Priya to her rapist, Nolan, so that he can own her outright. It is when Adelle gives these orders to Topher that she explains that he was hired precisely because he lacks morality, which both seemed like a somewhat fair depiction of Topher up to this moment in the show and is also something that is then falsified by Topher's subsequent actions. Instead of sending Sierra back, as a Doll, he sends Priya to Nolan, enabling her to kill him. Then Topher and Boyd clean up the dead body.

It is significant that Topher starts to regain his sense of self by disobeying orders. If he just goes along with what he is told no matter how bad it is, he is not being autonomous because he is not rationally reflecting on whether this is truly what he wants to do. The orders from up above that attempt to keep Topher doing immoral things for the profit of the Rossum Corporation are hindrances on Topher's autonomy.[51] Thus, Topher can seek out his autonomy by disobeying those orders and attempting to do the right thing because he wants to see himself as a morally good person. Topher's autonomy begins to show as he breaks from the narcissist idea that his actions at work can be separated from their results. Topher makes this break by disobeying his orders so that he can help Priya.

Topher shows his moral compass can point in the right direction by helping Priya. He then works at making things as right as possible by assisting with the clean-up, apologizing, and asking Priya what she wants after it is all over (to which she responds "a beer"). And then when Priya asks him, "Are we happy here?" Topher stutters to respond, "I ... you.... Most of you.... I have no idea" ("Belonging" 2.4). Topher's finally figures out that he has taken for granted the permissibility of his actions: he has no idea what he is doing to the Dolls. It was not that he was morally bankrupt, as Adelle suggested, but that he assumed he was not doing anything evil at work because that made it easier for him to excel at his job and take home a large paycheck—something that many people have to do, even if their paychecks are not really that large. Prior to the point where he helps Priya, Topher has not even started the process toward autonomy—he has no idea really by what values he should guide his life. But once the gravity of what Rossum is asking Topher to do hits him, Topher starts to ask the questions that he has to answer to work toward being autonomous. Is Topher helping the Dolls? What is his life about if he is hurting the very people whom he is working with? What's Topher's end goal? What are his values?

This experience with Priya/Sierra begins Topher's moral development, and—we would argue—enables him to start becoming autonomous. The problem is that Topher was shutting out an essential part of who he really was—his morality—so that he could fit in better at work. That suggests that it was not the authentic Topher we met in the first season, but a Topher whose values had been warped by a job that required him to be someone else—the amoral Topher. We see who Topher authentically is once he has more information to work with (once he knows what they are really doing at the Dollhouse). And that is when he begins to work against Rossum, regardless of how those actions will push back against him. He is overcoming his safe narcissism that supported the powers that be. We often find out what we autonomously most care about when we are pushed into situations that call for sacrifices. If we decide that we are willing to make the sacrifices, then we must really care.

Topher's moral transformation is further exhibited when he learns that Rossum is trying to develop technology to remotely program people, turning anyone into a Doll. Unfortunately, Topher also tells Adelle that he has figured out how to make the technology work. Andrew Zimmerman Jones argues that Topher cannot stop himself from fixing the tech, "as if he was programmed."[52] Though Topher is growing toward an autonomous embrace of morality, he clearly has already autonomously braced his drive for scientific excellence. It is probably this autonomous drive toward scientific excellence that obscures the fact that he is performing science for nefarious purposes. The Rossum Corporation gives Topher the job and the resources that enable him to do amazing science, and that both supports Topher's autonomy, with respect to the scientific work, and hinders it, since he probably would not autonomously choose to pursue evil with his science. We find out that this tension lies in Topher's values when Adelle hands over Topher's technology to Rossum, which means that Topher's technology will now enable Rossum to wipe every person's brain on the planet and make everyone into Dolls. As Topher later explains, "I'm the one who brings about the thought-pocalypse" (though he also considers the name "brain-pocalypse"—as he states, "I figure, if I'm responsible for the end of the world, I get to name it" ["The Hollow

Men" 2.12]). After Adelle turns over the technology, Topher is, as a moral person, angry about it, and he calls Adelle "the coldest bitch on this planet" ("Meet Jane Doe" 2.7). Adelle responds by slapping Topher and letting him know that, if he knows what is good for him, he "will follow every single one of my commands as if they were your heart's most deep desire" ("Meet Jane Doe" 2.7). Thus, Adelle attempts to push Topher back into being the amoral, obedient, and non-autonomous servant who simply follows orders as if they were his own deepest values.

Topher nonetheless follows his own path. Julie Hawk refers to him as the "sacrificial lamb of humanism," as in the end he autonomously chooses to die to bring an end to the thought-pocalypse.[53] When he prepares an explosion to end Rossum's control over everyone's minds (reverting each person back to their original minds), Adelle realizes that Topher will not survive the explosion he is planning. Topher responds, "Small price to pay.... I didn't want to cause any more pain" ("Epitaph 2: The Return" 2.13). Topher's autonomous choice is to accept the dire consequences of his prior immoral life.

It is important that when he was doing Rossum's bidding, Topher was doing it because he was ordered to and for the paycheck. He did not really think out the situation and was not rationally weighing what he was doing—in fact, he was engaging in self-deception to keep himself from realizing the enormity of the wrongs he was committing at Rossum. He was not autonomous since he was being irrational and engaged in self-deception. Topher becomes autonomous when he decides he is the one who will martyr himself to free everyone else from technology that he invented. Hence, through Topher's moral growth, we see a journey of overcoming narcissism and achieving autonomy.

Dollhouse then provides a plethora of characters who cannot possibly be autonomous, and perhaps a few characters who find their autonomy as they move away from the limitations placed on them by their society. While the Dolls cannot be autonomous because they have their values programmed into them, this representation is unfortunately not purely science fiction. As Anderson notes, "from day one we're influenced by the hopes, dreams, and expectation of other people in regards to who we should become ... there are well intentioned parents and teachers ... friends and lovers ... employers who want to channel our creativity and productivity into something they can sell, the government that monitors us."[54] In other words, we all have much of our value systems derive from sources like daily interactions, television, books, podcasts, news, etc. None of us are beyond external influence, most of us blindly take in these influences, and few of us, even when we know about the media's pervasive influence on our values, stop and reflect rationally on whether we wish to revise our value system. Hopefully none of us are as indebted to our media programming as much as the Dolls are, but we all have a good bit of programming.

As we saw with Topher, it is always possible to overcome one's programming and develop into a new self. Sometimes, this comes through a major life event that forces fresh reflection on our identities. Other times, new people enter our lives, as Echo does for Topher, and urge us to rethink what we believe and do, so autonomy is difficult for any of us, especially under the kind of hierarchal system we live under in a capitalist, statist society. There is, though, hope, and *Dollhouse* gives some glimmers of that hope as we will see by examining Echo's life after she becomes self-aware.

Echoes of Freedom

When Echo becomes self-aware as a Doll she is able to eventually connect to all of her various imprints. She then has to find an authentic self that is not a return back to Caroline, but is instead a new version of who Echo has become. Echo, in a way, achieves her own autonomy, but her autonomy includes a variety of individuals all living in the same body.

Throughout the series, the Dolls/Actives are referred to as being in a state of "tabula rasa," which means they are a blank slate because they have zero personality and are not really persons at all. Oluwafemi Morohunola explains that "in that state, everything that the Actives believed and felt disappeared."[55] St. Louis and Riggs note that as blank slates, the Dolls are innocent, as well as prey to manipulation in their highly suggestible states.[56] Significantly, two Dolls emerge out of these tabula rasa states and become self-aware: Alpha and Echo.

Beginning with Alpha, he is evil through much of the series, which could be related to his original personality as the violent criminal, Carl William Craft.[57] Perhaps the fact that Carl Craft is evil makes it easier for Alpha to overtake his blank slate and become self-aware—maybe his evil proves too powerful for him to stay a blank slate. It also could be that Alpha is simply able to adapt to his composite personality after having all of his 48 personalities imprinted into him at the same time. St. Louis and Riggs argue that "full awareness of all of his imprints does not imbue him with full consciousness, because it doesn't imbue him with a moral code."[58] While we think there is something right about this St. Louis and Riggs view, it is a controversial position to imply that autonomy requires a moral code.[59] We argued that Topher deep down was a moral person and so his autonomy required embracing moral duty—that position sidetracks the debate over whether autonomy generally requires a moral code because we believe that Topher's autonomy in particular does require a moral code. Maybe Carl Craft is not such a moral person, and it would then be controversial whether his autonomy requires a moral code. We will sidestep that issue here.

Regardless, it is clear that Alpha becomes self-aware while he is still evil. For much of the series that we witness as viewers, Alpha is both self-aware and evil, so we do not really know why Alpha becomes self-aware or how his self-awareness relates to his lack of morality. Eventually, Alpha seems to come around and is on Echo's side by "Epitaph Two: Return" (2.13). But this moral transformation also occurs off screen (between the events of the regular episodes and the Epitaph episodes that occur in the future). We know that Alpha becomes self-aware and later becomes moral. Since these key transformations are not explored on the show, Alpha's autonomy is not useful to analyze here.

Of greater interest here is Echo, whose journey of self-realization is depicted on *Dollhouse*. Echo, who is a distinct person from her original existence as Caroline, begins as a complete blank slate, but then grows into a composite personality that includes every person she had to be in her various engagements.[60] Nevertheless, she also is not merely a composite of those programmed personalities; rather, Echo is the central self that organizes and regulates the various personalities within her. As Julie Hawk puts it, while Echo "had a sense of many selves," she also "learned not only to recognize the imprints, but also to manipulate them to her advantage ... she refused to be simply the embodiment of someone else's desire and instead became someone who strove to tear down the structure that allowed this system to remain."[61] In other words, there is an Echo—a unique personality that exists above and beyond the composite of all the personalities within her. Echo is, as Ivy (Topher's assistant) calls her, a kind of superego ("Getting Closer" 2.11), or, as Topher calls her, a "house party that's going on inside your head" ("Getting Closer" 2.11). Echo's unique existence as a distinct person in fact explains why when she wakes up in the attic and is told that they use real names there, she responds, "My real name's Echo" ("The Attic" 2.10).

We also know there is a distinct Echo because Alpha points this fact out when he has captured Paul Ballard. Alpha explains to Paul that Echo has true, non-implanted love for Paul: "Those others, her feelings for them, they were imprinted, manufactured. But what she feels for you, it's different" ("A Love Supreme" 2.8). Consequently, Echo's love for Paul is distinctly hers: it is neither one of her composites, nor something that was merely programmed into her. It is something that the authentic Echo develops and then acts toward. Her love for Paul is one of the things that allows her to develop as an individual with her own life and, really, her own self.

It is worth pausing here to note the parallel between Echo and Spike (from *Buffy* and *Angel*) in this sense. While Angel has his soul forced upon him, Spike actually chooses to regain his soul because he loves Buffy, who he cannot be with while he is evil, so we see in *Buffy* and *Angel* that vampires are driven by a literal bloodlust and their lack of a soul makes them evil, yet it is Spike's choice to break this cycle and to take on a soul of his own, which turns him into a moral agent. Thus, love motivates Spike to find his autonomous and moral self, which didn't exist as such prior to him having a soul.[62] Spike and Echo both represent the power of love to motivate the creation of new selves. Hence, Spike and Echo are both autonomous in this sense since they choose to follow what they value most—the persons they love. We will return to this theme of the power of love when we discuss *Buffy* in chapters five and six.

Like Spike, Echo stands out as a paradigm case of someone who develops themselves in an autonomous fashion. Consider how a child who lacks a personality cannot truly choose their personality because they wouldn't know how (how would you decide whether you want to be introverted or extroverted if you were a child who understood neither idea?) and wouldn't have any basis to make choices or complain if others, such as their parents and teachers, made wrong choices on their behalf (your parents train you to be highly motivated, but later in life you wish you were lazier—such a complaint appears to be less credible when made by a child who would prefer to be lazy but has no idea what is at stake). Most of us reach adulthood and simply find that our early personalities have already been formed. Having a personality, we then, as young adults, develop in various chosen directions, potentially autonomously, after that, so almost all of us have a large part of our personality already formed when we become old enough to start making alterations. Most of us are unable as rational adults to start with a blank slate and carefully form our personality in any way we desire. Most of us have to make up our autonomy with a large amount of our values and our personality already given to us.

Echo, on the other hand, is a rational adult, with all the personality options made available to her through her previous imprints, and she can openly reflect on how she wants to move from blank slate to an autonomous Echo. Of course, even this process is not calm and deliberate for Echo. Obviously a lot is going on and Echo does not have the luxury to just sit down and spend long periods of time deciding who she wants to be. The point though is that Echo is given an opportunity that most of us do not have. There is no dominant personality that pushes Echo in any given direction. Even the Caroline personality appears to Echo as just one of many imprints for her to choose between. Most of us, in contrast, have a dominant personality coming out of childhood. We can change it and mold it, but that childhood personality cannot simply be treated as one out of many options. But Echo is a central mind that can weigh competing options and choose what works best for her. And so when she develops who she wants to be, Echo is making rational choices among a large range of options (in fact, a larger range than most of us are able to choose from since our experiences are more limited than Echo who is going on a wide range of engagements) and no options are prioritized for her in the way that our childhood options tend to be for us.

A good example of who Echo eventually chooses to be is given in her interactions with Joel Mynor. We first encounter Joel in "Man on the Street" (1.6), where he has hired out Echo to play his deceased wife. Joel's fantasy is to have his wife back for one day—the day when he intended to surprise her with a new house after making big money for the first time, though it is also the day when she died while driving to that surprise. It is Joel, perhaps more than anyone else, who makes the Dollhouse feel like it could be a positive thing on an emotional level (while there are other scenes where positives are mentioned, such as the ability to cure diseases like PTSD or paranoid schizophrenia, these positives feel like lies—that is not what the Dollhouse is *really* doing and we know it). It is Joel that explains to Paul that everyone has a fantasy—most of which are not really sick and twisted. For Joel, the Dollhouse was just a way to live out his fantasy, which allowed him one more day every year to spend with his wife.

We meet Joel again in "A Love Supreme" (2.8) where Alpha is hunting down and killing all the johns who hired out Echo. Since Joel did intend to sleep with Echo on his fantasy engagement, he is included on the list, and so Paul and Echo search out Joel to save him. After Alpha seemingly kills Paul, Echo fights Alpha, and Joel is saved, then Echo and Joel discuss Joel's engagement to a new woman. Joel has mixed feelings about discussing this with Echo, whom he sees (in a way) as his deceased wife, though he also obviously realizes she is a Doll. Echo, however, allows Joel to talk to Rebecca, the personality imprint of his deceased wife. Joel tells Rebecca that his fiancé is not meant to replace her and he expresses surprise that he is not yet past his grief. Echo, as herself, responds:

> ECHO: You don't get past it. It just … becomes a part of who you are.
> JOEL: *You* live on for me, and I'm so glad of that.
> MOMENTS LATER, ECHO TO PAUL ON LIFE SUPPORT: And *you* live on for me ["A Love Supreme" 2.8].

There's just so much going on in this scene. First, by this point, Echo is transitioning imperceptibly between her self as Echo and her various personalities. Second, Joel accepts that Echo is actually Echo, but also believes Rebecca is simultaneously in there in some meaningful way. Third, this scene says something very important about grief and accepting that the death of a loved one is not something you will ever move past, but is instead something that becomes part of you. In an important way, your value for your loved one is something you autonomously adopt, and accepting them as part of you even after they pass on is an autonomous way to deal with grief. Joel and Echo are both experiencing this autonomous moment of understanding themselves better through their grief for loved ones.

Finally, this scene makes a deep point about Echo's relationship with her implanted personalities. When she says Joel won't get past Rebecca, it is also a point about her own acceptance of the personalities within her. While there is a distinct Echo that is more than just her composite personalities, Echo is also made up of those personalities and who she is derives, in some important sense, from them. This point is symbolic of the fact that we all forge our autonomy within a society where so many people influence us, some for good and others for bad, yet we wish to incorporate and endorse all the positive influences around us and grow more into our selves based on how those good people around us see us. Even the people who negatively influence us also allow us opportunities for growth, which may include the autonomous decision to kick certain kinds of poisonous people out of our lives.

Echo accomplishes this ideal. She has a great deal of weakness and negativity within her various personalities, but she chooses to bolster the positive ones, and minimize the negatives. That is what we all must attempt to do even while under the heavy influences of the media. Like Echo, we are all challenged by heavy influence implanted into our minds. As Chomsky argues, these influences are quite often implanted through the media for the purpose of making us more receptive to giving into power and supporting the interests of the powerful. As Chomsky says, the powers that be are engaged in "the manufacture of consent, deceiving the stupid masses with 'necessary illusions,'" while diverting everyone's attention from the "institutional factors that determine the persistent and substantive content of these commitments [of thought control]."[63] Thus, the powers that be make sure that the people are deceived—confusing the interests of the powerful with their own interests—and fail to see the institutions at work behind the curtain that both manipulate their values and serve to replicate the power structure as it is. Part of this manipulation is the attempt to make us accept corporate and governmental influences in our lives as positive when in fact these influences tend to support their own interests, not ours. Hence, they are to be contrasted with the various positive influences in our lives, such as friends and family, whose attempts to influence us are meant to genuinely be for our own good.

Both positive and negative influences are unavoidable in real life. The media influence all of us. Even people who attempt to neither watch TV, listen to the radio, nor go on the internet, are almost certainly influenced by people who are media-connected. And not all media sources provide negative influences. It is up to each of us to figure out what media influences we wish to endorse, and which we wish to escape and avoid. We are all similarly situated to Echo in that we necessarily incorporate a countless number of external influences, but we must do the work to figure out who we are in the middle of all that chaos.

Echo figures out who she is amongst all her various influences: she is someone who is intent on destroying Rossum, preferably before Rossum can quite literally erase everyone's personalities and directly implant the ones of their choosing. Of course, that was, we must admit, Caroline's main goal which eventually led her to be coerced into taking the Doll agreement in the first place. We do not think this coincidence means that the Caroline imprint is the primary influence on Echo. Instead, we think that Echo is autonomously developing into a moral agent like Topher, and is motivated by love and grief. And Echo's morality happens to align with Caroline's: the biggest evil they see around them just happens to be the Rossum Corporation. Just as Echo represents all of us trying to find ourselves amongst the jumble of media influence, Rossum is a fairly straightforward, but exaggerated representation of that influence. After all, Rossum is attempting to literally wipe everyone's mind clean so that Rossum's influence can literally be imprinted on each person's mind. Rossum is an explicit and over-the-top version of what various media sources already implicitly do every day (in a more subtle fashion, of course). And, Echo's quest to destroy Rossum represents the moral option to replace the system of corruptive influence with a new system.

Thus, we can see in *Dollhouse* a call for a new system, which would look a lot like anarchism. As Chomsky explains:

> I think people should be able to live in a society where they can exercise these kinds of internal drives and develop their capacities freely—instead of being forced into the narrow range of options that are available to most people in the world now. And by that, I mean not only options that are *objectively* available, but also options that are *subjectively* available—like, how are people allowed to think, how are they able to think?[64]

Chomsky is seeking a society where people are not only able to choose from a set of objective options—such as careers and hobbies—but also subjective options—the ability to think as they feel best, as opposed to having their thinking implanted into them like they are Dolls. As Chomsky continues:

> Various blockages have been developed and imposed to prevent people from thinking in those ways. That's what indoctrination is *about* in the first place, in fact—and I don't mean somebody giving you lectures: sitcoms on television, sports that you watch, every aspect of the culture implicitly involves an expression of what a "proper" life and a "proper" set of values are, and that's all indoctrination.[65]

In our current society, according to Chomsky, we have indoctrination: our various media influences tell us what is proper. In doing so, they cut off options—both objectively in terms of things to do in life and subjectively in terms of ways to think and feel about the world. The powers that be convince us that it is okay to destroy the environment, to ignore the homeless, to work on building more weapons that can annihilate the world many times over, etc. In this sense, we are just Dolls programmed to sit by while power corrupts us all and quite literally destroys the planet and our authentic selves.[66] Chomsky instead envisions a new society, based on anarchism and socialism, "where people have the opportunity to decide freely for themselves what their needs are, and not just have the 'choices' forced on them by some arbitrary system of power."[67]

As Chomsky points out, the powers that be fear just such a system: "the idea that people could be free is extremely frightening to anybody with power. That's why the 1960s have such a bad reputation."[68] When people are left free to think for themselves, they will be unlikely to sacrifice their interests for the interests of the powerful. They will instead seek a society where everyone can be free, without requiring anybody become a sacrificial lamb for the profit of others. Thus, they will wish to stop being Dolls, and that desire will turn the people into a massive group of Echoes.

Our Society Needs a Treatment

Consent and autonomy are key components to figuring out how we wish our lives to go. We make consensual agreements with others to receive their assistance with projects that we cannot perform on our own—and life is largely only meaningful through projects that involve other people. But it is important that involving those other people in your life projects is done through their consent: not because they are coerced, pressured, or forced to agree due to bad situations or deep desperation. Life often requires that we work together on projects, but this is only done correctly—done consensually—when everyone freely, with adequate information, and competently agrees that the project is something they purposely wish to become obligated to jointly perform.

While freedom is too vague to be assured to be a good thing, autonomy involves a person pursuing and enacting values that they themselves endorse as good. While you may freely live a life of someone else's choosing, it will not be a fulfilling life if you did not choose it yourself. Autonomy involves figuring out what kind of life you wish to live and then living accordingly. Therefore, we all wish to ultimately have autonomous lives in meaningful ways.

Dolls are pretty much incapable of both consent and autonomy. While they are Dolls, they cannot consent to anything since they lack freedom.

Further, as Dolls, their values are programmed into them and so they cannot be autonomous. Insofar as they are Dolls, they cannot get their lives straight. They really do not have lives in any meaningful sense. They are merely depositories for Topher's programming.

Although this situation seems like science fiction, in a significant sense, we are all depositories for the media's programming. We learn many of our core values from our various media influences, such as the shows we watch, the books we read, the news we "learn" about the world from, etc. Many of these sources are pre-programmed to slant us toward the interests of the powerful people and corporations that run the state and society in general. Just as the Dolls are programmed to serve Rossum in *Dollhouse*, Chomsky argues that we are all programmed to serve our bosses, our companies, and our governments. Thus, *Dollhouse* shows us how we are all manipulated in societies under hierarchal control and struggle to have our autonomy respected.

Anarchists doubt the stability of a system where people cannot achieve autonomy and are constantly manipulated into nonconsensual agreements. They believe that humans are inclined to seek out meaningful freedom, which would be available under anarchism. In spite of the anarchist hope that people would seek out a society where autonomy is more easily discovered, history shows that humans are constantly slipping back toward hierarchy. After Joss Whedon made all of these shows and movies that consistently and substantially criticize hierarchy, even his own brand lapsed toward hierarchy in *Marvel's Agents of S.H.I.E.L.D.*, yet that show is much more complex than it first appears, and it too shows the pitfalls of hierarchy. Further, Whedon's other Marvel projects, the *Avengers* films, depict the natural draw toward equality and anarchist organization. Thus, we turn to Whedon's work with Marvel next to see the pull and push between hierarchy and anarchism.

Three

Tips for Organizing Anarchy
Marvel and the Push/Pull of Anarchism

Finding Shawarma in Tahiti

With *Angel* and *Dollhouse*, we saw the various problems associated with hierarchy, and the possibility of a better way through anarchism. If hierarchy is so bad and anarchism so ideal, one has to wonder why most of us are so attracted by the former, and a good bit frightened of the latter. Chapters one and two already provided some answers to these questions. In part, the powers that be wish us to feel exactly like that. And they have their means—especially the media—to propagate and replicate those feelings. Additionally and relatedly, we seem to just feel more comfortable with someone else in charge: freedom can be terrifying, whereas relinquishing control to hierarchy can provide relief. And, the system of power, both in contemporary times along with going back in history, works quite hard to make us identify that relief as coming in the form of cis, straight, middle-aged, white men, such as Phil Coulson.

After a long line of TV shows and movies that challenge the standard hierarchal routine, Joss Whedon made *Marvel's Agents of S.H.I.E.L.D.* (from here on, just *Agents of S.H.I.E.L.D.*), which, at least on the surface is a bit of a disappointment. It is not that *Agents of S.H.I.E.L.D.* does not have strong women (see especially Melinda May and Daisy "Skye" Johnson). Nor is it that *Agents of S.H.I.E.L.D.* does not have strong, underrepresented minority characters (such as Alphonso "Mack" MacKenzie and Elena "Yo-Yo" Rodriguez). The problem is that this diverse and intriguing cast operates under the leadership of a character—Coulson—who is quite intriguing and loveable himself, but who is also a typical representation of the powers that be in real life.[1] As Whedon scholar Samira Nadkarni puts it, Coulson is "a white male patriarch" and *Agents of S.H.I.E.L.D.* employs the trope of white, male heroism.[2] Unlike Whedon's other shows, the main protagonist of *Agents of S.H.I.E.L.D.* looks an awful lot like Whedon himself.

We should pause here to note that technically, Joss Whedon is not the show runner for *Agents of S.H.I.E.L.D.* The show runners are Jed Whedon, Maurissa Tancharoen, and Jeffrey Bell. Of course, as we stated in the introduction, in a philosophical sense, analyzing a TV show or movie through "Joss Whedon" is always misleading as all TV shows and movies, unlike most novels, are the products of multiple minds. Every show that Joss Whedon has made had a series of writers, producers, cast, and crew—all of whom surely contributed in countless ways to the successes and occasional disappointments that theorists, ourselves included, too easily attribute to Whedon as a kind of shorthand. And since Joss Whedon contributes in various ways to *Agents of S.H.I.E.L.D.* (as one of the creators, executive producers, writers, and directors), it is not completely wrong to continue this shorthand of considering *Agents of S.H.I.E.L.D.* to at least loosely be a Joss Whedon show. Further, all the actual show runners worked on previous Joss Whedon led shows: Jed Whedon and Maurissa Tancharoen worked on "Dr. Horrible" and *Dollhouse*, while Jeffrey Bell worked on *Angel*. Thus, Joss Whedon is an important central factor in all of these shows, and we are also using him as a shorthand device to stand for the larger teams that make the shows. In this respect, it is fair to include *Agents of S.H.I.E.L.D.* under our discussion, but with a caveat that it could be the least Joss Whedon series of the ones included.

Let's also pause a second time to consider other Whedon series where the main protagonist is a cis, straight white man. After all, "Dr. Horrible," *Angel*, and *Firefly* all have white male leads, yet each of those cases is interesting in its method for challenging the standard. Dr. Horrible is, of course, evil. Though we root for him, even he eventually realizes that he is in fact evil. Angel and Mal Reynolds are typical white males and are even putative leaders of their respective groups of investigators/bandits, yet in each case, their leadership is presented as problematic, complex, and their groups tend toward an improved and more egalitarian structure (or at least as we argue in the chapters about those shows). Angel eventually recognizes that he cannot really be the leader of either Angel Investigations or Wolfram & Hart, and the others, especially Cordelia, Gunn, and Wesley, challenge his leadership and often establish the need for more equality. Similarly, while Mal insists on being the leader of his crew, it is clear that others, such as Inara and Book, have more egalitarian perspectives that are preferable to Mal's self-involved hierarchy (as we will see in the next chapter).

Phil Coulson is one example of a Whedon hero who is a white male leader whose leadership is largely presented as positive. Whedon scholar Jennifer Beckett describes him "as the quintessential 'good spy.' Calm, cool, collected, and immaculately suited, he is the model of efficiency and, importantly, we are never given cause to question his actions and by extensions those of S.H.I.E.L.D."[3] Coulson's leadership actually feels reassuring: we the audience, along with almost all of the characters who work with him, trust that Coulson will figure out what to do and will ultimately lead the good guys to victory. Coulson is our protagonist, our boss, our hero, our guide, our father, and our white male savior.[4] While the depiction is comforting, it is also highly problematic, especially since it is so familiar. It normalizes a specific way of thinking about and viewing of the world: one that upholds racial, gender, and structural hierarchies.

In a similarly disconcerting fashion, S.H.I.E.L.D.—the key spy agency that *Agents of S.H.I.E.L.D.* revolves around, whose acronym stands for Strategic Homeland Intervention, Enforcement, and Logistics Division—itself is presented as a positive institution that serves justice. In *Angel* and *Dollhouse*, we saw the significant difficulties that occur when trying to trust institutions that wield extreme powers. S.H.I.E.L.D. nevertheless is just such an institution: it finds, manages, and controls the powerful Inhumans. And just as we trust Coulson, we also largely trust S.H.I.E.L.D. In this sense, *Agents of S.H.I.E.L.D.* seems to go against the anarchist trend by championing both an institution and a typical leader-type. In fact, Grant Ward even refers to Skye, before she joins S.H.I.E.L.D., as one of the "pseudo-anarchist hacker types" ("Pilot" 1.1), so S.H.I.E.L.D. is presented as a good institution, and the outsiders, such as Skye from the "Pilot," are presented as the problematic anarchists.

Further, as with many superpower shows, comics, and movies, the *Agents of S.H.I.E.L.D.* storylines are often metaphors for bigotry: people with superpowers, many of which are useless superpowers, are seen as different and strange, and thus are oppressed, yet many of the key operators we meet in S.H.I.E.L.D. are regular humans. Clearly, there is some mixture as S.H.I.E.L.D. has essential personnel that have superpowers, including one-time S.H.I.E.L.D. Director Jeffrey Mace, as well as many characters, such as Skye, who develop from being regular humans to Inhumans, yet given the significant role of so many typical humans in leading S.H.I.E.L.D. and running S.H.I.E.L.D. operations, it cannot be ignored that the show has a bit of a white savior feel: the oppressed can only be saved through the assistance of the good oppressors, which reinforces the agency of the oppressors and the passivity of the oppressed. Whedon scholar Jennifer Beckett notes that "there is something comforting in the idea that while buildings may explode and aliens can swoop down and invade there is always someone better, a team of someones, there to save the day."[5] The problem is that the team saving the day seems to represent the oppressors. Whedon scholar Samira Nadkarni weaves all of these threads together, and explains that the many elements in S.H.I.E.L.D. appear "distinctly tied to a narrative of colonization," one that specifically upholds American hegemony.[6] Again, this is complicated, but *Agents of S.H.I.E.L.D.* raises concerns that must be noted.

In spite of these issues, *Agents of S.H.I.E.L.D.* has layers of complexity that keep the show from being fully problematic. It turns out that S.H.I.E.L.D. was actually a front for the evil organization of Hydra and while Coulson is largely a positive leader, many of his superiors are themselves corrupt and evil. As the show develops, S.H.I.E.L.D. must operate as an underground organization, where it is much less of a stand-in for statist or hierarchal views, and becomes more amenable to (though never perfectly suited for) anarchist theorizing. Ultimately, we have reason to be more critical of *Agents of S.H.I.E.L.D.* than any of Whedon's other shows, but it nevertheless represents both the honest comfort that is provided by hierarchy, and it also depicts some key problems that befall an attempt to cling too much to hierarchy. In other words, we have an inclination—which has surely been inculcated by the media—toward hierarchy and away from anarchism, and *Agents of S.H.I.E.L.D.* depicts that inclination.

There is, however, another inclination pushing in the other direction, which we learn from Peter Kropotkin. Kropotkin (1842–1921) was a Russian aristocrat, philosopher, revolutionary theorist, and anarchist. He was imprisoned for his activism, and escaped, spending many of years in exile in France, England, and Switzerland. He supported a society free of a central government and based on voluntary associations of self-governing communities. Kropotkin explains:

> The [anarchist] conception of society just sketched, and the tendency which is its dynamic expression, have always existed in mankind, in opposition to the government hierarchic conception and tendency—now the one and now the other taking the upper hand at different periods in history. To the former tendency we owe the evolution, by the masses themselves, of those institutions—the clan, the village community, the guild, the free medieval city—by means of which the masses resisted the encroachments of the conquerors and the power-seeking minorities.[7]

In this quotation, Kropotkin notes a tendency, which we see in *Agents of S.H.I.E.L.D.*, toward endorsing hierarchy and even toward finding it comforting. But there is also a dynamic tendency toward freedom, which we observe in the making of clans, guilds, and other groupings that are based on equality and freedom for everyone, as opposed to giving into the alleged authority of the power-seeking conquerors. One freedom-inclined group that Kropotkin failed to mention would be the Avengers.

The tendency to freedom inevitably arises for the Avengers. It is inevitable because the Avengers cannot have a clear leader: each one of them is sufficiently powerful and intelligent that their opinions and thoughts must be heard and incorporated. At times, especially in *Avengers: Age of Ultron*, this unity of independents leads to trouble—there is no reason to think that anarchism would be without problems. In fact, any clan of equals will have issues. The point, though, is that given who the Avengers are as individuals, they cannot give up their autonomy and distinct voices when it comes to seeking the right thing to do in their circumstances. Of course, significantly, we all should see the world in similar fashions: we are all too important to yield our autonomy and distinct voices. We all should have equal says in the decisions that impact our lives and that involve our own moral duties. The Avengers are superheroes and so it makes no sense for them to accept hierarchal control of their lives and decision-making from above. But why should it make sense for any of us? Therefore, in depicting the dynamic tendency toward anarchism for superheroes, the *Avengers* films tell us a lot about how we should develop the confidence to embrace our own freedom and autonomy.

In this chapter, by looking at *Agents of S.H.I.E.L.D.*, the two Whedon-led *Avengers* films, and the works of Kropotkin, we will be able to track the opposing tendencies that cause a push from and pull toward anarchism. While it is necessary to see the pull away from anarchism, as manifested in everyone enjoying Coulson as a character and rooting for an institution like S.H.I.E.L.D., it is important to note that truly respecting ourselves and seeking our own autonomy requires that we all see ourselves as the Avengers see themselves: as capable, strong, and moral individuals who can make the right decisions if given the opportunity to do so.

Slipping Toward Hydra

Peter Kropotkin believed that history contains a plethora of evidence of various forces at play that push away from and pull toward anarchism—and, specifically, anarchist communism. Kropotkin himself was an anarchist communist who believed that the anarchist society would be a socialist one, where the means of production belonged to the people, and a communist one, where the people did not work for wages, but instead shared in the products and surpluses of their labor. As Kropotkin says of anarchist communism: "In common with all socialists, the anarchists hold that the private ownership of land, capital, and machinery has had its time; that it is condemned to disappear; and that all requisites for production must, and will, become the common property of society, and be managed in common by the producers of wealth."[8] For Kropotkin, the producers of wealth are all of us: we each work in a diverse variety of ways to contribute to wealth production, whether we are the ones laying the roads that deliver the materials, driving the trucks on those roads, emptying the trucks, putting the materials together, planning the construction, or teaching many of these individuals philosophy or history so that they are better critical thinkers as they work; we all do our own parts to produce the eventual positive outcome. Through our collaborative effort to improve the world, as Kropotkin says, "we are beginning to think of society as a whole, each part of which is so intimately bound up with the others that a service rendered to one is a service rendered to all."[9] We all are deserving of receiving rewards, and so it does not make sense, for Kropotkin, to try to calculate wages based on who contributed how much to the overall job.

We are driven toward anarchist communism, for Kropotkin, for a variety of reasons, just as we are driven away from it for other reasons. In terms of the former, Kropotkin explains in *The Conquest of Bread*:

> We [anarchist communists] hold further that Communism is not only desirable, but that existing societies, founded on Individualism, *are inevitably impelled in the direction of Communism*. The development of Individualism during the last three centuries is explained by the efforts of the individual to protect himself from the tyranny of Capital and of the State. For a time he imagined, and those who expressed his thought for him declared, that he could free himself entirely from the State and from society.[10]

People yearn for freedom, but this freedom is denied by the power of capitalism and the state. Individuals believe that they can gain their freedom by finding their lone paths of escape away from that constricting power of bosses and states. Each man soon finds out though that, "without the help of all, he can do nothing."[11] We cannot, then, move away from our lack of power within the hierarchal society to a situation of unfettered individualism, where each individual is out for him or herself. We humans are inherently complex creatures who need to live among other people since we need help for much of what we hope to achieve in life. Individualism is an attractive response to hierarchy (it would be nice to quit your job and go at life on your own with no boss), but it is ultimately a doomed one (you won't last long going at life on your own in the modern world): meaningful human lives eventually require other people.

On the other side, Kropotkin continues, "we have all been brought up from our childhood to regard the State as a sort of Providence; all our education, the Roman history we learned at school, the Byzantine code which we studied later under the name of Roman law, and the various sciences taught at the universities, accustom us to believe in Government and in the virtues of the State providential."[12] Even as we recognize the power that hierarchal organizations hold over us, we must acknowledge that we have been taught that this power is only used for good. Jennifer Beckett refers to this dynamic as "offering us a securitized reflection of the world around us."[13] As we will soon see, even the TV show *Agents of S.H.I.E.L.D.* presents the governmental organization of S.H.I.E.L.D. as a good one that can save us (though with clear complications, which will largely hold our interest here). In other words, we initially have the inclination to move toward individualism first and then eventually toward anarchist communism later, yet we have been taught so many times that the actual solution lies in the type of hierarchal organizations that are in fact suppressing our freedom and autonomy. As Kropotkin tells us, "each politician, whatever his colours, comes forward and says to the people, 'Give me the power, and I both can and will free you from the miseries which press so heavily upon you.'"[14]

Thus, the individual seeking reprieve can either retreat back down to subjugation by accepting the hierarchy's control over him or he can reach up to a society where all are free, as in anarchist communism. Though there surely has been and will be a good deal of back and forth over the course of history, Kropotkin confidently believes that people will inevitably be drawn to the freedom of an anarchist communist society. To see this push and pull in action, it is useful to see how it is depicted in Joss Whedon's Marvel works, starting with *Agents of S.H.I.E.L.D.*

Agents of S.H.I.E.L.D. begins with a voice-over that tells us, "The secret is out. For decades, your organization stayed in the shadows—hiding the truth. But now we know they're among us: heroes and monsters. The world is filled with wonders" ("Pilot" 1.1). S.H.I.E.L.D. is meant to be a secret organization that helps protect both regular humans (from the monsters) and the more irregular humans (from the monstrosity that lies within humanity in general). Hence, its secrecy appears to be reasonable: they are protecting the world both from real dangers and from the potential panic that could result from people knowing about these dangers. Grant Ward explains S.H.I.E.L.D. in the following fashion: "We're the line between the world and the much weirder world. We protect people from news they aren't ready to hear. And when we can't do that, we keep them safe" ("Pilot" 1.1). Thus, S.H.I.E.L.D. is there to protect us all from the news we can't yet handle.

This setup is a fairly trite TV device used to force secrecy into the show's background to create tricky situations for the characters to handle. In reality, it would surely be better for the people at large to know what dangers they face so that they can democratically determine for themselves how to handle those dangers. That way, abuses of power could be averted and transparency would thrive (this idea also fits with what Whedon scholars refer to as a need to question the lack of oversight over security agencies[15]). Thankfully, prior to the events of the TV series, in the first *Avengers* film (to be discussed later), the Avengers very visibly and publicly fought Loki and the Chitauri, revealing the existence of both superheroes and super villains to the world. Consequently, S.H.I.E.L.D. is not necessarily a secret organization during the run of the show, but it also is not very democratic.

Instead, S.H.I.E.L.D., especially in the early episodes, appears to have a fairly routine and overtly hierarchal structure. Here are a few Season 1 examples of S.H.I.E.L.D. leadership: Phil Coulson is in charge of his team of agents in the field; Victoria Hand runs the S.H.I.E.L.D. base Hub; Anne Weaver runs the S.H.I.E.L.D. Academy of Science and Technology; and Nick Fury is the Director of S.H.I.E.L.D. Finally, although it is not a significant part of the TV series, in the Marvel movies, including *Avengers* and *Captain America: The Winter Soldier*, S.H.I.E.L.D. is housed under another, large organization, the World Security Council. To sum up, S.H.I.E.L.D. has both a clear hierarchy and attempts to maintain secrecy. That means that both the agents at the bottom of that hierarchy and the people of the world do not determine what S.H.I.E.L.D. does even though S.H.I.E.L.D. makes decisions that impact everyone.

Beckett notes that "S.H.I.E.L.D.'s role has always been as a kind of CIA/NSA that deals with threats to the Marvel Universe."[16] But it is similar not just in scope, also in secrecy: S.H.I.E.L.D. is like many secret organizations, such as the CIA, NSA, KGB, MI6, etc., that claim to do good but who do not wish to have their activities witnessed by the prying eyes of the people for whom they are allegedly doing good. That alone should give us reason to be automatically suspicious of S.H.I.E.L.D.: we, the people, cannot know for sure that they are doing good, even if they claim to be, because we cannot really make that judgment for ourselves as we do not know what they are doing. That is not to say that they are not doing good, but that their good, if it is being done, is left mysterious and solely up to their own discretion and regulation. The judgment of the few is substituted for the judgment of the many: the people who run S.H.I.E.L.D. decide what's good, and the people must simply sit by and hope S.H.I.E.L.D. decides correctly.[17] Beckett notes this problematic arrangement, and concludes that it might be "at the root of the problem."[18]

Such a system is, of course, quite common among hierarchal, statist societies. The powers that be ask the people to simply trust them: they can make these decisions best, and we, the people, can be saved from having to panic at the thought of making our own decisions. This idea is highly problematic, as Kropotkin explains: "The absorption of all social functions by the State necessarily favoured the development of an unbridled, narrow-minded individualism. In proportion as the obligations towards the State grew in numbers the citizens were evidently relieved from their obligations towards each other."[19] When the state claims it can best make decisions for the people, then the people feel as if they are relieved of their moral duties to each other. That false sense of relief can both be comforting (since it is easier to assume others will do your moral work for you) and lead to unbridled individualism where each is only out for themselves. The powers that be do the people a favor by making the key decisions about what justice and safety require for everyone. But it is no real favor: it leaves the people less prepared to make moral judgments of their own and, relatedly, less prepared to watch the state or other institutions that are supposedly making moral judgments on their behalf. As Kropotkin warns, "The result is, that theory which maintains that man can, and must, seek their own happiness in a disregard of other people's wants is now triumphant all round in law, in science, in religion."[20]

As we can see, such a system is ripe for corruption, which is great for Hydra. If there is no public oversight, and the key decisions are left up to the powers that be, then the circumstances are put in place that allow the powers to make decisions that most benefit themselves, as opposed to benefiting society. Two things need to be made clear about this claim. First, the claim does not require the over-generalization that everyone who has power is necessarily bad. As we saw when examining *Angel* and *Dollhouse*, the anarchist points to institutional problems as more worrisome than bad individuals. The idea is not that everyone who has power just coincidentally happens to be bad. The point instead is that institutions tend toward self-preservation. Institutions support and set social, economic, and legal rules that favor their institutional tasks. Individuals are promoted within institutions when they likewise act in ways that meet with the institutional values and assist with the accomplishment of institutional tasks. It need not even be conscious or purposeful: individuals who get ahead will be the ones that fit and enhance the institutional structures that they inhabit. Some of those people will purposely think and act as the institution requires so that they can get ahead. Others will simply implicitly and subconsciously take on institutional values. Thus, some people in power will prioritize the values of the powerful because they intentionally wish to do so. Other people in power will do so without much thought because their fitting within institutional power is what allowed them to gain or keep power in the first place. Hence, not everyone in power is bad, but almost everyone in power will act to support power.

Second, the corruption need not derive from the powers that be: the lack of greater oversight also allows room for external corruption to take over. In a hierarchal society that has secret organizations in power, there is a tendency for bad actors to seek out and discover ways to empower themselves through those secret organizations in large part because no one is watching. It is much easier for evil to rise to the top of a secret organization than to rise to the top of an organization with public oversight (though evil, of course, can find a way in either case).

Hence, it is revealing and significant that even though S.H.I.E.L.D. is presented as a do-good, heroic institution, it is in fact thoroughly infiltrated by Hydra. And through John Garrett (who turns out to be the Clairvoyant), Hydra's infiltration goes to the "tip top" of S.H.I.E.L.D. ("Turn, Turn, Turn" 1.17). And when Coulson tells him, "I would die before serving Hydra, you sick son of a bitch," Garrett responds, "I hate to tell you, but you've been serving Hydra all along" ("Turn, Turn, Turn" 1.17). And this is the key point: Hydra completely infiltrated S.H.I.E.L.D., and so when Coulson and others were earlier working for S.H.I.E.L.D., they were in fact unknowingly working for Hydra and presumably contributing indirectly to evil all along. That is the problem with the blanket assumption that institutions are good: when we are merely cogs or bystanders, we really do not fully know what the institutions are up to. S.H.I.E.L.D. is presented as good throughout the first season, but that entire time, Hydra secretly was running S.H.I.E.L.D.[21]

Thus, in "Turn, Turn, Turn" (1.17), when we learn that Hydra has taken over S.H.I.E.L.D., it is interesting to see an episode where both Coulson and Victoria Hand are convinced that the other one is Hydra, even though neither is. Having been betrayed from within the hierarchy, each character swiftly moves from inherently trusting hierarchy to immediately and completely distrusting it. This instability is quite familiar: many of us tend to both seek out hierarchy for guidance while we also are quite quick to see the flaws in our economic and political leaders. At one moment, you sufficiently trust the government to handle the energy crisis. In the next moment, you are not at all surprised when it is exposed that politicians receive so much money from the energy corporations that they actually exasperating the energy crisis. Or—perhaps closer to everyday issues—you trust the company you work for to do good things with the product of your sweat-pouring labor, but then you are not surprised when your boss is a buffoon who ends up wasting your best ideas and efforts. We both have a deep and somewhat abstract trust of the vague hierarchy ("I'm sure *the government* will fix this problem" or "I'm sure *my company* will make the right call"), while we are constantly faced with real-life, up-close-and-personal counter examples ("*My congressperson* is a lying, stealing idiot" or "*My boss* is a know-nothing jerk").

Even when Hydra has taken over S.H.I.E.L.D. and they all have every reason to distrust hierarchy, Hand argues for distrusting Coulson based on the fact that he has "disobey[ed] a direct order, multiple counts" and "fail[ed] to report the crimes of his protégé" ("Turn, Turn, Turn" 1.17). Thus, even as the hierarchy is letting them down, Coulson is seen as suspicious because he has failed to completely adhere to the hierarchy in the past (which in retrospect was corrupted by Hydra) and was loyal to his people as opposed to reporting them. Hand emphasizes that Hydra is untrustworthy because "they hide in plain sight. They earn our trust, our sympathy. They make us like them" ("Turn, Turn, Turn" 1.17). It is Hand's trust and sympathy of individuals that she has grown to find worrisome and blameworthy, as opposed to her inherent trust for institutions. Hand is placing blame on her faith in people, though it was the institution that allowed Hydra to take over. Hydra worked since World War II to infiltrate S.H.I.E.L.D. and gain promotions, all while S.H.I.E.L.D. was hidden from public oversight and democratic control. It is not the institution or its hierarchal bent that Hand blames, but her own trust, her own sympathy, and the people, like Coulson, who didn't sufficiently follow the orders of the institution that turned out to be corrupt.

As John Garrett explained to Coulson, Victoria Hand and Coulson were both working for a malevolent organization all along and so there is no value in following orders. There was no real gain for subsuming their autonomy to S.H.I.E.L.D. since, as it turned out, S.H.I.E.L.D. was using them all for Hydra's evil intentions. Protecting our autonomy is essential particularly because when we allow others to dictate our actions—especially when those others are distant from or unknown to us—we have conceded our ability to make good decisions for ourselves. You work for S.H.I.E.L.D., and it turns out you are allowing Hydra to make moral decisions for you. And, Hand eventually figures this out as she explains to Coulson, "You and I may be the highest ranking S.H.I.E.L.D. agents who aren't Hydra or dead, not that that means anything now. So stay in touch, Agent Coulson," to which he responds, "I guess you can call me Phil" ("Turn, Turn, Turn" 1.17). Later, Skye would put the point much more succinctly; they are "not Agents of S.H.I.E.L.D., just Agents of Nothing" ("Providence" 1.18). In a short amount of time (though a lot happened in that brief period), Hand has figured out that it is time for her to shed the institution and to embrace a personal connection: she trusts Phil, and they can start the good fight together. Of course, she figures this out too late as Ward murders her shortly thereafter, exposing himself as Hydra as well.

Coulson figures it out, too. He still wishes to do what's right, and he clings a serious amount to the idea that doing good is done through an organization, yet Coulson also will fight for justice regardless of the situation, as we see in an exchange with Eric Koenig. Coulson wants to leave the secret base that Koenig has brought him to (for Coulson's own protection) because Hydra has allowed all the S.H.I.E.L.D. prisoners to escape another base, the Fridge. Koenig tells Coulson that he can't leave because "there are protocols," to which Coulson responds, "Since the entire agency's pretty much collapsed, maybe now's not the time to stand on protocol" ("The Only Light in the Darkness" 1.19). Therefore, the collapse of S.H.I.E.L.D. allows Coulson to realize, more than ever before, that it is paramount to go with his decision of what's best as opposed to simply trust institutional protocols that are not based on the particular circumstances of the moment. Coulson explains to Koenig that there is a danger of violence and people could die, and "I still consider it my duty to be the shield that protects them" ("The Only Light in the Darkness" 1.19). Coulson is going to act for justice, with his team, regardless of whether he is in the organization because shielding people from harm is more important than the S.H.I.E.L.D. institution.

There is further evidence that Coulson may have learned a larger message from the dissolution of S.H.I.E.L.D. when he argues with Lincoln Campbell through much of Season 3 about following orders. For much of that season, Coulson, now director of S.H.I.E.L.D., is, predictably, arguing that

Lincoln needs to learn the importance of following orders without question. That position is decidedly not anarchist. Anarchists believe each person should have their own autonomy and there is no justification to ask anyone to follow orders without question, yet in the big final showdown between Hive and Coulson in the Season 3 finale, there's this exchange:

> HIVE: We're two sides of the same coin, Coulson: commanders leading soldiers.
> COULSON: The only difference is, when you give an order, your followers have no choice but to obey. But when I gave my team the order to stay behind, they just wouldn't listen ["Ascension" 3.22].

In this exchange, Coulson goes against the position he has been holding in his exchanges with Lincoln for the whole season. He is quite proud that his team did not follow orders when acting against orders was necessary to save the day. That kind of independent, autonomous thinking is what is necessary to actually save the world. In fact, it is ultimately Lincoln who autonomously takes over and decides for himself that he will enact the ultimate sacrifice and die to save the world. This ending of Season 3 suggests that S.H.I.E.L.D. under Coulson's direction may have improved, at least in some respects. We will return to what follows after these events, in Season 4, in the next section.

It is not that S.H.I.E.L.D. was always or thoroughly a bad organization. When analyzing Hydra's infiltration of S.H.I.E.L.D., it is worth concentrating on the fact that S.H.I.E.L.D. was meant to be a good organization, but its secrecy and hierarchy still allowed for Hydra to infiltrate it.[22] For Kropotkin, this situation is analogous to state socialism, as Marxists would advocate. Kropotkin can agree with Marxists on the ultimate goal: they share the goal of ensuring the freedom of all of the people through the elimination of hierarchy. However, Marxists and anarchists fundamentally disagree on how to achieve that goal. Anarchists believe in immediately moving from the capitalist state to anarchism, whereas Marxists believe in a gradual transition that moves from the capitalist state to a socialist state (accepting some level of political hierarchy to assist with the transition away from economic hierarchy). The Marxists argue the anarchist plan is unrealistic (as the transition would be too sudden), while the anarchists believe the Marxist plan accepts too much hierarchy and will inevitably give way to a different source of evil. In other words, the anarchists believe that a socialist state will attempt to do good, like S.H.I.E.L.D. does, but will devolve into evil, just like when Hydra takes over S.H.I.E.L.D.

In his book *The Conquest of Bread*, Kropotkin worries that state socialism makes progress while setting up new problems: "The State Socialism of the collectivist system has certainly made some progress. State railways, State banking, and State trade in spirits have been introduced here and there. But every step made in this direction, even though it resulted in the cheapening of a given commodity, was found to be a new obstacle in the struggle of the working-men for their emancipation."[23] The problem for Kropotkin is that they are just replacing one form of hierarchy (capitalism) with another (the socialist state). While this change has its positives (it may make some commodities cheaper and easier to obtain), it also continues to entrench power, so when the people seek to empower themselves, they will simply have a different opponent: instead of the capitalists, they will simply have to fight the communists.

In his 1887 "Anarchist Communism: Its Basis and Principles," Kropotkin further explains that "anarchists recognize the justice of both the just-mentioned tendencies towards economic and political freedom, and see in them two different manifestations of the very same need of equality which constitutes the very essence of all struggles mentioned by history."[24] The anarchist does not see any real difference between economic and political freedom. Sure, philosophers can make a theoretical distinction between them: we can pick out economic freedom as freedom with respect to money, labor, and business, and we can pick out political freedom as freedom with respect to democratic rights and fundamental liberties of thought and conscience, yet this theoretical distinction breaks down in real life. Free speech requires that neither your government nor your employer can restrict what you wish to say, contrary to the capitalist state where your employer can restrict your speech and contrary to the socialist state where your government can do so. The freedom to act autonomously further requires that neither your government nor your employer can force you to act against your will with threats of either imprisonment (as a socialist state might allow) or loss of means for living (as a capitalist state might allow).

Hence, just as the anarchist speaks against the restrictions of freedom from the capitalist state, Kropotkin adds that the anarchist must say to the state socialist, "You cannot modify the existing conditions of property without deeply modifying at the same time the political organization. You must limit the powers of government and renounce parliamentary rule."[25] Thus, state socialists contradict themselves: they cannot obtain their goal of economic freedom without providing political freedom because these are merely a theoretical distinction. What it means to be free necessarily means having both economic and political freedom.

For Kropotkin, state socialists attempt to do good (by providing economic freedom), but in their confusion, they simply do more bad (by restricting political freedom). While S.H.I.E.L.D. attempts to protect Inhumans, they do so through a secret organization that is run by numerous people who are not Inhumans. And, in fact, it is rather clear that people who wish to abuse and use Inhumans were easily able to make it up the S.H.I.E.L.D. ranks and take over.[26] They assumed that an organization run mainly by humans in secret could do the right thing for Inhumans, but such an organization can easily become corrupted just as the state socialists actually did in much of world history after Kropotkin's passing in 1921.

Shielded Images of Hierarchy

In addition to the time that S.H.I.E.L.D. turns out to be infiltrated by Hydra, *Agents of S.H.I.E.L.D.* provides two other telling instances of what's wrong with hierarchy in Season 4. Season 4 begins with the Ghost Rider episodes where S.H.I.E.L.D. is run as a more standard, fairly realistic hierarchal and bureaucratic organization. These episodes mock the very idea of S.H.I.E.L.D. as a hierarchal organization, which is both useful for our current analysis and a bit strange. We say it is strange because, of course, these episodes are showing what hierarchal organizations, like S.H.I.E.L.D., realistically look like, which just emphasizes how earlier seasons are downplaying the sorts of problems one would typically face with this kind of organization in real life. Season 4 of *Agents of S.H.I.E.L.D.* strengthens the anarchist analysis in its final episodes where the show is renamed "Agents of Hydra." When we move to a computer-generated world where Hydra is winning, we once again see a more realistic examination of the problems of hierarchal society. Thus, in Season 4, we get depictions of serious problems with hierarchy that other seasons of *Agents of S.H.I.E.L.D.* may have downplayed. Let's begin with the Ghost Rider episodes.

As Season 3 ends, the S.H.I.E.L.D. team has defeated Hive, but is somewhat left in shambles. Daisy has left S.H.I.E.L.D. and is now a vigilante, referred to as "Quake." In previous episodes, and after it was revealed that Hydra infiltrated S.H.I.E.L.D., Nick Fury made Coulson the Director and gave him the assignment of rebuilding S.H.I.E.L.D. Now, at the end of Season 3, Coulson is no longer director of S.H.I.E.L.D., having been replaced by the previously mentioned Jeffrey Mace.

As Season 4 begins, bureaucracy has taken over S.H.I.E.L.D., and it is especially rigid and opaque as illustrated through a color-coded system that is titled, "the Spectrum of Security."

> May: Why do I, level red, have to go through you, level orange, to request hardware? Shouldn't red be higher than orange?
> Simmons: Well, orange encompasses both red and yellow, so.... It's hard to explain, but the Director didn't want to use numbers because he didn't want any team member to feel less than.
> May: Well, you do have a higher clearance than me.
> Simmons: Only in most instances.
> May: I feel less than ["Ghost" 4.1].

This exchange perfectly exhibits bureaucracy as many people who work for large corporations or government organizations experience it. It is attempting to do something that no one asked for (replacing numbers with colors), the reasoning (to make sure no one feels "less than") is suspicious at best, and the result is both highly confusing (no one can tell how the colors interact) and undermines the very reasoning provided (ultimately, you can find the hidden hierarchy just the same).

Scholars connect this kind of bureaucracy with "administrative evil." Administrative evil refers to how bureaucracy is used to mask the evil performed on the job so that good people go to work and perform labor that seems innocuous, but that ultimately results in the corporation, or governmental organization, performing evil deeds.[27] Bureaucracy, like this Spectrum of Security color-code, is a method of control through confusion.[28] If people do not really understand their proper place in the hierarchy, they do not know how to even question the hierarchy. And if they do not question the hierarchy, then they simply do as they are told without questioning—abandoning their autonomy because it is too confusing to try to figure out the bureaucracy. In other words, the system wins.

Further, in "Meet the New Boss" (4.2) we are directly introduced to this bureaucracy and the basis for it. May and Coulson are made to wait to meet the new Director as he is stuck in a meeting. Coulson suggests the meeting might be them "discussing new ways to implement bureaucracy," and he and May comment that the room looks "like it was decorated by someone who needs to unclench" ("Meet the New Boss" 4.2). They believe they are meeting with the new Director because Coulson sanctioned a mission to search for Skye without authorization, but new Director Jeffrey Mace is not worried about that, as he explains to them: "She was your friend. Loyalty's a good thing" ("Meet the New Boss" 4.2). The problem is not directly with Mace: he is a good leader, and he develops into a positive character in the show. Like with previous seasons, S.H.I.E.L.D. is meant to be a good organization that has good leadership, and this seems like a fair assessment of Mace's term in office.

At the same time, it is Mace's job to bring S.H.I.E.L.D. back into the public view, and so he is significantly concerned with public relations (PR) and optics. May scoffs at the idea of "optics," and Mace explains it to her, "The way things look, the package we present," to which she tells him, "I know what it means. It just seems trivial" ("Meet the New Boss" 4.2). Of course, May is correct, yet optics was something that the secret S.H.I.E.L.D. could take for granted. As S.H.I.E.L.D. attempts to become a legitimate, but public institution, they have to care about what people think, which they unfortunately interpret as providing a managed and produced image as opposed to just being honest with the public and allowing the public a fair say in the operation of the agency. Sherry Ginn argues that controlling, manufacturing, and limiting knowledge and/or information is a method of maintaining control in a variety of instances in Whedon's shows.[29] The same can be said here. In the early seasons, S.H.I.E.L.D. was able to control their image through their secrecy, but they ultimately lost control over their entire organization because of that secrecy. Therefore, Jeffrey Mace's S.H.I.E.L.D. has to be concerned with optics. Control is now expressed through meaningless bureaucratic rules, all meant to present a produced but reassuring image to the public.

During Mace's tenure at S.H.I.E.L.D., public image matters because suddenly S.H.I.E.L.D. needs to receive funding—a convenient fact waved away in earlier seasons in an unrealistic fashion. Obviously, any large organization needs money to do its work. Throughout the series, S.H.I.E.L.D. spends an enormous amount of money, and it only makes sense that they need to obtain that money from somewhere. As it is a governmental organization, S.H.I.E.L.D. clearly needs to obtain money by kissing up to Congress, which is what Mace asks Coulson to do. When Coulson balks, Mace explains, "we both know why I have this job. But what I don't have is the anonymous, unlimited funding you seemed to have before ... to build billion-dollar airplanes. No, our budget hinges on the U.N. and the Sokovia Accords and on impressing the House Appropriations Committee" ("Meet the New Boss" 4.2).

This plot point is *inherently* realistic. Of course S.H.I.E.L.D. would have to obtain money from Congress to operate! And of course obtaining money from Congress requires kissing up to the Congress people with power on the relevant committees. And—again, of course—kissing up to these Congress people will involve S.H.I.E.L.D. doing things from time to time that are not in the interest of justice or the common good, but in the interest of making the right people happy. Real life organizations have real life problems, like budgets and making the right people happy. It is much easier for early seasons to concentrate on S.H.I.E.L.D. using all of its institutional resources to fight evil, but in real life, institutional resources come at a cost, and that cost is usually a bunch of its own, incorporated, unavoidable evil.

While Mace is largely a good leader, the bureaucracy he implements eventually comes back to haunt them. Mace tells May and Coulson that his slogan is: "a team that trusts is a team that triumphs" ("Meet the New Boss" 4.2). And since S.H.I.E.L.D. has previously been infiltrated, Mace's S.H.I.E.L.D. is run through a bureaucracy that corrodes away at that very trust, which is plausible since you cannot fully trust everyone in a large organization—as proven by Hydra's earlier success. This tension is exhibited through S.H.I.E.L.D.'s lie detector tests. Simmons, who remains a key operative at S.H.I.E.L.D. and a true believer in how Mace runs it, has to take regular lie detector tests. Unfortunately for Simmons, Fitz (at this time, they are in a relationship) reveals that he is keeping secrets from her. Simmons is both upset at the secrecy and at the fact that she now has information, such as the creation of the android, Aida, that she cannot hide from her regular lie detector test. Simmons' difficulty directly derives from Fitz's. Simmons only has this problem of needing to keep the secrets insofar as Fitz had earlier obtained secrets himself. We all have secrets though. But the lie detector tests mean that Fitz could not share secrets with Simmons, and so the trust between them eroded. Mace's own slogan is undermined by his actions. The bureaucratic S.H.I.E.L.D. is not a place where trust can grow.

Therefore, we see through Mace's bureaucracy why hierarchy erodes good organizations. In the first season, the erosion occurred because evil was able to slip into leadership behind the veil of secrecy. In the beginning of the fourth season, we again have good leadership in Mace, but goodness is prey to the corrupting forces of bureaucracy. The realistic need for funding means kowtowing to people in positions of political power. The attempt to ensure that everyone is trustworthy erodes the ability of individuals to trust each other. As realistic as these problems for hierarchy are, *Agents of S.H.I.E.L.D.* may deliver its strongest statement against hierarchy when we transition to an alternative reality where Hydra has won the fight.

At the end of Season 4, Aida, the android, has trapped the minds of the S.H.I.E.L.D. agents in a simulation (the Framework) where Hydra has won and Aida herself, as Madame Hydra Ophelia, is running things. In this reality, brainwashed Coulson acts as a teacher, and attempts to brainwash the students with hierarchal thinking:

> COULSON: This is a dangerous world. The Cambridge incident proved that. To understand this, you have to imagine individuals over the state. It was a mess. People were divided. They had their own truths, their own media, their own agenda…
> [Coulson goes on to describe how the weak state allowed an Inhuman into the country, before he continues on as follows:] But what inspires me is the way our country reacted, the way we came together. When no one would tell us the truth, Hydra stepped forward. They brought us law and order, purpose. They galvanized us for the good of the state over individual interests. They…. Yeah, Burnell.
> BURNELL: But, sir, isn't it true that Hydra came from Nazis?
> COULSON: That's not true. Never say that ["What If…" 4.16].

Coulson then explains that Burnell is being tricked by propaganda, but that just shows the importance of separating "fact from innuendo" ("What If…" 4.16). This speech represents the view that a Hydra sympathizer would endorse. It is also the view that an unjust, totalitarian state would endorse. The primary position of that Hydra view is that we must value the state's position over that of individuals. The Hydra view is the exact opposite of the anarchist view. The speech explicitly rails against an anarchist view where individuals would think for themselves and pursue their own interests autonomously. The Hydra view, as seen from Coulson's speech, is that independent thinking is a threat. Preference is given to state sponsored narratives, which are propagated through the state apparatus. That is why Coulson reprimands Burnell to never say that Hydra came from Nazis—Burnell's independent thinking could prove uncomfortable or embarrassing to the state's viewpoint by pointing to the heinous, but obvious connection between Hydra's image of the state and that of the Nazis.

Aida's Framework depicts the complete success of hierarchy. While there is much in *Agents of S.H.I.E.L.D.* that presents hierarchy as fine, it is Hydra's success within the Framework that shows the ultimate representation of pure law and order hierarchy, and it is dreadful and malevolent. Thus, throughout *Agents of S.H.I.E.L.D.* we see the ways in which a good organization falters and corrodes toward evil. By the end of Season 4, we see a computer program version of the worst-case scenario: law and order hierarchy is fully preserved, and it is a dystopian presentation of evil ruling the world, so while we do note that there is a mixed bag of analysis in *Agents of S.H.I.E.L.D.*, the series also provides a regular display of how hierarchy trends downward. Furthermore, this display is complimented by two Marvel movies where heroes work together and trend upward toward anarchism.

Avenging Is Order

The Avengers are, by and large, natural anarchists. That does not mean that they espouse anarchist theories.[30] It does not even mean that they would endorse the label if asked, yet there are three things that are inherently true of the Avengers. First, they are autonomous individuals who do not bow down to the orders of someone with whom they disagree. Instead, they make their own judgments and act in the way that they deem is best. Second, insofar as they are Avengers, they work as a team. Even though they are autonomous individuals, they are not lone warriors who act on their own without a sense of community. They are Avengers—a team of super individuals who put aside their differences to come up with communal solutions to problems that threaten the entire world. That brings up the third and final point: Avengers act for justice. They do not use their superpowers for personal greed, but instead use them to bring justice to the world in morally permissible ways.

You put all three points together, and you have anarchism. Anarchists seek a community of individuals whose individual rights and liberties are respected, but who look out for the justice of the community as a whole.

Anarchists recognize each person's freedom ought to be respected, provided that doing so is consistent with a like-freedom for all others. Anarchists do not follow orders from the powerful few when they disagree with those orders. Instead, they use their own judgment to do what is right, and, like the Avengers, are willing to engage in self-sacrifice for the greater good of justice. As Kropotkin says, "the sense of justice, or equity ... brings the individual to consider the rights of every other individual as equal to his own."[31]

We see this understanding of anarchism in the definition that Kropotkin uses in his entry on anarchism for the Encyclopædia Britannica:

> Anarchism is the name given to a principle or theory of life and conduct under which society is conceived without government—harmony in such a society being obtained, not by submission to law, or by obedience to any authority, but by free agreements concluded between the various groups, territorial and professional, freely constituted for the sake of production and consumption, as also for the satisfaction of the infinite variety of needs and aspirations of a civilized being.[32]

For Kropotkin, anarchism does not involve submission or obedience to any hierarchal authority, but instead involves making free agreements between civilized persons for the sake of satisfying everyone's various needs and aspirations. The Avengers would not submit or obey someone simply because that person was in authority, especially if they felt that person was asking them to do something wrong. Further, where there is harmony among the Avengers (and sometimes they are surely not in harmony), it is because they have a free agreement to work together to pursue justice. The Avengers meet Kropotkin's definition.

To what extent, though, does it make sense to call the Avengers "anarchists" when they would not consider themselves to be anarchists? That's a fair question, and we need not insist on the label here to make our larger point. Namely, even if the Avengers would not consider themselves to be anarchists, their organization and values fundamentally align with anarchist views.[33] In this way, the Avengers represent the distinctive tendency we all have toward anarchism. If we had the confidence in ourselves that the Avengers do, then maybe we would not submit so easily to power. If we recognized the demands of justice on us as the Avengers do, maybe we would not allow power to manipulate us so often. As Kropotkin points out, the power of anarchist communism simply requires that we see others who are brave enough to enact it, and then we will be driven toward it: "how can we doubt that this force (already so powerful) will enlarge its sphere of action till it becomes the ruling principle of social life?"[34] The Avengers represent who we all should become, and who we will become as soon as we witness powerful examples of people willing to sacrifice themselves for the good of justice.

It is useful here to examine a conversation between the Hulk/Bruce

Banner, Captain America/Steve Rogers, and Iron Man/Tony Stark. In this conversation, Banner is wondering why Stark wasn't brought in on the Tesseract project, and what S.H.I.E.L.D. is really doing with the secret development of this energy source. Stark explains that he should be able to answer Banner's question since he is using Jarvis to hack into S.H.I.E.L.D.'s secret files, which causes Rogers to exclaim:

> ROGERS: Yet you're confused about why they didn't want you around?
> STARK: An intelligence organization that fears intelligence? Historically, not awesome.
> ROGERS: I think Loki's trying to wind us up. This is a man who means to start a war, and if we don't stay focused, he'll succeed. We have orders, we should follow them.
> STARK: Following is not really my style.
> ROGERS: And you're all about style, aren't you? [*The Avengers*].

The conversation concludes with Banner asking Rogers if he recognizes that it "smells a little funky." Notice here, that even though Captain America believes in following orders, Stark represents a completely contrasting view: following orders is not Iron Man's style. Sarah Zaidan characterizes Stark as someone with a "sharp and curious mind" and the "determination to learn from a project's mistakes and improve upon them for the next iteration."[35] In other words, Stark confidently recognizes his own intelligence and trusts his own moral instincts. If it seems like S.H.I.E.L.D. is up to something "a little funky," then Stark is going to check up on S.H.I.E.L.D. to ensure that he does not unintentionally contribute to some immoral plot. His moral instincts thereby protect Stark from complicity with any potential secretive evil done by S.H.I.E.L.D.[36] In fact, they protect him so much that he is going to hack into S.H.I.E.L.D. and figure out what they are up to on his own.

While Rogers appears to be in favor of unquestioningly following orders in this situation, the truth is a bit more complex. Rogers is the one Avenger who is the most suspicious of their capture of Loki. Loki surely gave himself up purposely and is up to something (as the movie later confirms). The others are not sufficiently suspicious, and Rogers is trying to warn them that they should be, so while Rogers is urging the following of orders, he is also doing so because that supports the view that he currently prefers: suspicion of Loki over suspicion of S.H.I.E.L.D.

More significantly, Rogers does not in fact follow orders, but instead snoops around on his own because Stark's "computer was moving a little slow" (*Avengers*). They discover that S.H.I.E.L.D. has been using the Tesseract to build weapons of mass destruction to fight aliens. In other words, once they learned that aliens like Thor and Loki existed, S.H.I.E.L.D. began preparing ways to kill them, as opposed to considering possibilities for cooperation, diplomacy, or trade. As Samira Nadkarni explains, this treatment replicates neo-colonial and imperial hierarchies and biases.[37] Within this system of power, the institutional and governmental reaction to a larger universe out there was that they needed to find ways to violently react to that discovery.

Thor astutely points out that it is because Earthlings started working with the Tesseract that they drew Loki's attention and caused the problems they are currently facing: "It is the signal to all the realms that the Earth is ready for a higher form of war" (*Avengers*). Fury only responds that the Asgardians started it (by coming to Earth first), even though he previously acknowledged that Thor and his people only want peace. Stark points out: "Nuclear deterrent ... 'cause that always calms everything right down" (*Avengers*). His sarcasm is easy to spot, though Fury is able to aptly respond, "Remind me again how you made your fortune, Stark?" (*Avengers*). Of course, Stark's own past is steeped in profiting from weapons, and so his hands are not entirely clean here.

They all then descend into fighting, leading to Banner saying, "I mean, what are we, a team? No, no, no. We're a chemical mixture that makes chaos. We're ... we're a time-bomb" (*Avengers*). The typical connection of chaos to anarchy is not lost on us here. Anarchism is not about everything being smooth and easy. As we will discuss shortly, Loki offers free and easy lives through his dictatorship over the whole world. If Earth simply lets Loki rule us all, then we at least wouldn't have to bother with elections, political parties, making laws, or even making our own moral decisions any more. Anarchism involves independent personalities making their own choices about what each believes is best, and that means there will be disagreement and difficulty, but that is the cost of freedom. There is no one person who gets to make the final call. Everyone has the freedom to express and even pursue their best judgment. Disagreement is inevitable, though if done respectfully and with an eye toward morality, then it can be resolved to as much satisfaction of each person as possible. On the other side, Loki fittingly represents the push back toward the comfort of having one person make all the decisions.

Loki is the perfect anti-anarchist villain of the first film. As the film starts, Fury initially challenges Loki, who assures him that he is there to help the world:

> LOKI: I come with glad tidings of a world made free.
> FURY: Free from what?
> LOKI: Freedom. Freedom is life's great lie. Once you accept that ... in your heart ... you will know peace [*The Avengers*].

Loki explicitly offers submission. He will remove the burden that freedom causes by simply taking away everyone's freedom. As we have seen, it is often comforting and easy to just accept hierarchy and allow others to make decisions for you. Loki offers someone for the whole world to obey unquestioningly in exactly this fashion.[38]

Loki later expands on this idea to a group of humans who have kneeled before him rather than be killed:

> Is not this simpler? Is this not your natural state? It's the unspoken truth of humanity, that you crave subjugation. The bright lure of freedom diminishes your life's joy in a mad scramble for power, for identity. You were made to be ruled. In the end, you will always kneel [*The Avengers*].

Loki represents the position of hierarchy where he is the powerful one and everyone else submits. And, to be honest, Loki's position portrays a certain way that the world currently appears. We all give in to states and corporations, accepting their rule over us instead of seeking our own freedom. We accept subjugation, some of us more than others, to rule from above, even if we pretend that this subjugation amounts to "freedom." It is not true freedom though as we would find out if we attempted to live contrary to the various rules that we are expected to submit to. We are not free, for instance, to take foods and goods that no one else is using. We are not free to live in a house that is not selling. We are not free to write new books about Mickey Mouse even if we stay consistent with the Disney characterization. We are not free in numerous ways, including ways that would involve harming no one else. Instead, we must kneel to the state and the corporations who demand we act in certain ways and not in others.

Perhaps that is why the Avengers make clear that they are not soldiers. Hawkeye/Clint Barton tells Black Widow/Natasha Romanoff that she is "a spy, not a soldier" (*Avengers*). Then, shortly after that, Rogers and Stark have this conversation about Coulson's death:

> ROGERS: Is this the first time you've lost a soldier?
> STARK [loudly]: We are not soldiers! [Then regular voice] I am not marching to Fury's fife.
> ROGERS: Neither am I! He's got the same blood on his hands as Loki does [*Avengers*].

It is made clear that the sense in which they are not soldiers is that neither is following Fury's orders.[39] They will each make their own decisions and have no desire to subjugate themselves to Fury or to anyone else. This point is emphasized when Rogers notes the similarity between Fury and Loki. Both are looking to make others follow them. While Fury may have better intentions, he still acts within an assumed hierarchy and expects others to follow orders. And, further, Fury's S.H.I.E.L.D. falls into the same trap of structural violence as Angel's Wolfram & Hart or Coulson's S.H.I.E.L.D. Where hierarchy is assumed to be justified, it is easy to infer that violence is likewise justified to promote the interests of that hierarchy. As Nadkarni puts it, in *Agents* of S.H.I.E.L.D. and the Marvel Cinematic Universe, hierarchy reinforces the framework of a totalitarian and problematic state through the subjugation of others.[40] Thus, both Fury and Loki are looking to weaponize the Tesseract and control others. While the differences between them obviously matter, so do the similarities.

Notice that when Rogers asks the NYPD for help in the final showdown against the Chitauri, the policeman asks him, "Why the hell should I take orders from you?" (*Avengers*). They are not really orders, though: Rogers has simply identified the best plan of attack. The same thing happens when the Avengers are assembled together and Rogers provides the strategy. It is not that Rogers is ordering the others to act as he wishes them to. Instead, they need a joint strategy, and he has come up with one that they all believe in and can get behind. Anarchism is not about chaotic individuals each doing their unconnected things, which would cause constant conflict. Anarchism seeks communal planning and joint activity, but where everyone agrees to the overall plan as opposed to being simply ordered to follow it.

Even Fury eventually comes to see this point as he refuses to follow the order to issue a nuclear strike against Manhattan, instead telling them: "I recognize the council has made a decision, but given that it's a stupid ass decision, I've elected to ignore it" (*Avengers*). Fury then refuses to follow a stupid ass order, preferring instead to go with his own, morally preferable judgment, which allows for saving all the lives that would be extinguished if he had ordered the nuclear strike. He even goes so far as to shoot down one of the two planes that attempts to take off to nuke Manhattan. And by the next movie, when Stark says, "You're not the Director of me," Fury even responds, "I'm not the Director of anybody. I'm just an old man, who cares very much about you" (*Avengers: Age of Ultron*). Fury is headed toward a full transformation away from hierarchy.

After the Avengers have won the day, it is Fury who then grants them their freedom. He tells the World Security Council that he would not be tracking them, he is allowing Thor to take the Tesseract and Loki, and, as one member of the Council put it, he is unleashing "the Avengers loose on the world" (*Avengers*). At the end of the first *Avengers* film, the Avengers are not agents of S.H.I.E.L.D., they do not answer to the World Security Council, and there is no written contract. When Maria Hill asks Fury how they can be sure that the Avengers will come back, he responds, "Because we'll need them to" (*Avengers*). Significantly, they have no need to be aligned through a hierarchy that binds them because the Avengers are aligned through doing what's right. As Kropotkin explains, "In spite of the narrowly egoistic turn given to men's minds by the commercial system, the tendency towards [Anarchist] Communism is constantly appearing, and influences our activities in a variety of ways."[41] The Avengers overcome their egos because they must work together for justice. Therefore, Fury's belief that they will return when needed is a hopeful ending for the first *Avengers* movie. Of course, ego will rear its ugly head when we arrive at the *Age of Ultron*.

Trusting People with Dark Sides

Agents of S.H.I.E.L.D. shows us that even when institutions attempt to do good, doing so through hierarchy inevitably pulls us down toward restrictions of freedom and perhaps pulls us all the way down to the point where good turns out to be evil. *Avengers* shows us that if we confidentially recognize our own value as agents (as superheroes do) and acknowledge our duties to justice, then we are pushed up toward anarchist organization and activity. *Avengers: Age of Ultron* (from here on, just *Age of Ultron*) starts with another pull downward through Tony Stark's hubris. Hubris means excessive pride or self-confidence; it denotes arrogance and conceit. In other words, hubris is a great description for Stark's attitude. This depiction represents a likely tension: just as the Avengers have the confidence that they will not accept being ruled, they also can have the hubris to think that they ought to rule. That is why it is important that Hawkeye's wife, Laura Barton, warns him, "You need to be sure that this team is really a team" (*Avengers: Age of Ultron*). It is this tendency to hubris that initiates all the trouble in *Age of Ultron*.

After the Avengers have captured Loki's scepter, Stark asks to study it. He explains to Bruce Banner that his purpose is to use the scepter to develop artificial intelligence and create Ultron. Banner asks him if Stark's plan excludes telling the other Avengers, to which Stark agrees:

> STARK: Right. That's right. You know why? Because we don't have time for a city hall debate. I don't want to hear the "man was not meant to meddle" medley. I see a suit of armor around the world.
> BANNER: Sounds like a cold world, Tony.
> STARK: I've seen colder. This one ... this very vulnerable blue one? It needs Ultron.... Peace in our time. Imagine that [*Avengers: Age of Ultron*].

As they go back and forth through this exchange, we see that Stark has taken over the role of S.H.I.E.L.D., complete with all of its problematic hierarchy.[42] In *Avengers*, Fury and S.H.I.E.L.D. seek out weapons of mass destruction in case bad aliens invade. Here, in a clear parallel, it is Stark who seeks out Ultron for the purpose of protecting the world in case bad aliens invade. In both cases, S.H.I.E.L.D. and Stark make these decisions undemocratically—decisions that tend toward violence as a first resort to a merely possible problem. We the viewers know that Thanos is out there and is a big bad (a big bad is the term for the main villain in any Whedon show or film), yet from the characters' perspective, aliens could turn out to be mostly good (as

Thor and the Asgardians appear to be) or bad (as the Chitauri appear to be). It certainly seems worth waiting to meet the aliens that come next—if any ever do—before deciding that they must be dealt with through violence. As Rogers explains to Stark later, "Every time someone tries to win a war before it starts, innocent people die. Every time" (*Avengers: Age of Ultron*). The quick turn to violence is no better, and is usually much worse, than waiting until violence is absolutely necessary.

Stark, however, is not patient. He wishes to harness the power of Loki's scepter—which has only been the cause of problems in the past—to create artificial intelligence to install peace on Earth. Of course, we already saw that Loki's not-very-benevolent promise was likewise peace on Earth. Hence, we are already prepared to be suspicious of Stark's plan for peace, and it does indeed blow up in his face as the film progresses. What is important here though is that he is making this decision on his own: he has no interest in waiting for debate, and has no desire to hear the other side (knowing full well that Rogers and Thor would surely argue that he should not meddle). Stark's hubris has pulled him back down to a statist position where he takes on the role of the state and makes the key decision for everyone else.

Even when Stark is confronted about building Ultron, immediately after the rest of the team meets him, Stark refuses to take moral responsibility. Rogers tells him that "the Avengers were supposed to be different than S.H.I.E.L.D." (*Avengers: Age of Ultron*), but Stark's hubris blinds him from seeing the similarities. Instead of worrying about his plan, he simply reminds them that he saved the day in the previous fight (in *Avengers*) by carrying the nuclear warhead through the wormhole. Stark perhaps correctly argues that he did not fully create the Ultron that is clearly going to cause them trouble: he may have initiated something, but it seems as if the scepter finished the work somehow. Nevertheless, he also argues, in spite of the evidence of Ultron's evil, that ultimately he is right to create Ultron since they "need this" (*Avengers: Age of Ultron*). It is Stark's decision, he makes it alone (with only a bit of discussion with Banner), and even when it is obviously going bad, he does not accept moral responsibility.

Ultron is, of course, bad. He presents a similar hierarchal position as both Loki and, as we have just seen, Stark. Of course, Ultron directly derives his position from Stark, as he makes clear when he replays a tape of Stark's voice when explains his purpose is to be "a suit of armor around the world" (*Avengers: Age of Ultron*). Wanda Maximoff/Scarlet Witch notes this very connection between Ultron and Stark when she asks Rogers, "Ultron can't tell the difference between saving the world and destroying it. Where do you think he gets that?" (*Avengers: Age of Ultron*). Ultron offers peace in our time just as Stark sought, but clearly he offers it through his own rule. That, though, seems not too far from Stark's attempt to build Ultron and hope he would provide peace in our time, presumably through Stark's leadership. As Ultron tells the assembled Avengers, he knows they meant well, but "you just didn't think it through. You want to protect the world, but you don't want it to change. How is humanity saved if it's not allowed to … evolve?" (*Avengers: Age of Ultron*). Thus, Ultron offers peace, but through a new world of his design (and one without the Avengers, whom he correctly identifies as killers).

And when the Avengers get together with Fury and discuss their plan against Ultron, Fury makes clear that their best tools are themselves:

> ROMANOFF: Well, this is good times, boss, but I was kind of hoping when I saw you, you'd have more than that.
> FURY: I do. I have you. Back in the day, I had eyes everywhere, ears everywhere else. Here we all are, back on Earth, with nothing but our wit, and our will to save the world. So stand. Outwit the platinum bastard [*Avengers: Age of Ultron*].

While the Avengers are superheroes, their ability to represent regular humans is made almost explicit by them facing an enemy who is much stronger than them. Just as the Avengers can stand against Ultron through teamwork and their wits, humans must eventually build a new kind of society with little else. As Kropotkin puts the same point more eloquently, "men at last attempt to free themselves from every form of government and to satisfy their need for organization by a free contract between individuals and groups pursuing the same aim."[43]

Stark's creation of Vision, out of Jarvis, is not significantly different than the creation of Ultron. This time, both Banner and Thor seem to give at least implicit approval, but Stark's decision was purposely kept from any larger discussion once again, and Rogers is left completely in the dark. Stark does not seem to have sufficient basis to believe Vision would be different than Ultron, but he continues on, nonetheless, through a bit of blind hope. Thor likewise is placing his trust in a vision about the Mind Stone. It is less clear why Banner goes along, other than his own blind hope.

The Avengers do, nonetheless, get lucky with Vision. Vision says, "I am on the side of life. Ultron isn't" (*Avengers: Age of Ultron*). Vision though seems to have his own set of self-doubts. He acknowledges, "Maybe I am a monster. I don't think I'd know if I were one. I'm not what you are, and not what you intended. So, there may be no way to make you trust me, but we need to go" (*Avengers: Age of Ultron*). And then he picks up Thor's hammer on the way out. Thus, their trust in Vision is secured through whatever mystical powers provide Thor's hammer with the magical ability to determine worthiness. *Age of Ultron* then heads toward a conclusion where things are initially working out based on luck, in spite of Stark's hubris.

Rogers nonetheless recognizes that deep, moral questions remain: "Ultron thinks we're monsters and we're what's wrong with the world. This isn't just about beating him. It's about whether he's right" (*Avengers: Age of Ultron*). And when they do fight Ultron in Sokovia, they set as their primary goal making sure that they save the people of Sokovia. They place saving others as their priority, risking their own lives in the process. That is the spirit of anarchism, according to Kropotkin: "those who man the lifeboat do not ask credentials from the crew of a sinking ship; they launch their boat, risk their lives in the raging waves, and sometimes perish, all to save men whom they do not even know. And what need to know them? 'They are human beings, and they need our aid—that is enough, that establishes their right— To the rescue!"[44] The Avengers then prove their worthiness not through a mystical hammer or a presumption that they are on the side of what's right. Instead, their worthiness is established through the fact that they work together in a collaborative fashion to save the endangered human beings around them (without ever asking those people whether they have credentials that show they are worth being saved). To put it simply, the Avengers show their worthiness by acting as anarchists.

Pulling a Team into Shape

The Marvel editions of Whedon's works have clear ebb and flow to them. *Agents of S.H.I.E.L.D.* and the *Avengers* films move back and forth between problematic representations of hierarchy to clear instances of Kropotkin's notion of mutual aid. Kropotkin explains that he does not expect people under anarchism to be motivated by love or even sympathy. He instead describes "a feeling infinitely wider than love or personal sympathy—an instinct that has been slowly developed among animals and men in the course of an extremely long evolution, and which has taught animals and men alike the force they can borrow from the practice of mutual aid and support, and the joys they can find in social life."[45] We ought to be motivated by a sense of solidarity that encourages us to provide mutual aid to each other. It is "Mutual Aid and Mutual Support" that Kropotkin says is "a feature of the greatest importance for the maintenance of life, the preservation of each species, and its further evolution."[46] People who engage in mutual aid are committed to helping each other simply because it is the right thing to do, regardless of whether they love or sympathize with those other people. Both the agents of S.H.I.E.L.D. and the Avengers believe in mutual aid, consistently risking their lives over and over to aid others, who are not known to them, simply because doing so is right.

Clearly, Kropotkin does not believe that true mutual aid resides in a hierarchal setting. Where we listen to the orders of others, instead of determining our moral obligations for ourselves, then we become morally lazy.

We no longer act on mutual aid, but instead act on individualism, where each person is out for themselves. *Agents of S.H.I.E.L.D.* depicts good people as members of a clearly hierarchal organization. As such, we see the flaws inherent in the system. Hydra is able to infiltrate S.H.I.E.L.D. such that S.H.I.E.L.D. corrodes its own goodness as its leaders are not as moral as the agents who are on the streets fighting evil, yet through it all, the main S.H.I.E.L.D. team— Coulson, May, Skye, Fitz, Simmons, Mack, Yo-Yo, and others—maintain committed to mutual aid. While the organization spans from good to evil, the individuals that make up the lower end of the hierarchy (and Coulson) fight to be good on a consistent basis. The core team is helping others just because it is right, even if the hierarchy breaks down and no one is ordering them to help others.

The Avengers likewise have their struggles. On the one hand, their insistence on making their own judgment calls allows them to avoid many of the trappings of hierarchy. The Avengers will not give in and do only as S.H.I.E.L.D. orders. They instead consistently do what they believe to be right and just. Of course, when their hubris expands, as Stark's definitely does, they risk moving away from joint cooperation and are pulled back down toward unbridled individualism.

Throughout Whedon's Marvel works, we see a push and pull that shows the temptation of hierarchy while also showing the call of the righteous path of mutual aid. Having said that, it must be noted that there are two general sides of anarchism. While we have seen many anarchists who would fall under anarcho-socialism—including Kropotkin the anarcho-communist as well as Robert Paul Wolff, Henry David Thoreau, David Graeber, William Godwin, and Noam Chomsky—there is another side. Anarcho-capitalists embrace the individualism that Stark can be seen as representing (especially in *Age of Ultron*). Anarcho-capitalists join anarchism and capitalism together in a way that they believe truly represents what anarchism should be. And, to be entirely honest, *Firefly* has a fairly clear anarcho-capitalist feel to it—at least on the surface. To see that the anarcho-capitalism does not run deep, we will next take you out to the black.

Four

The Black Reaching Out

Anarcho-Capitalists vs. Anarcho-Socialists on Board the Firefly[1]

The Call from the Black

We have now seen anarchist critiques of hierarchy by examining *Angel* and *Dollhouse*. Through analyzing *Agents of S.H.I.E.L.D.* and the *Avengers* films, we have also seen that there are competing social tendencies both toward and away from anarchism. Our studies of Joss Whedon's works thus far have led us to understand several claims that anarchists make about what is wrong with hierarchal society and why it makes sense for us to look for an anarchist turn. We have yet tried to examine positive anarchist principles in action. To start this task, which will take up the remainder of the book, we will now discuss *Firefly*. Our initial goal will be to figure out what the central theme of *Firefly* is, which would then tell us something about what positive claims we can derive from investigating Whedon's films and TV shows.

A number of *Firefly* commentators have argued that the television show presents a libertarian message.[2] Libertarianism, roughly, refers to any political ideology that places a primary and substantial value on human liberty. Libertarianism includes a wide range of views on both the ideological left and ideological right, though the term tends to refer more to right-wing views in American political parlance.[3] Right-libertarianism also ranges across multiple views that differ with respect to the role they assign to the state: minimal statist libertarians are not anarchists since they support a limited role for a state provided that the state only serves to protect the liberty of individuals to do as they please, while anarcho-capitalists, who are perhaps extreme libertarians, embrace both anarchism and capitalism.

Even though these scholarly *Firefly* commentators prefer the open-ended term, we are more interested in anarcho-capitalism in particular, which is more consistent with the libertarian aspects of *Firefly* than other libertarian theories would be. These commentators argue that *Firefly* represents a positive portrayal of some version of libertarian philosophy, which could mean that it supports the rights of individuals over those of social groups or society itself, bases morality in self-ownership and consent, and/or rejects strong positive obligations to help others simply because they are in need. Since the show also depicts a rejection of the state, it would not merely be a general right-libertarian show, but would more likely be an anarcho-capitalist show in particular. Thus, we are merely being more specific when we question whether *Firefly* is really an anarcho-capitalist show. We will continue to use "libertarian" as an umbrella term that encompasses all kinds of right-libertarian views, with "minimal statist" standing in for right-libertarians that are not anarchists and "anarcho-capitalist" meaning anarchist-right-libertarians.

Assuming it makes sense to discuss the most central message of a TV show as complex as *Firefly*, much in the show speaks in favor of a general libertarian interpretation, and in particular an anarcho-capitalist one. First, the lead character, Captain Malcolm "Mal" Reynolds is clearly a libertarian of some kind: he stands for individual liberty and against governmental interference in individuals' lives. Jayne Cobb is an even stricter libertarian and is most likely an anarcho-capitalist. Jayne is the John Galt of space: Jayne will bow out of any activity in which he does not see the "profit" or "percentage."[4] Jayne certainly would never, for instance, intentionally give away money for the sake of helping a bunch of mudders.

Not only are some of the main characters libertarians, but the big bad in the show—the Alliance—is the typical libertarian/anarcho-capitalist villain: an all-powerful government looking to spread its meddling throughout the 'verse. If you were looking to write an anarcho-capitalist tale, you would need to invent a villain just like the Alliance. When you add in a theme song that sounds like the lyricized premises of an anarcho-capitalist argument, you quickly see why astute commentators see *Firefly* as a libertarian show, and you can imagine that it just might be an anarcho-capitalist show.

In spite of this credible stance, there are difficulties for the libertarian interpretation. First, Joss Whedon is no libertarian. The rest of his oeuvre is thoroughly anti-libertarian or at least inconsistent with libertarian values.[5] We saw, through *Angel* in Chapter Two, that structural violence is not merely a problem due to the government, but due to hierarchy in general. Poverty is a particularly nasty form of structural violence that capitalism makes possible. By examining *Dollhouse* in Chapter Two, we saw a capitalist villain, the Rossum Corporation, that undermined our autonomy in a way that makes consent—a lynchpin of libertarian morality—unable to convey true moral obligations. Thus, contrary to libertarian philosophy, Whedon's *Dollhouse* provides an argument that corporations endanger consent in particular and libertarian morality in general. Further, in our previous chapter, we discussed the *Avengers* films and saw that a libertarian arrangement, which would endorse a clear hierarchy as long as that hierarchy was not political, was ineffective and nearly impossible when it came to Superheroes trying to work together. We will later see, in our next two chapters, that *Buffy* certainly does not endorse libertarian values. Therefore, it would at the very least be odd if *Firefly* embraced values that all of Whedon's other shows unmistakably reject.

More importantly, *Firefly* does not present a consistent vision of libertarian philosophy.[6] Much of *Firefly* flies in the face of libertarianism. While Mal has some libertarian principles and provides libertarian critiques of the Alliance, his actions speak more loudly than his words. Even though Mal's penchant for self-sacrifice for the sake of others, especially in his crew, is technically consistent with libertarianism, it certainly is not the best way to represent strict libertarian values. Besides Mal and Jayne—the latter of whom, frankly, is largely comic relief—the other main characters are far from libertarians. In particular, given Whedon's strong commitment to feminism, it would be odd to derive the show's message from its two least feminist characters. As we will see, the female characters and the feminist male characters represent non-libertarian values that would align more with an anarcho-socialist outlook.

Hence, against the standard interpretation that the show represents a libertarian perspective, we will argue that *Firefly* is best understood as an anarcho-socialist show. We explain away the libertarian or anarcho-capitalist elements of the show in two ways. First, anarcho-socialism and libertarianism share a deep distrust of the state, which means that some seemingly libertarian elements are actually ambiguously indicative of both anarcho-socialist and libertarian interpretations. Second, the libertarian characters are genuinely libertarian, but they are actively engaged in moral character development that will bring them much closer to anarcho-socialist outlooks.

Furthermore, through this interpretation of *Firefly* as an anarcho-socialist show, we will understand that Whedon's messages and characters across all of his works are best analyzed through an anarcho-socialist lens. Many of Whedon's key female characters, including Buffy, Cordelia, Echo, Kaylee Frye, and Inara Serra, and feminist male characters, including Giles, Angel, Hoban "Wash" Washburne, and Dr. Simon Tam, act according to anarcho-socialist values and attempt to enact small versions of anarcho-socialist communities within their respective groups of fighters. Thus, we look to raise and then settle the debate over the central theme of *Firefly* to show that not only is this show more anarcho-socialist, but that this outlook provides a superior perspective for understanding Whedon's works in general.

Stealing from the Rich, Selling to the Poor: The Theories

Libertarianism starts with the notion that each person owns his or her self, or, as anarcho-capitalist David Friedman simply puts it, "everyone has the right to run his own life."[7] Let's call this the "self-ownership claim."[8] A person's self includes her mind and body. If a person owns her self, then she can do whatever she wants with her mind and body, as long as her action is consistent with every other person owning his or her own self in the same way. It is wrong for River Tam to hit Jayne Cobb even with her own hand because that interferes with Jayne's right to protect his own body. Shepherd Derrial Book, however, has the right to grow his hair as long as he likes, no matter how much he risks it all caving in: he has the right to place his own brains in "terrible danger" (River, "Jaynestown" 1.7).

While self-ownership is a central tenet of both left and right libertarians, right-wing libertarians believe that owning one's self entails the ability to own objects, either through meeting some simple test for first obtaining the object (being the first one to grab it, use it, change it, etc.) or by obtaining the object from another person through a justified transfer.[9] Once a person takes ownership in an object, her rights extend to that object: the person can do whatever she desires with the object as long as it is consistent with the same extended self-ownership for all others. As minimal statist Robert Nozick states it, "My property rights in my knife allow me to leave it where I will, but not in your chest."[10]

Finally, libertarians accept that there are freely chosen trade-offs of liberty: sometimes you allow others to infringe on your liberty in one way for the sake of an increase in liberty in another way. To this end, individuals enter into consensual exchanges of liberty. As Nozick points out, just as a person can choose to cross his own moral and personal boundaries, he can also "give another permission to do these things to him.... Voluntary consent opens the border for crossings."[11] For example, Badger can consent to give Mal a certain amount of Badger's own money in exchange for Mal consenting to use Mal's self, his ship, and others who have consented to work for him, to gather some goods for Badger. Since they consented to this arrangement, neither is impermissibly crossing the others' boundaries. Each allows boundaries to be crossed (Mal can take some of Badger's money and Badger can demand some of Mal's labor) in exchange for increases in liberty elsewhere (Mal receives money and Badger receives goods as a result of the labor of Mal and crew).

While there are a large variety of right libertarian views, the strict libertarian argues that the above three points (self-ownership, property, and consent) exhaust morality.[12] Libertarians would accept the moral permissibility of doing anything that results from self-ownership, legitimate property acquisition, and consent. A person's actions are perfectly permissible if they only involve their selves, their legitimate property, anything they received from the consent of others, and their actions do not infringe on the similar rights of others. Such a moral theory would not allow clearly immoral acts such as murder (violates self-ownership), theft (violates property), and kidnapping someone (lacks consent).

Libertarian moral theory does not require helping others. As Friedman says, "I oppose welfare programs that support the poor with money taken by force from the taxpayers."[13] He later adds, "A libertarian society would have no welfare, no Social Security system. People who wished to aid others would do so voluntarily through private charity instead of using money collected by force from the taxpayers."[14] In both quotations, Friedman shows that he is interested in protecting individuals from being made to pay taxes that they did not voluntarily consent to—which would deprive them of their property (the money to be taxed). He is not interested in making people contribute to helping others who are in dire situations, such as the impoverished and the elderly. Libertarian morality requires that people are only asked to do what they consent to do, and so helping others is not morally required. Thus, libertarians do not accept a taxation system where the taxes are used to help others since such a system, according to Friedman, "insists on collecting the taxes whether or not I want the services."[15] No one can be blamed for not choosing to use their self-ownership or property ownership to help others in need if they do not wish to do so. Helping others, according to libertarians, is simply a desire that some people wish to act on, while others have no such desire.

The minimal statist does not believe in a state that would enforce positive duties of morality since the libertarian denies there are such duties. Therefore, there are no systems for social security, welfare, education, or any other similarly helpful government provisions. The minimal state only includes governmental systems, such as courts, the military, and police forces, that protect and enforce self-ownership, property rights, and consensual agreements. As Nozick states in the thesis for *Anarchy, State, and Utopia*, "Our main conclusions about the state are that a minimal state, limited to the narrow functions of protection against force, theft, fraud, enforcement of contracts, and so on, is justified."[16]

The anarcho-capitalist points out that this minimal statist position creates the very same problem as a welfare statist position.[17] The welfare state represents the liberal position that the state should support the welfare of the citizenry through programs such as education, health care, parks and recreation, etc. In both cases, people are being made to give up their property (in the form of money paid in taxes) for communal goods that they did not consent to provide for the whole society. While minimal statists argue that the state is necessary for these minimal functions of ensuring rights are protected, anarcho-capitalists argue that such a position violates rights just like that of the welfare statists: you cannot be forced to help others without your consent. Therefore, being made to pay for someone else's police protection is just as wrong as being made to pay for their education. Anarcho-capitalists argue that they are the only morally consistent libertarians.

Turning next to the anarcho-socialist position, we will look at the Mexican anarchist Ricardo Flores Magón (1874–1922). Magón was influenced by Peter Kropotkin's *The Conquest of Bread* and he organized with the Industrial Workers of the World, an international labor union. He was one of the theorists and social activists that sparked the Mexican Revolution (1910–1920). Magón also edited the Mexican anarchist newspaper, *Regeneración*.

Magón sees anarchism not only as the solution to an over-bearing political hierarchy, but also to an economic hierarchy that just as much attempts to control people's lives. Accordingly, he calls for the people to obtain their economic liberty, which entails

> the ability to make a living through working, without having to depend on anybody, an ability that can be obtained only—understand this well—by making the lands, the houses, the machinery, the means of transportation and the warehoused goods, by means of expropriation, the common property of all, men and women, without discrimination based on race or color.[18]

Thus, for Magón, it is not enough that governmental officials do not manipulate and control their subjects, it is also necessary that company bosses and the bourgeois class are not agents of manipulation and control. In his "Letter from L.A. County Jail," Magón explains what anarchists already know: in a society where the people own the land and the means of production, the workers will show camaraderie and "mutually exchange their products."[19] For anarcho-socialists the critique of the state is not far from the critique of capitalism. As Magón says, "Without economic liberty, it's not possible to enjoy political liberty."[20]

For anarcho-socialists, a justified society must lack systematic hindrances to liberty, regardless of whether those hindrances are political, economic, social, or other. Just as there are many kinds of libertarians, there are likewise many anarcho-socialists, including anarcho-collectivists, anarcho-communists, anarcho-syndicalists, and anarcho-feminists.[21] Each of these views agrees that the people's liberty should be infringed neither by political nor by economic means, but they disagree on how society ought to be arranged.

There is one important agreement among anarcho-socialists: anarchism entails not establishing property rights that allow anyone to have the power to manipulate and control others.²² For libertarians, like Friedman, the private property rights of individuals are human rights.²³ Magón, though, disagrees: "The right to property is an absurd right because it originates in crime, fraud, and the abuse of force."²⁴ Instead of seeing private property as foundational, anarcho-socialists ask how private property came to be. Humans, after all, did not originally evolve into creatures that already owned property. Anarcho-socialists believe that either nothing was originally owned or that the world was originally owned in common, as in all humans owned all of the world together. That is the starting point for anarcho-socialists, and, as we saw, libertarians do not necessarily disagree. The libertarian simply believes that we move from either non-ownership to private ownership through some act, such as a person declaring that they own something or being the first to use that thing.

If we all owned the world together, then someone declaring one day that they now owned some particular thing (even if they are first to use it) would be stealing that thing from everyone else. Imagine someone just yelling out one day that they now own Maui when the previous day everyone in the world shared ownership over Maui or Maui was just not a thing that could be owned at all. We can even imagine this person was the first to land on Maui. If that person did not forcefully protect their claim to Maui, they would surely just be laughed at ("You don't really own Maui, you fool"). If that person used force to protect their claim to Maui, they have simply stolen Maui from the rest of the world by force. Just as the libertarian sees taxes as a forceful and even violent taking of property, the anarcho-socialist sees the appropriation of the commons as literally violent. Magón explains:

> The right of a single person to territorial property was born in the attack of the first ambitious person who brought war against a neighboring tribe in order to subdue them into servitude, putting the land which this tribe cultivated in common under the control of the conqueror and his captains. Thus, it was through violence, through the abuse of force, that private territorial property was born.²⁵

For Magón and the anarcho-socialists, the creation of private property then was based on the violent acts of individuals who overtook peoples who had previously shared property in common.

A further key point that anarcho-socialists share is the idea that an anarcho-socialist arrangement of society, regardless of the particulars, will result in a moral sense of community that is based on mutual aid and solidarity. Magón explains solidarity by calling it "the consciousness of the common interest, and the actions that follow from this consciousness."²⁶ By sharing property and being beholden to no leadership, the members of the anarcho-socialist community will make their own moral decisions, see their fellow comrades as joined with them as a team, and will find solidarity in their common interests. According to Magón, the recognition of this solidarity "should unite the human species into a single intelligent and active force."[27] We see such powerful force through solidarity in each of Whedon's shows. We will see that *Firefly* exhibits just this kind of solidarity, though it is masked by a forced hierarchy that, at first look, appears to be more libertarian.

As should be clear, the anarcho-capitalist and the anarcho-socialist will have quite strong complaints about each other. The anarcho-capitalist will deny that the anarcho-socialist really counts as an anarchist since the anarcho-socialist limits liberty when it comes to things such as the liberty to own factories and huge plots of land. The anarcho-socialist, in response, doubts the anarcho-capitalist's commitment to anarchism and respect for liberty since the anarcho-capitalist allows the liberty of the workers to be squashed to increase profits for their bosses. The anarcho-capitalist would respond that the worker consents to a limitation of her liberty in exchange for the boss consenting to pay wages. The anarcho-socialist would respond that the worker's agreement is not consensual since it is an exploited agreement that is only made within a morally unacceptable power hierarchy. The anarcho-capitalist will challenge the idea that *this* power hierarchy is immoral since no libertarian rules of morality are violated by the boss's exploitative actions. While the individual moves within this debate provide useful information about each position, obviously the two sides are unlikely to find an ultimate agreement.

We can bring in two interconnected distinctions to highlight these stark differences: negative vs. positive liberty and negative vs. positive duties.[28] A person enjoys negative liberty if no person intentionally interferes with her ability to act. Libertarians prize negative liberty as a direct consequence of the self-ownership claim: if you own yourself, then you are truly free if no one interferes with your ability to act. Someone can enjoy maximal negative liberty and be unable to accomplish anything worthwhile in their lives. Imagine, for example, a person who falls into a pit and cannot get out. Though there is little he can do in his dire situation, no one is interfering with him in the pit, so the person dying away in the pit retains all of his negative liberty.

Positive liberty refers to the freedom to perform acts of some substance. Libertarians argue that no one should have their negative liberty violated to help others obtain positive liberty.[29] If a person does not wish to give money to an important cause that will promote positive liberty, then it would be wrong, according to libertarians, to interfere with her negative liberty by coercing the person, such as through a coercive taxation system, to help the positive liberty cause. Libertarianism would allow that the person could freely choose to donate to the cause, but neither can charity be required nor can it be blameworthy not to give. The choice to give is simply a free expression of self-ownership that warrants neither moral praise nor moral blame.

The anarcho-socialist supports a society where both negative and positive liberty are enjoyed.[30] This seemingly inconsistent result is simply achieved by denying the extension of self-ownership. People own themselves, and so their negative liberty is violated when you interfere with their person. Objects, however, are shared in common so that all people can use the objects necessary to enjoy their positive liberty. As noted, the libertarian will think that a person cannot be free if they cannot *control* objects. The anarcho-socialist, on the other hand, will argue that a society where everyone has negative liberty, but only the powerful few enjoy positive liberty because they control the vast majority of objects, is a horribly unfree society for everyone save for those few. As Italian anarchist Errico Malatesta put it, "That aspiration towards unlimited freedom, if not tempered by a love for mankind and by the desire that all should enjoy equal freedom, may well create rebels who, if they are strong enough, soon become exploiters and tyrants, but never anarchists."[31]

As noted, anarcho-socialists, like Magón or Malatesta, believe that in an anarcho-socialist community, there will be senses of solidarity and mutual aid where individuals accept positive duties to help each other.[32] A positive duty requires the agent to do something to meet it, where inaction can be sufficient to meet a negative duty. "Give to those in need" is a positive duty. "Do not kill, steal, or cheat" are negative duties. The positive duty to help others would not be enforced in an anarcho-socialist society: anarchism lacks legal and political enforcement mechanisms. Instead, anarcho-socialists believe that agents will recognize their positive moral duties when their moral values are no longer warped by a paternalistic state that invades our ability to think clearly about moral matters. When people live under a state that is constantly saying that it will take care of people and make their moral decisions for them, people become morally lazy. The anarcho-socialist believes that people will awaken to their moral codes if left to think for themselves. These moral codes will include both positive duties to help others achieve their positive liberty and negative duties to respect negative liberty.

To put it all simply, anarcho-socialists and libertarians (including both minimal statists and anarcho-capitalists) agree that a powerful, central government is an unjustified intrusion on people's lives. They disagree on what should replace it. Minimal statists would prefer a minimal state while anarchists of both types seek to remove the state from society entirely. Anarcho-capitalists and libertarians would both require a capitalist system that included private property. Anarcho-socialists would support a system of communal property instead.

Having seen the theories, we can now return to examining *Firefly*. Since libertarians and anarchists alike are anti-state, *Firefly*'s critique of the Alliance in itself may not settle which approach provides a superior interpretation of the show. Consider the moment in the film, *Serenity*, when River complains that the Alliance meddles: "People don't like to be meddled with. We tell them what to do, what to think. Don't run. Don't walk. We're in their homes and in their heads and we haven't the right. We're meddlesome." That is a telling comment from River that sheds quite a bright light on the film's and the show's message, yet libertarians and anarcho-socialists alike agree that states are too meddlesome. Thus, this moment points equally in all of those anti-state directions.

To figure out the correct interpretation of the show, we need to concentrate more on the differences between the competing interpretations. The differences come out when key characters are morally called upon to act for the positive liberty of others. Hence, to test the dueling interpretations, we should examine how the characters react to positive duties to support the positive liberty of others.

No More Sadistic Crap Legitimized by Florid Prose

Positive duties may provide the key for judging the competing libertarian and anarcho-socialist interpretations of *Firefly*. If so, the main dynamic to study could be the one between Mal and Simon, with the former being a libertarian while the latter certainly is not. Simon embraces positive duties to the point of giving up everything he owned for the sake of his sister. Thus, Mal and Simon provide a telling contrast specifically on the issue of positive duties.

Starting with Mal, Whedon has already acknowledged that Mal is a libertarian,[33] and Mal clearly embraces libertarianism. For example, there are all those wonderful lines where Mal is openly critical of government, such as when he says, "That's what governments are for—get in a man's way" ("Serenity" 1.1) or "That sounds like the Alliance. Unite all the planets under one rule so that everybody can be interfered with or ignored equally" ("The Train Job" 1.2). While these lines are indicative of libertarianism, they would not unequivocally distinguish between libertarian and anarcho-socialist interpretations.

What marks Mal as distinctly libertarian is how he runs his ship. After first buying Serenity, Mal explains to Zoe that Serenity can provide their freedom: they can "live like people. A small crew—them as feel the need to be free. Take jobs as they come. And we'll never have to be under the heel of nobody ever again. No matter how long the arm of the Alliance might get, we'll just get us a little further" ("Out of Gas" 1.8). But Mal's heel will, at least a bit, be on his crew as he will enjoy greater freedom on his boat, which he definitely sees as an extension of his self-ownership. When Lawrence Dobson shoots Kaylee, Mal decides he would kill Simon and River if Simon, whom he blames, does not save Kaylee's life. When Wash responds, "Can we maybe vote on the whole murdering people issue?" Mal tells him, "We don't vote on my ship because my ship is not the rutting town hall" ("Serenity" 1.1). From Mal's libertarian viewpoint, owning the ship allows him to order around the people who agreed to work for him, and, thus, agreed to limit their liberty rights in exchange for some of his money.

It is less clear whether Mal would count as a minimal statist, an anarcho-capitalist, or somewhere in the middle. He voluntarily fought for the Browncoats (an association of independent planets that each had their own governments) during the Unification War. His military service could signal that he at least supported minimal planetary governments. It could also simply be that he stood so strongly against the Alliance government that he signed up to fight with their opponents. It is not entirely clear why Mal joined the war. The closest we get to an explanation is in the comic, *Those Left Behind*, when Whedon, during "A Brief History of the Universe," mysteriously explains, "He joined out of belief and nothing more."[34] While Mal's specific libertarian belief system remains an open question, he is certainly not an anarcho-socialist since anarcho-socialists would believe that Mal infringes on his crew's freedom by recreating a hierarchal system within Serenity.

While Mal may be a clear libertarian, Simon presents a significantly different perspective. It is not necessarily inconsistent with libertarianism for Simon to give up everything, including his life as a doctor in Capital City on Osiris, to save his sister. Libertarians clearly can care about their family members or choose to engage in self-sacrifice. Libertarianism simply does not make self-sacrifice a moral duty or even worthy of special moral praise; a positive duty to sacrifice for others is inconsistent with libertarian self-ownership. The question, then, is whether Simon helps his sister out of a positive moral duty or simply chooses to do so for personal reasons, such as brotherly love.

Since Simon likely acts out of both love and duty with respect to River, their relationship is not fully instructive here. To get a more edifying picture, let us examine Simon's manner of dealing with Jayne. There is unlikely to be any love lost between these two as Jayne betrays Simon by trying to sell him to the Alliance in "Ariel" (1.9). From Jayne's perspective: why not? There's a reward for turning Simon in, and Jayne has made no consensual agreement with Simon. While it would be an infringement on Simon's and River's negative liberty, Jayne would likely rationalize it as a justified infringement since they are fugitives. Jayne pretty much explains this perspective in the film, *Serenity*, when he says, "No offense, Doc. I think it's noble as a grape the way you look to River. But she ain't my sister and she ain't your [Mal's] crew. Oh, and neither is she exactly helpless. So where's it writ that we got to lay down our lives for her?" Therefore, for Jayne, he has no personal connection to River, does not really consider her to be part of the crew, and there's nothing really written in the moral rules, in his judgment, that says he ought to risk his life for Simon and River.

Once Simon realizes that Jayne has betrayed them, he waits until Jayne is on his examination table and under the knife to deliver this speech:

> You're in a dangerous line of work, Jayne. Odds are you'll be under my knife again. Often. So I want you to understand one thing very clearly. No matter what you do or say or plot—no matter how you come down on us—I will never ever harm you. You're on this table, you're safe. Cause I'm your medic ["Trash" 1.11].

Simon sees himself as under immense positive duties. Whether his patient is someone he loves or is a serious threat to him and his sister, he will go beyond the doctor's negative obligation of "do no harm," and will strive to meet his positive duty to help others in need. Simon believes he has positive duties even when it is Jayne under his knife, which truly shows Simon has a strong belief that morality extends beyond the limitations that libertarians place on it.

While Jayne repeatedly attempts to betray Simon, Mal does not. Far from it, Mal in fact changes because of Simon's influence. Remember that Mal is more than happy to turn Simon over to Dobson in "Serenity" (1.1). Mal is quite relieved that Dobson is after Simon, and offers to lock Simon in a cell until the Alliance can take Simon away, yet when Dobson says he considers everybody on the ship to be culpable, Mal responds, "Well, now. That has an effect on the landscape" ("Serenity" 1.1). So, clearly in the first episode, Mal acts as a libertarian might: if turning in Simon protects Mal, his crew, and his ship, then he's happy to do so since he doesn't see himself owing any moral duty to Simon.

Throughout the rest of the series, Mal feels it would be wrong to betray Simon simply because Simon is part of Mal's crew. Consider Simon's inquiry into why Mal returned to save him and River in "Safe":

> SIMON: Captain, why did you come back for us?
> MAL: You're on my crew.
> SIMON: But you don't even like me. Why'd you come back?
> MAL: You're on my crew. Why are we still talking about this? ["Safe," 1.5].

Of course, even an anarcho-capitalist can find this discussion unproblematic. An anarcho-capitalist could say that Mal has chosen to highly value his crew to the extent that he is willing to risk his own life for them. This personal choice need not require pre-existing positive duties. It is also possible that Mal feels that he has made a consensual agreement to protect Simon and River when he took them aboard.

In response to these interpretations, neither mere personal choice nor prior consent seem to explain Mal's strong sense of duty toward the Tams. First, the risk is both very substantial and very real. Mal is doing everything he can to avoid the Alliance, and taking on River and Simon brings him right onto the Alliance's radar. Mal will obviously struggle to avoid capture and likely death now that he is harboring River and Simon. While it is possible that someone can simply choose, without any moral motivation, to take on substantial risk for others, it is not very likely to this extent for people with whom Mal has so little connection.

Second, Mal felt he made no consent that required allegiance to Simon when he was willing to sell the Tams out to Dobson. At no later time in the show does Mal ever explicitly consent to protect Simon and River. Further, there is nothing for him to personally gain by consenting to protect them, and everything to lose by doing so. It is highly unlikely that a rational libertarian would ever consent to this deal, so it is unlikely that Mal consents to protect the Tams.

Mal appears to owe Simon nothing from a libertarian perspective, but Mal seems to realize that he owes positive assistance to Simon for some grander reason, as Book suspects. Book attempts to inquire why Mal is helping Simon since clearly Simon is not paying enough to be worth the trouble he and River bring with them:

> BOOK: I'm wondering why a man so anxious to fly under Alliance radar would house known fugitives. The Alliance had her in that institution for a purpose whatever it was, and they will want her back. You're not overly fond of the boy. So why risk it?
> MAL [SARCASTICALLY]: Only because it's the right thing to do…
> BOOK: I'm beginning to wonder if you yourself know why you're doing it ["The Train Job" 1.2].

Shepherd Book, on the surface, represents the religious perspective of the show. Deeper down, Book represents substantial moral thought: he believes in significant moral commitments, including positive duties, which he does not believe necessarily derive from religion. Here, Book senses that Mal has a moral code that goes beyond the limited libertarian morality. Mal does not merely choose to help the Tams since, as Book is careful to note, Mal does not even like them and they endanger Mal's cherished freedom. Book sees that Mal recognizes the same inner conflict, though Book suspects that the libertarian Mal does not fully comprehend where his strong sense of positive duty comes from. Mal does clearly realize that he *must* risk everything—his life, his crew's lives, and *even his liberty*—to save these siblings that he does not even like.

The libertarian interpretation of Mal lies on the surface instead of running down deep. This point does not deny the claim: Mal really is a libertarian on the surface, but Book and others see a deeper version of Mal—deeper than even Mal sees. Consider how Kaylee scoffs at Jayne's suggestion that Mal is waiting for the right moment to turn River into the Alliance:

> Kaylee: That's not funny.
> JAYNE: He ain't stupid. Why would he take on trouble like those two if there weren't no profit in it, hmm? Captain's got a move he ain't made yet, you'll see ["The Train Job" 1.2].

Kaylee, notice, sees Mal in a distinctly non-libertarian fashion. Kaylee knows that Mal will never turn River in. Mal is a libertarian on the surface, and the commentators who point that out are quite right at that level, yet deep down, as Book and Kaylee see, Mal is an anarcho-socialist who just does not know it yet—Simon and the rest of the crew have to bring it out of him.

A More or Less Killing Mood

To further argue that the show is anarcho-socialist, we will next turn to specific episodes. Starting with "The Train Job" (1.2), we see a significant deviation from libertarian principles in how the characters respond to a failure of consent between Adelai Niska and Mal. As we will see, Mal not only does not respect consent in the way that a libertarian ought to, but he strongly prioritizes positive duties over his consent—which makes no sense from a libertarian moral outlook.

The consensual arrangement between Niska and Mal is not standard since it does not meet all the typical requirements for consent. For an agreement to be consensual, it must be, at the very least, freely made, made by competent agents, and adequately informed. In this case, Niska and Mal are freely agreeing, competent agents, but Niska does not inform Mal what they will be stealing for him:

> NISKA: Are you going to ask me what it is I need?
> MAL: As a rule, no.
> NISKA: Yes. Good! You have reputation. Malcolm Reynolds gets it done is the talk ["The Train Job" 1.2]

Thus, it is a legitimate consensual arrangement because the one condition for consent not met, the information condition, is explicitly waived. Mal's waiver of the information requirement becomes a major plot point that sets up the moral predicament. However, due to the waiver, Niska has actually received Mal's genuine consent to steal six crates of Pescaline D, which is a medicine desperately needed by the people of Paradiso due to the fact that so many people there suffer from Bowden's malady. Intuitively, there appear to be two moral values in conflict: on the one hand, Mal ought to uphold his consent, while, on the other hand, one ought to help strangers who desperately need medicine. If Mal fails to uphold his consent, he fails a negative duty to Niska, yet sick people in desperate need create a positive duty to help. Since the libertarian embraces the former value, while denying that the latter value obligates at all, the episode provides a useful test for the two competing interpretations.

One libertarian, P. Gardner Goldsmith, writing on this episode, praises Mal for choosing the latter: "when he realized how much harm he was doing to the poor people living under Alliance tyranny who were dependent on the drug to survive, Mal actually chose to *give up* his booty in favor of what was right."[35] While this choice implies that Mal is breaking his consent, Goldsmith explains that he compensated for this issue: "to stress Mal's strong moral stand, he then handed his payment for the job back to Niska's agents."[36]

Unfortunately, Goldsmith tells us little about what implement in the libertarian's moral toolkit allows for this intuitively correct conclusion. Instead, Goldsmith provides a libertarian perspective on how the local sheriff is better placed to make decisions for the local people.[37] The problem is that there is no such moral tool available to libertarians. We could say that it is wrong for Mal to steal, with which any libertarian would agree, but then it would have been wrong to steal without knowing what he was stealing in the first place. The show assumes, in part for the narrative structure, that Mal can steal and count as the good guy. Otherwise, neither self-ownership nor property rights explain why Mal can violate his own consent. Mal agreed to limit his liberty for the deal that Niska offered. Once he limited his liberty in that fashion, he was obligated, *through his self-ownership*, to keep his consent exactly as he agreed to do. That is, Mal's consent involves the creation of an obligation to use Mal's self-ownership as Niska saw fit insofar as Mal was acting on Niska's behalf. Libertarian moral theory does not allow him to violate the consent just because doing so would help others—such a move places a positive duty (to help the sick) over a negative one (Mal cannot violate the rights that Niska incurred through their consensual exchange).

Further, Mal cannot simply reconfigure the deal and return the money as Goldsmith suggests: such a drastic change of terms would now require Niska's further consent. Imagine that I promise to sell you my car on Tuesday for payment today. Further imagine that when Tuesday comes, I tell you that I have changed my mind and will not be selling you the car, but I give you the money back. This repayment does not change the facts that you need the car on Tuesday, you cannot find another car in time, and I have held onto your money and prevented you from buying another car elsewhere while you waited for Tuesday. Most importantly, I would be violating my consent insofar as I promised to give you a car and not money on Tuesday. It is an entirely new exchange if I simply give you the money back since no car is being handed over. If I then insist that I held my end of the bargain while you continue to not have a car, I am simply lying to you. Libertarian moral philosophy would entail that Mal should uphold his consent and he cannot do that simply by returning the money.

At the same time, we, the viewers, have strong moral intuitions that Mal *must* give the medicine back to the people of Paradiso. The basis for our intuition is simply that the sick people desperately need it: they would not be able to live meaningful lives—or any lives—without it. To put the point clearly, the positive duty to provide positive liberty to the sick ought to motivate Mal. The desperate need of strangers intuitively trumps past consensual agreements. At least, that is both what an anarcho-socialist would say and why we, the audience, are so relieved that Mal returns the medicine. Moreover, this explanation is precisely what Mal provides when he explains why they are taking the cargo back, which is surprising to both Jayne and Wash:

> JAYNE [WHO HAS BEEN DRUGGED BY SIMON]: What? What do you mean "back"? I waited for you guys!
> WASH: What are you talking about? What about Niska? Won't this put him in more or less a killing mood?
> MAL: There's others need this more ["The Train Job" 1.2].

It is because "others need this more" that Mal returns it. It is not that his self-ownership involves valuing the gift of Pescaline D. Mal has not entered into any kind of consensual deal with the people of Paradiso—they are strangers to him. It is *their need* that creates a positive duty that Mal morally must fulfill. It's almost as if, as Malatesta the anarchist put it earlier, Mal has been tempered by a love for mankind.

The libertarian in this scenario must commit to the value of consent since the consent was well made: Mal was free to refuse the job, they were all competent adults, and he chose not to be informed. The show, though, forces Mal into a situation where he must realize that the moral value of positive liberty overcomes that of consent. In the end, it is not even a close call:

> SHERIFF: These are tough times. A man can get a job. He might not look too close at what that job is. But a man learns all the details of a situation like ours. Well, then he has a choice.
> MAL: I don't believe he does ["The Train Job" 1.2].

Thus, when confronted with a tough choice between libertarian moral values (which would unquestionably side with consent) and positive moral duty (which would unquestionably side with helping sick people), it turns out not to be a tough choice for Mal at all. He chooses the non-libertarian value because deep down he is not nearly as much of a libertarian as he believes he is.

Stealing Away Our Pain

In "Jaynestown" (1.7), the mudders of Canton represent the kind of people that the famous libertarian author Ayn Rand's heroes, such as John Galt or Howard Roark, would feel are moral troublemakers for expecting assistance with their positive liberty. As we learn in the episode, Jayne never intended to help the mudders: he accidentally dropped money on them while betraying his partner, Stitch, in a frantic escape to save his own life. Even though Jayne had no intention to save the mudders, they lionize him as a hero.

The mudders, who live in Canton, represent a vivid picture of the results of structural violence, as we discussed in Chapter Two. The mudders farm the mud on Boss Higgins' Moon, where there is clearly a shortage of work options. We learn from their song "Hero of Canton: The Ballad of Jayne Cobb" that the Magistrate takes one dollar to every five cents that they earn. Given their geographic situation, it is hard to imagine them finding superior employment, and so their options are severely limited by their circumstances. Anarcho-capitalism does not find the exploitation of the bad circumstances of others to be morally worrisome since capitalism allows employers to pay low wages to employees without regard to why the employees need to take low wage jobs. Therefore, anarcho-capitalism will likely condone taking advantage of the mudders and leaving them living in deplorable conditions, yet anarcho-socialism finds the exploitation of others' difficult circumstances to be so morally problematic that anarcho-socialists seek to devise a society where such situations simply cannot arise, such as through communal property.

The anarcho-capitalist though has an available response to this interpretation of the episode. Canton is a "company town," which implies that Higgins is both the state and the employer. Anarcho-capitalists would rebel against such an arrangement since they believe that states corrupt the market system. They would argue that it is because Higgins is the magistrate and represents the state that he can use the power of the state to force a coercive labor situation on the mudders.

It is unclear in the episode how much work Magistrate Higgins' governmental role is playing on the mudders' situation. Even if he did not control the state, they would still be easily exploitable because the main labor available on the moon appears to be farming mud. And if Boss Higgins simply owned the land and the mud on it, then he would still be able to reap a huge percentage of the profits for himself and pay the mudders next to nothing, yet since the show complicates this relationship with the company town scenario, we cannot place too much emphasis on it either way.

More telling is the episode's pivotal moment when a mudder sacrifices his life for Jayne. When this moment occurs, Stitch had just exposed Jayne as a fraud. Then, when Stitch shoots at Jayne, the mudder, without any thought, jumps into the bullet's path, giving up his life in exchange for Jayne's. This ultimate act of self-sacrifice completely confuses Jayne:

> JAYNE: Don't make no sense. What ... why the hell'd that mudder have to go and do that for, Mal? Jumpin' in front of the shotgun blast? Hell, there weren't a one of 'em understood what happened out there. They're probably stickin' that statue right back up.
> MAL: Most like ["Train Job" 1.7].

Jayne cannot understand someone who so strongly accepts positive duties that they would give up everything—life included—for another person. Although we cannot know for sure why the mudder did this, we, the viewers, are not likely to find it as inexplicable as Jayne does. At the end of the day, Jayne was a fraud, which has to be a disappointment, but he does not deserve to die. We are not baffled, as Jayne is, by the ultimate self-sacrifice because we simply see the mudder as a good person—someone who truly deserves a statue.

"Jaynestown" therefore presents an enigma for Jayne's anarcho-capitalist mindset. Jayne's own bewilderment represents the shortcomings of libertarian moral philosophy in general. The mudders have jobs, and yet they are seeking heroes who would recognize a positive duty to help them. The mudders endorse the kind of self-sacrificing morality that libertarianism eschews. Anarcho-socialism, on the other hand, can critique seemingly consensual work relations that leave the workers impoverished, while also upholding self-sacrificing moral requirements as honorable and often necessary. Of course, to the anarcho-capitalist Jayne, that just don't make sense.

Who'd Help Us?

As a final episode that chiefly concerns positive liberty, let's discuss "Heart of Gold" (1.13), where everyone on Serenity is willing to fight to save prostitutes from Rance Burgess on the moon of Deadwood. Zoe even explains to the crew that each one must decide whether they want to assist since the job will be dangerous and payment was uncertain:

> JAYNE: Don't much see the benefit in getting involved in strangers' troubles without a up-front price negotiated.
> BOOK: These people need assistance. The benefit wouldn't necessarily be for you.
> JAYNE: That's what I'm saying ["Heart of Gold" 1.13].

Jayne, however, immediately changes his mind when he finds out that the people they will be saving are prostitutes. As soon as they arrive Jayne asks, "Can I start getting sexed already?" ("Heart of Gold" 1.13). Jayne will get paid—he is not acting simply for the positive liberty of others. All the others, though, consent to the mission because, as Book explains in a way that clearly indicates an appreciation for positive duty, the benefit will be for others. An anarcho-capitalist would have to explain this scenario by claiming that the crew just enjoys helping others and/or risking their lives. Of course, since they are risking their lives and most of the characters respond poorly to danger, this interpretation is a stretch at best. Instead, it makes more sense to think that the crew, including Mal and only excluding Jayne, recognizes a duty to promote the positive liberty of others, even when that requires their own risk and uncertain payment.

During the episode, Mal does eventually sleep with Nandi, who is a former Companion and now the prostitutes' madam, but their sexual encounter appears to be based on mutual attraction and does not seem to be payment for services. This point nevertheless allows for an important digression about the inadequacies that plague the relationship between Mal and Inara. Inara privately weeps when she learns that Mal and Nandi had sex. Inara clearly has feelings for Mal in spite of the fact that he regularly mistreats her. Our position is that Mal is a surface-level libertarian who is growing into more of an anarcho-socialist, which represents who he truly is, deep down, yet this interpretation is consistent with Mal being a significantly flawed character, which is depicted through his inability to fully cognize his deeper moral character and his mistreatment of others, as judged mostly from an anarcho-socialist morality.

In particular, Mal is no feminist, but anarcho-socialist morality, replete with positive duties, requires a commitment to help people who suffer at the hands of the patriarchy as well as other forms of oppression. That Mal is not a feminist follows from his mistreatment of Inara. Among other problems, Mal repeatedly disrespects his consensual agreements with Inara, such as by entering her shuttle without her permission. Further, he refers to her with language that he knows she despises, such as by repeatedly calling her a "whore" (even after consenting to not call her that ever again in "Out of Gas" 1.8). Through some of his sexist behavior, Mal is failing both libertarian and anarcho-socialist standards since he fails to uphold consensual agreements, yet Mal is further failing higher anarcho-socialist standards since he is not giving Inara the proper respect that she is due, regardless of whether he consented to treat her in certain ways.

All of these points are complicated, psychologically speaking, due to Mal's inability to articulate or accept his strong, romantic feelings for Inara.[38] That, however, in no way excuses his behavior. Just as Mal is unable to fully see himself as an anarcho-socialist and feminist, and instead clings to being a libertarian, Mal's sexism establishes him as a purposely and overtly flawed lead character whose views should not straightforwardly represent the show's actual views.[39]

Transitioning from a flawed hero to a thoroughly bad villain, Rance Burgess, it is worth pondering over what makes Rance so atrocious. We know that Rance is rude, sexist, and willing to hurt anyone to attain his child, but what makes him truly evil? Rance's main claims to villainy relate to his greedy attempt to run everything without concern for how his actions indirectly lead to the poverty of others. Nandi makes this point entirely clear:

> Rance Burgess has money enough to build a city, a real community. Keeps people living like this so he can play cowboy—be the one with the best toys. Turn this moon into a gorram theme park ["Heart of Gold" 1.13].

Notice in Nandi's explanation, Rance's main crime appears to be that he has taken libertarian values too far: he has all of this money that he uses to buy useless toys, instead of helping the impoverished people around him. Nandi's complaint about Rance comes down to the fact that he fails to recognize his positive duties, and instead takes his self-ownership to mean he can do whatever he wants with his money—which, of course, just is the anarcho-capitalist position.

It is worth noting that Rance's situation could arise in a manner that is entirely fitting with anarcho-capitalist principles. Rance has some good fortune, makes some wise investments, fully utilizes his character skills of being cunning, cutthroat, and determined, and he finds himself as the richest man in their community. With the power that comes with that position, he manipulates and controls those around him—provided that he only does so in ways that they end up agreeing to because their bad circumstances do not give them any other choice. Once Rance consolidates money and power, he has no moral responsibility, according to anarcho-capitalism, to do anything to help anyone else. He uses his money—which would be enough to "build a city, a real community" ("Heat of Gold" 1.13)—to buy toys for his amusement while others around him suffer in poverty. According to libertarian morality, Rance has done nothing worrisome, yet to us as the audience, he is one of the worst villains on the show.

If we are meant to trust Nandi—and her death would not be as impactful if we were not meant to—then *Firefly* is likely using her words not to support a libertarian interpretation of the show, but to warn us of the dangers of libertarian systems, especially ones as extreme as anarcho-capitalism. Like "The Train Job" and "Jaynestown," "Heart of Gold" represents just one of many cases where the crew of Serenity finds themselves carrying out positive duties in support of others' positive liberties. On numerous occasions, *Firefly* goes against the spirit, if not the letter, of libertarianism in general and anarcho-capitalism in particular by bringing us characters who believe it is morally incumbent on them to help others in need just because those others are in need. We have already seen Simon strongly recognizes his positive duties. We will now turn to two more characters at the moral center of the show: Book and Kaylee. Each in turn will similarly show strong commitments to positive duties to support the positive liberty of others.

The Good Book's Poems and Songs

As previously mentioned, Shepherd Book can be seen as one of the moral centers of *Firefly*. In "Bushwhacked" (1.3), it is Book that finds the humanity in the reavers and insists on helping put the dead to rest. In "The Train Job" (1.2), Book is not only interested in praying for the crew, but also is hesitant to do so because he knows that Mal would not approve. Book is also willing, in "War Stories" (1.10), to assist in the firefight even though the *Bible* is against killing. He justifies doing so by noting that the *Bible* is "somewhat fuzzier on the subject of kneecaps" ("War Stories" 1.10). Finally, Jayne quotes him in a tense moment toward the end of the film, and the quotation tells us everything we need to know about Book: "Shepherd Book used to tell me, 'If you can't do something smart, do something right'" (*Serenity*).

Throughout the series, Book represents not only a moral point of view, but also a moral perspective that is complex and interesting in a way that befits the show. He does not simply mimic the moral viewpoint of his religion, but instead seeks out nuance that applies to the crew's specific circumstances in rational and reasonable ways. While it would be unusual for a shepherd to represent the moral views of an atheist like Joss Whedon, Book is not a usual character (we know that Book is not what he appears to be: he has Alliance connections ("Safe" 1.5), and Jubal Early confidently asserts that he is no preacher ("Objects in Space" 1.14).

In the film, *Serenity*, Mal and Book have a second conversation, closely mirroring the one from "The Train Job" (1.2), over Mal protecting Simon and River. In this one, Mal is explicit that he doesn't understand why he didn't leave River behind, to which Book responds:

> BOOK: It's not your way, Mal.
> MAL: I have a way? That better than a plan?
> BOOK: Only one thing is gonna walk you through this, Mal. Belief.
> MAL: You know I always look to you for counsel, but sermons make me sleepy, Shepherd. I ain't looking for help from on high. That's a long wait for a train don't come.
> BOOK: When I talk about belief, why do you assume I'm talking about God? [*Serenity*].

In this exchange, we once again, like in "The Train Job," see Mal doing the right thing, but not really knowing why he did it. Mal embraces his positive duty to help the Tams, but it is Book, much more than Mal, who clearly understands that Mal performs these moral actions because he deep down recognizes his positive duties—even if Mal, the surface-level libertarian, does not understand that yet. Further, we see that although it is assumed that Book is a moral man because of his religion, his faith in "belief" is not necessarily rooted in religion.

The topic of belief comes up again when Book is dying after having shot down an Alliance ship:

> BOOK: Not very Christian of me.
> MAL: You did what's right.
> BOOK: Coming from you, that means almost nothing.
> ...
> BOOK: I don't care what you believe! Just believe it. Whatever you have to [*Serenity*].

Book's very last words are urging Mal to believe in something, whatever it is. While Mal is on a journey of self-discovery, *Shepherd* Book has been guiding him along that path. He initially jokes in his death scene, here, that Mal's affirmation that he did what was right amounts to almost nothing. Though it is a joke, it is indicative that Mal's path is not yet complete insofar as his belief system continues to come up short. We can speculate that although Mal has a critical belief system that accurately finds fault with the Alliance, he has yet to find something positive to believe in, which represents a shortcoming of libertarian morality. Without belief in the positive duty to assist others, life becomes more self-involved and potentially less fulfilling. Book is not pointing Mal to belief in God, but to believe in a more substantial morality, whatever its source.

Shepherd Book is a proper guide for Mal's journey because we see that Book has gone on this journey himself in the comic *The Shepherd's Tale*.[40] Book, whose father was abusive while his upbringing was impoverished, started out by just looking for a way to get away from his home and escape the reach of the Alliance's police forces.[41] At that time, Book had a distinctly libertarian perspective on life. Young Book explains: "You see, this life is a fight and if you sit still, someone will get the drop on you…. I won't let it happen."[42] Instead, according to young Book (who sounds a good bit like the older Mal), "I'll protect myself, take what I need, and keep moving. Because it's every man for himself."[43]

In spite of this early outlook on life, Book quickly grows to embrace self-sacrifice and positive duties. Book ends up acting as a mole within the Alliance: he serves as an officer who appeared to be seeking his personal glory by attempting to win the war *in one day*.[44] Instead of a glory hound, Book acted as an infiltrator, risking his life to damage the Alliance from within: his seemingly rash acts were in fact a ruse to kill four thousand Alliance men.[45] Book's brave but relatively small act is reminiscent of Team

Angel trying to act against structural evil from within. Book the mole, just like Team Angel the legal team, acted from a place of morality and fought against evil in the way that seemed best at the time. Even though Book began in difficult circumstances, he decides, early on, to risk everything to help the fight against the Alliance.

Perhaps the most illuminating moment in Book's journey of self-discovery is when he turns to religion. While Book as a mole was serving to promote the positive duties of others by taking on the Alliance, he did so by killing people who worked for the Alliance, including not just soldiers but also doctors, teachers, and other support staff.[46] The moment when he realizes that there's another, better way for him to help others is when he is eating a bowl of chicken soup. Further reminiscent of Angel's early epiphany, the chicken soup leads to Book's more intricate epiphany. For Book to have the chicken soup, a chicken had to live and die, a bowl had to be constructed and put before him, a table had to be made and placed there to hold the bowl, a floor was necessary to support the table, the floor and its building had to be placed on Earth, the entire galaxy needed to exist for Earth to have a place in the galaxy, and the universe and existence in general had to be there to support the galaxy.[47] The interconnectedness of the universe all came together to feed Book, giving him life.[48] As such, Book, who immediately asks himself what he is to do with this life, turns to religion.[49]

Book has come to see the universe as interconnected. This perspective is meant to serve as a sharp contrast with his younger, more libertarian viewpoint. Young Book stood against the world, acting on his own with only an interest for preserving his negative liberty. Instead, this older Book realizes that he is one small bit of an interconnected world—and thus, just as Malatesta the anarchist advised, he must do his part to help all the other bits, just as they all, in various fashions, find ways to support him. Positive duties are not a hindrance that Book is forced to live with, but a key to understanding his place within the universe.

Book goes on a journey from libertarian mindset to a belief in something bigger than himself, which clearly includes positive duties to help others. Part of Book engaging in that positive activity involves leading Mal on a similar journey. We learn from Book that these journeys play a significant part of *Firefly*'s story. We can confirm this perspective by examining another character that represents the moral center of the show: Kaylee Frye.

New People Got Stories

Kaylee is *Firefly*'s moral compass: whatever way she points on a moral issue is probably the show's intended moral message. Kaylee is naturally a moral person. She is not always the best judge of character since she places too much faith in people (as we will see), but viewers are hard pressed to find a time in the show where Kaylee does not care for others. Kaylee has a pure sincerity that provides a peek into the show's moral heart.

We can tell where Kaylee's heart lies: she sees goodness in Simon. Even though Simon can be unpleasant to Kaylee, she consistently returns to him since she sees he is a good person who would sacrifice to help others. She sees this goodness right away, in "Serenity" (1.1), because of his profession:

> KAYLEE: You seem so young. To be a doctor.
> SIMON: Yeah. You're pretty young to be a ship's mechanic.
> KAYLEE: Know how. Machines just got workings, and they talk to me.
> BOOK: That's a rare gift.
> KAYLEE: Oh, not like being a doctor. Helping fix people, that's *important* ["Serenity" 1.1].

Simon's first impression is positive because doctors *help people*. Of course, plenty of people become doctors for the money, but Simon, for whatever reason, has left that behind by traveling to the outer worlds. While Mal is suspicious of Simon, Kaylee's optimistic view of people allows her to be impressed and think the best. Of course, we know she is right: Simon gave it all up to save his sister. And, so it is Kaylee, not Mal, who reads Simon correctly.

It does take a while, of course, to figure out that she is right about Simon. In "Serenity," we initially side with Mal's suspicions. When Dobson shoots Kaylee, Simon initially refuses to save her unless Mal flees away from the Alliance, yet as soon as she is able, Kaylee immediately reads the situation positively and is forgiving:

> KAYLEE: [Simon] wasn't gonna let me die. He was just trying to.... It's nobody's fault. Okay? Just promise me you'll remember that?
> MAL: I'll keep it in mind.
> KAYLEE: You *are* a nice man, Captain. You always looking after us. You just gotta have faith in people ["Serenity" 1.1].

Kaylee knows who Simon is immediately and implicitly trusts him. And just like Book, Kaylee plays a key role in leading Mal through his moral journey. She urges him to have faith in people, pushing him away from his isolationist, libertarian bent, and toward a communal, anarcho-socialist perspective. Kaylee not only has faith in Simon's moral foundations, but also in Mal's: both are nice.

In "The Message" (1.12), Kaylee cares about another character, Private Tracey Smith, who betrays his own consent. Tracey is in the middle of transporting organs inside his body. When he breaks his consent, Tracey has no acceptable excuse from a libertarian perspective: someone has offered him more money to buy the organs. His reason for needing more money is not personal greed but because Tracey "could get my folks off that rock they've been forced to live on, set them up some place better, some place warm" ("The Message" 1.12). Tracey fails to follow through on his consent because he needs to help his parents out of a bad situation.

What's Kaylee's response to Tracey's violation of consent? "That's real nice," she says ("The Message" 1.12). Kaylee genuinely means it: she immediately likes Tracey. She may have judged his character too soon (he ends up blowing the whole mission because he fails to trust the Serenity crew), but she agrees with his point. Kaylee supports the idea that you should sacrifice the value of consent when it comes to helping your parents. Kaylee's moral code supports positive duties to help others, and thus she supports both Simon and Tracey.

There is one significant discussion when Mal first meets Kaylee that appears to metaphorically represent libertarianism. At the time, Bester is the mechanic for Serenity and he invites Kaylee on board for a sexual hook up. The exchange starts with Bester explaining to Mal that they can't take off because their secondary grav boot is shot. Kaylee disagrees:

> KAYLEE: No it ain't. Ain't nothing wrong with your grav boot. Grav boot's just fine.... Your reg couple's bad. Don't serve much of a purpose anyway. Just tends to gum up the works when it gets tacked. So I figure why even have one? Better to just take your g-line, plug it straight into the port pin-lock, and that should, uhh.... [Engine starts] There ["Out of Gas" 1.8].

Amy Sturgis argues that this scene metaphorically represents the libertarian's stance against governments.[50] The reg couple, on this interpretation, stands for the government: it doesn't serve any real purpose, and instead "just tends to gum up the works." Sturgis argues that the rest of "the works" from the ship's engine represent liberty, which is "easy to take for granted if one possesses it."[51] Of course, our argument is that *Firefly* really is an anti-state, pro-liberty show, but one can interpret it that way without holding that it is deep-down a libertarian show. Instead, as Kaylee's hard-wired goodness indicates, the show represents the hope for a social arrangement that lacks a state, but that works out through moral arrangements between a community of individuals who, like Book and Kaylee, show solidarity with each other. It is worth noting that, even after being called a "prairie harpy," Kaylee acts out of goodness and steps in to help out a stranger in need, in a truly collaborative manner. She doesn't wait until she has a contract to get paid for helping Mal; she just promotes Mal's positive liberty by enabling him to fly his ship without any request for reimbursement. Kaylee, like Book, both represents the moral center of the show, and that moral center points toward anarcho-socialism.

Missing What's Solid

With all of this support for positive liberty on the show, it is important not to dismiss the show's critique of the state. Consider this brief exchange:

> INARA: You are always breaking the rules, no matter what society you're in. You don't get along with ordinary criminals either, which is why you are constantly getting in trouble.
>
> MAL: You think following the rules will buy you a nice life, even if the rules make you a slave ["Shindig" 1.4].

The state creates rules by which to organize society. Perhaps the state claims to be doing so benevolently and paternalistically. Nevertheless, history consistently confirms that the people who run the state ensure that the rules are fashioned to protect and promote their interests. Libertarians and anarcho-capitalists can watch this exchange with complete agreement with the point: governmental rules make you a slave. The state's rules are hindrances and obstacles to individuals attaining their freedom and living as they see fit. *Firefly* is surely taking a stance against meddlesome state rules.

The exchange however runs deeper. The initial reading of Inara's sentence is that Mal always breaks governmental rules, no matter what society he is in. In that sense, "society" has a narrow meaning: it means a civilized society with a governmental structure. On that reading, Inara's making a point of saying that Mal is a good libertarian who refuses to abide by governmental rules.

There is, nonetheless, a wider reading of "society." Inara's own example is that Mal even breaks the rules of criminal society. Here, "society" refers not just to state-run societies, but to any loose organization of individuals who inhabit a shared community. With this wider reading, Mal's response becomes more enlightening: it is not just the rules of the government that make you a slave, but rules of any hierarchal society. In fact, labor rules make more sense here than governmental rules: it is when the worker thinks that following company rules will buy her a nice life that the worker simply becomes a wage slave. As anarcho-socialist Ricardo Flores Magón put it, "The worker today is as much a slave as the chattel slave was yesterday, with the only difference being that the worker can choose his boss."[52] This laborer works harder and harder for the company, never really attaining the promotions and raises that she deserves, until she is finally laid off because doing so is more profitable than allowing her to reach retirement. The worker, like the citizen, ends up following rules until they become slaves of the hierarchal system of which they are mere cogs.

Mal's response, not just to Alliance rules but to rules in general, is to become an outlaw. Magón would approve: "Throughout history, the liberties conquered by the human species have been the work of outlaws who took the law into their own hands and tore it to pieces."[53] For the most part, Mal and crew are not quite trying to tear the law into pieces, but they are looking for their own way to preserve their own liberties, out in the sky.

The anarcho-socialist critique of society is more thorough, which makes it both more fitting of *Firefly* and of Joss Whedon's works in general. It is, according to Magón, the only society that guarantees the positive right to live: "The right to live is the basis of all rights, and consists of the right that all human beings have to take full advantage, simply by the fact of being alive, of all that exists, with no other obligation than that of allowing other human beings to do the same."[54] Mal's journey of self-discovery will eventually lead him to realize that life is not about maintaining hierarchy on his ship, but about building a community of trust and solidarity dedicated to each person's right to live. It is clear that he is starting to get this point when he explains to Saffron after he finally gets the upper hand on her: "You got all kinds of learning, and you made me look the fool without trying, and yet here I am with a gun to your head. That's cause I got people with me, people who trust each other, who do for each other and ain't always looking for the advantage" ("Our Mrs. Reynolds" 1.6).

Therefore, through *Firefly*, we come to see how this show represents an anarcho-socialist standpoint, yet as we saw at the start, that's an umbrella term that includes numerous anarchist theories. To get more specific, we will next turn to the TV show that started it all and provides us with the most specific understanding of a positive anarchist theory. We will next examine anarcha-feminism in *Buffy, the Vampire Slayer*.

Five

Anarcha-Feminist Scoobies
Buffy's *Slaying Critique*

WWBD

"In every generation there is a Chosen One. She alone will stand against the vampires, the demons and the forces of darkness. She is the Slayer" ("Welcome to the Hellmouth" 1.1). While there are certainly moments where Buffy Summers feels lonely, she is never really alone. Buffy is not just the Slayer—she is also a member of the greatest assembled group of vampire and demon fighters ever assembled: the Scoobies. And the Scoobies represent the concluding argument of our book. The previous chapters were largely critical: *Angel* critiques structural violence; *Dollhouse* critiques limitations to our consent and autonomy; *S.H.I.E.L.D.* critiques the stability of hierarchy; and *Firefly* critiques a libertarian approach to anarchism. It is here, with the Scoobies, that we finally find a positive picture: the Scoobies are paradigm anarcha-feminists, and they represent the tradition quite well.

In standing up to injustice, structural violence, sexism, hierarchy, and all the other big bads of real life, Buffy slays the patriarchy and battles the problems associated with the state. Her methodology is rooted in egalitarianism, gender equality, and cooperation. Buffy as slayer embodies anarcha-feminist principles and *Buffy the Vampire Slayer* (from here on, *Buffy*) represents anarcha-feminist principles in action.

Clearly, *Buffy* is the quintessential Joss Whedon show. It is not only his first major show, but it also enjoyed the longest run. For this reason, we cannot devote a single chapter to *Buffy*. Instead, we will break apart the show into its critical and positive anarcha-feminist elements. This chapter will deal with the critical moves, concentrating on the feminist critique of patriarchy and the anarchist critique of hierarchy. While much has been written about the former, the latter is on display throughout the series, such as through critiques of high school, the Watchers Council, the Initiative, the Watcher/Slayer relationship, and, of course, the hierarchal vampires themselves. In the next chapter, we will see how Buffy and the Scoobies put the positive anarcha-feminist vision into action.

Finding the Glass Half Full and Filling It

But before we get ahead of ourselves, lets lay down the groundwork with some brief definitions. You wouldn't go on patrol without understanding how to use Mr. Pointy, would you?

Feminism is a movement seeking to establish and defend equal political, economic, and social rights for women. Historically speaking, at one point or another, that meant fighting for women to get the vote (political rights), advocating that women could control their money and property (economic rights), arguing that women should be allowed to represent themselves in court (legal rights), etc. Additionally, feminism works to establish equality between men and women and to dismantle problematic stereotypes that hinder human behavior and authentic self-development. For example, there are tropes that women have to act in girly ways or wear pink, or that boys should not express emotion. Feminists are there to express that it's absolutely okay if, say, a woman is not at all a girly girl or if a man is super communicative and emotive.[1]

Remember Xander Harris saying, "I laugh in the face of danger and then I hide until it goes away" ("Witch" 1.3)? Masculine gender norms would require that Xander act in a manly fashion and readily stand up to threats in aggressive ways. But feminism allows Xander to find his own way of dealing with a threat, whether that's avoidance or spouting sarcastic remarks to deal with the stress of fighting against evil. In other words, feminism supports people's choices to be, and act in accordance to, their authentic selves—and not simply adopt some social construct that they've been told to embrace. Furthermore, feminists recognize that the patriarchy (any system, institution, or group that works to advance the superiority of men or masculine ideals or norms) restricts all humans. The patriarchy does this through rewarding and promoting such stereotypes and gender norms as the ones we've been discussing, as well as through instituting hierarchies that restrict access to power or marginalize certain groups. For example, the patriarchy indoctrinates us in how to perform gender, limits our sexuality and/or gender identity, imposes unattainable beauty standards, or essentializes women as commodities for the sexual pleasure of men.

There are many kinds of feminists, and there is not one recognized way to solve the problems resulting from the patriarchy, especially as these troubles are further complicated by the consequences of capitalism or the state.

But anarcha-feminists offer a solution: dismantling both the state (the anarcha part) and the patriarchy (the feminist part) to achieve equality and justice for all. In the United States, anarcha-feminism is best understood as having started around the turn of the century with three women: Lucy Parsons (c. 1853–1942), Voltairine de Cleyre (1866–1912), and Emma Goldman (1869–1940), who all added a feminist dimension to the anarchist-socialist narrative that was developing at the time.

Let's briefly meet each one. Lucy Parsons was an American activist, labor organizer, and anarchist. She wrote on women's rights and labor rights, and was a contributor to the anarchist newspaper, *The Alarm*, which was one of the most well-known anarchist publications of the time period. She worked on it with her husband, Albert Parsons. She is one of the founders of the Industrial Workers of the World organization, an international labor union founded in Chicago in 1905. Voltairine de Cleyre was an American writer and anarchist. She argued against capitalism and in support of women's rights. She supported the idea of a stateless society without the use of force. Her essays were published after her death in Emma Goldman's publication *Mother Earth*. Emma Goldman was born in Russia and then migrated to the United States. She was an anarchist and political activist. She supported women's rights, social rights, and safe, fair labor practices. She founded the anarchist journal *Mother Earth* and published many works, including an autobiography, *Living My Life*.

For these anarcha-feminists, true liberty requires freedom from any hierarchal power, and not just from the state's, but also from the hierarchy of capitalism or the patriarchal family. For anarcha-feminists, no one should control how we think, how we behave, what gender norms we take up, etc. As Parsons sums it up, "My mind is appalled at the thought of a political party having control of all the details that go to make up the sum total of our lives."[2] Parsons counsels that we should support the development of liberty in every individual, so that these agents might judge for themselves what's going on in every scenario that comes up in their lives, and so they might have the freedom to develop their own views unencumbered by outside pressure.

It is not sufficient, for the anarcha-feminist, to be free from coercion from the state and the capitalist, women must also be free from the coercion of their fathers, husbands, and men in general. They must be allowed to develop as full autonomous adults, and not live under the coercion of restrictive gender norms. Parsons, de Cleyre, and Goldman interwove what was called the called "sex question" (understood as issues revolving around gender equality, women's rights, sex and sexuality, etc.) into the fabric of anarchism, thus founding anarcha-feminism.[3]

Anarcha-feminists combine the anarchist critique of the state and hierarchy with a special emphasis on the feminist critique of the patriarchal hierarchy, along with offering a feminist vision for a stateless society that moves beyond the limitations placed on us by gender norms, sexism, heterosexism, and bigotry of any kind. Thus, when envisioning a better world, the answer that anarcha-feminists provide is based in equality and collaboration, and not in hierarchy. Acting morally for the benefit of all—men and women alike—is the cornerstone of anarcha-feminism. And that is exactly how Buffy and the Scoobies operate. As such, we will now explore how *Buffy the Vampire Slayer* embodies this anarcha-feminist response.

Welcome to the Hellmouth

How does one navigate the Hellmouth? High school? Life? Through established hierarchies? Well, that's what Cordelia Chase thought, as she tested Buffy on the first day of school, giving her advice such as "You wanna fit in here, the first rule is: know your losers. Once you can identify them all by sight [glances at Willow Rosenberg] they're a lot easier to avoid" ("Welcome to the Hellmouth" 1.1).

At the beginning of the series, as Jes Battis describes her, Cordelia is a "self-centered, acerbic, and popularity-obsessed teenager."[4] She is the Queen Bee who offers friendship to Buffy on her first day, after determining that Buffy is sufficiently worthy of Cordelia's attention. In Season 1, Cordelia sees school (and life) as a popularity contest based on superficial things, such as expertise on whether vamp nail polish is still in or whether the softer side of Sears makes for acceptable clothing.[5] While Cordelia's behavior reveals what's known as relational aggression (aggression expressed through manipulating and/or harming someone's relationships or social standing),[6] it also indicates that Cordelia sees herself as powerful within the school community—she enjoys the benefits of high school hierarchy. The fact that Cordelia is at the top of the social scale, and can offer acceptance to a newcomer—"If you hang with me and mine, you'll be accepted in no time" ("Welcome to the Hellmouth" 1.1)—only underlines how hierarchy works to privilege or marginalize different groups. Here, Cordelia is marginalizing Willow. But Cordelia doesn't stop there. Later, she competes with Buffy over love interests, including Owen and Angel. She even ridicules Buffy: "Buffy, love the hair: it just screams street urchin" ("Halloween" 2.6). Cordelia's disdain applies widely throughout Sunnydale High School. Some folks she scorns; others she ignores so thoroughly that they literally fade out of existence. Remember Marcie Ross? If not, you can thank Cordelia ("Out of Mind, Out of Sight" 1.11).

As we have seen, anarchists worry about these types of hierarchical arrangements, where some groups are harmed while others are privileged because of some arbitrary social order enforced through manipulation and coercion. Under such arrangements, as anarcha-feminist Emma Goldman put it, "the minds of men are in confusion"[7]; the only way out of the confusion is to celebrate and appreciate individual worth and self-expression.[8] That is exactly what Buffy does when she recognizes Willow's humanity and strikes up a friendship with her, in spite of risking Cordelia's acceptance in doing so. Buffy is not interested in maintaining a ranked, popularity based pecking order; rather, she is interested in forging meaningful relationships.

Goldman further adds that "the strongest bulwark of authority is uniformity, the least divergence from it is the greatest crime ... it is everywhere present, in habits, tastes, dress, thoughts and ideas ... few have the courage to stand up against it. He who refuses to submit is at once labeled 'queer,' 'different,' and decried as a disturbing element."[9] The world Goldman depicts—even though she was discussing political, economic, and cultural life at the turn of the century—is applicable to Sunnydale High. Here, Cordelia enforces what is deemed as acceptable in habits, tastes, or clothes, and she mocks those who don't fit the standards she has set. When needed, Cordelia relies on relational aggression to influence and control others, so as to get them to fall in line. Or she just turns them into outcasts. In the real world, the same model works when upheld by the patriarchy: binary social constructs of proper behavior for men and women are emphasized and rewarded—such as beauty norms for women, where women have to be hot and sexy and embrace fashion trends—and those who do not fit these constructs are marginalized. Harmony Kendall and Cordelia are deemed pretty and so are at the top of the social scale; Willow is not. Anarcha-feminists offer the solution to this marginalization: rejecting arbitrary gender norms and thinking for oneself instead. As de Cleyre passionately beseeches each woman: "Look at some fashion-slaved woman, her waist surrounded by a high-board fence called a corset, her shoulders and hips angular from the pressure above and below, her feet narrowest where they should be widest, the body fettered by her everlasting prison skirt, her hair fastened tight enough to make her head ache and surmounted by a thing of neither sense nor beauty, called a hat"—and then judge for yourself the ridiculousness of the beauty standard.[10] In other words, anarcha-feminists insist on independence of thought and on self-expression.

But it is not just about fashion, but about mindlessly reproducing social norms and unthinkingly upholding gender constructs. As de Cleyre critiques, "Look how children grow up ... little girls must not be tomboyish, must not go barefoot, must not climb trees, must not learn to swim ... little boys are laughed at as effeminate, silly girl-boys if they want to make patchwork or play with a doll."[11] Buffy embodies a rejection of these norms: as she weaves between tombstones and delivers kicks in the air, she actively forges her own identity as an active fighter, and not a dainty damsel.

Importantly, Buffy exemplifies a rejection of hierarchical thinking: she does not give into social pressure and insists on figuring things out for herself. As Buffy moves away from the social recognition Cordelia offers and builds a strong friendship with Willow instead, she operates from a place of respect for someone else's personhood, and lays the groundwork for a collaborative, reciprocal relationship with fellow students. This pattern also follows for the other Scoobies as well. In fact, as Rhonda V. Wilcox notes, "it is a distinct element of the heroism of *Buffy*'s teen protagonists that they will not go to any lengths to avoid 'loser' status."[12] In this manner, Buffy eschews authority and relies on appreciative and respectful interactions instead of a blind reliance on what's considered cool. Hence, she follows anarcha-feminist principles when rejecting the hierarchy embodied in high school life.

Cordelia's disdain and disrespect for others shows the problems associated with hierarchy.[13] Fortunately, the path Buffy forges allows for this standard to be replaced by collaboration and friendship, as the Scoobies' egalitarianism can overcome hierarchal constraints. As Wilcox puts it, they "pursue what they see as right."[14]

It's a Whole Sucking Thing

As we have seen what separates anarcho-socialism, which is an open category that includes anarcha-feminism along with other anarchist views, from anarcho-capitalism is that anarcho-socialists critique hierarchy in all forms, especially the state. In *Buffy*, the analogs to hierarchy are provided through vampire culture.[15] Both the state and vampires develop their own immoral codes and rigid hierarchical arrangements to enforce their way of doing things; both expect everyone else to accept these measures or face the violent consequences.

As Lucy Parsons argues, corrupt states establish hierarchy through laws, sham elections, or through dictating "the kinds of books that shall be used in our schools and universities; [with] government officials editing, printing, and circulating our literature, histories, magazines and press."[16] In this manner, folks learn how to think in the ways that the party in power wants them to, and in the words of Parsons, the state will come "to crush the opposition, and silence the voice of the minority."[17] In other words, due to the authority of those in power, individual autonomy is squelched.

For their part, vampires also have an established hierarchy, rooted in their evil deeds and siring. When a vampire sucks the blood of a human, if that unfortunate individual is correspondingly allowed to suck from the vampire, then that person also becomes a vampire. "It's like a whole big sucking thing," Buffy explains ("Welcome to the Hellmouth" 1.1). That newly created vampire is indebted to their maker, who has power and control over the vamp they've just created. A social order is thus created through the act of siring.[18] In the key line of vampires for *Buffy*, the Master sired Darla, Darla sired Angelus, Angelus sired Drusilla, and Drusilla sired Spike. These vampires function within a strict hierarchy, and they are bound together not just through their sire-line, but also through the fact that the very act that establishes them as vampires—the sucking of their blood—lacked consent and was coercive. Vampires are literally bred into coercive hierarchy. Their consent, autonomy, and individuality are made irrelevant by the mere existence of the greater hierarchy that they simply must fit within.

For instance, Darla and Angelus sired Drusilla against her will. On a whim, Darla presented an innocent young woman to her lover, Angelus: Drusilla was this "surprise," or rather, a powerless commodity to be toyed with:

> ANGELUS: Did you find me a saint?
> DARLA: Better than that... She has the sight.
> ANGELUS: Visions? She sees the future? She is pure innocence, yet she sees what's coming, she knows what I'm going to do to her ["Dear Boy" *Angel* 2.5].

Now obsessed with Drusilla, Angelus stalks her, kills her family, and tortures her. Eventually, he sires Drusilla.[19] Just as political autonomy was infringed upon by the state, personal autonomy is infringed upon by the vampires. In Drusilla's case, after her encounter with Angelus, she lost her personhood and agency. The arrogant and aggressive Angelus perceived the human Drusilla as a plaything, something to be objectified, controlled, and conquered. Because of the asymmetry imbued in her and Angelus' positions, Drusilla had no will of her own and no chance of escape. As Angelus says of her: "It was over the moment I saw her. She was my opposite in every way. Dutiful daughter. Devout Christian. Innocent and unspoiled. I took one look at her and I knew. She'd be my masterpiece" ("Dear Boy" *Angel* 2.5). Due to the power differential at work, Drusilla fell prey to Angelus, and had her humanity first ignored and then robbed from her. Through her eventual transformation to vampire, she ceased to be her own person and became bound to her maker. Her chance to will the course of her life ceased as she became a vampire. Even as a vampire, Drusilla becomes bound to Angelus, again functioning as a non-autonomous individual. Anarchists worry that agents in the real world are controlled by the state, as they are guided in upholding certain values and discouraged from pursuing others, be it dress, speech, or "repression of one's real sentiments and the repetition of formal hypocrisies."[20] Thus, the state (like the vampire) violates autonomy.

This erasure of autonomy is imbued in every vampire relationship we've seen in the Buffyverse. As former humans, the newly sired vampires did not consent to their transformation. But their autonomy was overruled because of the power differential—the hierarchy at work. Darla had chosen to die from syphilis when the Master sired her. Sure, she received immortality in the deal, but she was not informed of what would happen and did not have the chance to make that choice for herself. Likewise, Drusilla seduced Spike before she bit him, but he never really understood that he was about to be made into a vampire. The hierarchy intrinsic in the power imbalance between the maker and the new vampire underlines the oppressive and constricting nature of the arrangement. In other words, hierarchy in the vampire realm literally robs one of one's soul: it condemns someone to an evil path that they might not choose on their own.

If vampires work together, they are organized in hierarchical packs, with an especially brutish vampire at the top of that scale. The Master, for example, is the leader of the Order of Aurelius, and he expects total obedience from his followers:

MASTER: Ah, Colin… You failed me. Tell me you're sorry.
COLIN: I'm sorry!
MASTER: There. That wasn't so bad, was it? Hold on… [He stabs his finger into Colin's eye.] You've got something in your eye ["The Harvest" 1.2].

The Master rules through fear and brutality. A vampire leader maintains his power through intimidation and viciousness. The state similarly intimidates those under its jurisdiction. As Parsons explained above, the state uses various means to stifle opposition or to privilege certain groups. Moreover, it uses "sheriffs, policemen, courts or jailors" to enforce its authority and its desires.[21] Emma Goldman put it best: "the State itself is the altar of political freedom and, like the religious altar, it is maintained for the purpose of human sacrifice."[22] What she means is that the state uses oppressive methods to ensure it is not challenged in any fashion; as Goldman and other anarchists explain, the state rests on the "surrender of the liberty of the individual or small minorities."[23] Those who disobey are punished through the machinery the state maintains, or in Parsons' words, "the prisons, scaffold and armies."[24] The state uses soldiers and the police to violently react to foreign and domestic dissidents. Similarly, vampires use other vampires, especially ones that they have sired, to ensure that they are not challenged and to literally seize the liberty of humans by either turning them or murdering them.

Furthermore, the state cuts off free expression from those under its auspices. Goldman explains that the state uses the modern school system to "break the will of the child, and then to pound, knead, and shape it into a being utterly foreign to itself."[25] In other words, children are taught to think along the lines that the state endorses, thereby stifling opposition from the cradle to the grave through propaganda. Similarly, we saw how the state turns individuals into willing followers, through the media, in the *Dollhouse* chapter. For *Buffy*, this brainwashing is illustrated through the existence of a psychic link between the sire and their progeny. Through this extrasensory bond, the master-vampire feels and controls the sired-vampire. Through this intimate invasion, any sense of personal autonomy or independence is obsolete.

That Way from the Beginning

In our chapters on *Angel, Dollhouse,* and *Agents of S.H.I.E.L.D.*, we saw how hierarchal institutions ultimately end up doing evil, even when some of those institutions, such as S.H.I.E.L.D. or the Angel-run Wolfram & Hart, are meant to do good. We see this same pattern in *Buffy* with two institutions that claim to be acting to help save the world: the Watchers Council and the Initiative.

Hierarchy and its attendant evils are present not just in vampire culture, but also within the Watchers Council. An organization purportedly designed to fight evil, the Watchers Council, with offices from Munich to Rome and Melbourne, has its roots in the Shadow Men. In this case, the Watchers Council is a stand in for the welfare state: it claims to be good, but it still insists on hierarchy, and it imports and replicates its own morally problematic codes, especially sexism. In other words, the welfare state wants to proclaim, "Yes, we are a state, but we are democratic and we look out for everyone's best interests," yet as we saw in the discussion of *Agents of S.H.I.E.L.D.*, the problems of the hierarchy are not escapable by simply proclaiming goodness. We will draw the same conclusion for the Watchers Council, which is also particularly patriarchal.

According to Quentin Travers, a director of the Council, the structure of the group is explained as follows: "The Council fights evil. The Slayer is the instrument with which we fight. The Council remains. The Slayers ... change. It's been that way from the beginning" ("Checkpoint" 5.12). Citing history and the way things were as an excuse, Travers is basically reducing the Slayers to tools. Slayers are not seen as individuals with needs and wants, but simply as instruments to use at the Council's will. The Slayers, who are told what to do and are expected to do it, are victims of an unfair power differential where they are given all of the responsibility and none of the authority.

According to philosopher Martha Nussbaum, this type of treatment is a specific kind of objectification, called instrumentality. Instrumentality is defined as the treatment of a person as a tool for the objectifiers' purpose.[26] According to Nussbaum, instrumentality can be immoral or benign. For it to be benign, the instrumental relationship needs to contain consent, as well as respect and reciprocity. For example, two friends agree to carpool. One friend drives the other to work and back. They agree to take turns doing the driving every couple of days, and each one is thankful and appreciative for the break they get while they are not driving; to show their appreciation, they even make a contribution toward gas money. In this case, the person who is being driven is using the other as their tool or instrument to get to work and back home, but this case of instrumentality is non-problematic because the two friends consented to this arrangement freely (thus meeting the consent requirement), are going to switch off on the driving (thus meeting the reciprocity requirement), and are courteous and grateful for the work of the driver (thus meeting the respect requirement). This case of instrumentality is benign.

However, the Council's usage of the Slayers is problematic instrumentality: Buffy has the powers and responsibilities of the Slayer thrust upon her, when she'd much rather be a regular high school teenager. The Council uses her as a weapon without checking with her wishes. Upon first meeting Rupert Giles, Buffy passionately informs him that she's retired from slaying; she is choosing to just be a regular teenager and not have to spend all of her time fighting for her life ("Welcome to the Hellmouth" 1.1). Later on in Season 1, in "Never Kill a Boy on the First Date," the same struggle is still apparent: Buffy wishes to be a regular teen, one who is free to explore her life choices, and maybe even date. But she is stuck in the role that has been imposed on her, and has to give up on her date with Owen to patrol the cemetery. Even when trying to set up a second date, negotiating with Giles for a night off is quite complicated, and Buffy's frustration with her Slayer role is obvious:

> BUFFY: I haven't had a day off in a while.
> GILES: True...
> BUFFY: And a cranky Slayer is a careless Slayer!
> GILES: Buffy, maintaining a normal social life as a Slayer ... i-is problematic at best ["Never Kill a Boy on a First Date" 1.5].

While the date eventually takes place, we are left with the idea that Buffy is unhappy with the pressure she is living under as a Slayer. After all, Buffy did not freely enter this arrangement of fighting evil—she is struggling with her new identity. Thus, the consent requirement is missing in her instrumental treatment.

The reciprocity requirement is likewise missing from the relationship. Council members watch and perhaps assist Slayers, but they are not actually engaged in hands-on fighting. They even have Special Ops teams to do their dirty work—they don't do any of the physical/violent labor themselves. Additionally, this case of instrumentality becomes increasingly problematic as we note that the Council is definitely not respectful of its Slayers, so that requirement is also missing. On her eighteenth birthday, Buffy is required to undergo the Cruciamentum, an ordeal that purposefully and methodically weakens the Slayer to test her prowess against a vampire while fighting from a position of physical disadvantage. Prior to the commencement of the test, the Slayer is injected with chemicals that dull her powers; she is supposed to be kept in the dark about the true reasons behind this weakening and about the coming challenge. Buffy experiences not only this physical weakening, but also a loss of self-confidence as she grapples with the unexplained loss of strength, where she can't even defeat a human who is pestering Cordelia.

> BUFFY [a little desperate]: You're not getting the big picture here. I-I have no strength. I have no coordination. I throw knives like…
> GILES: A girl? ["Helpless" 3.12].

Of course, it is Giles who is drugging her. It's also Giles who drops this casual sexist remark. And he is doing it all because he is listening to the authority of the Council: he does not question the problematic methods and antiquated tests that the Council uses, out of a blind sense of trust and faith in the hierarchal institution of the Council. He is not using his own rationality or moral sense. According to anarchists, this blind following of supposed authority is exactly where hierarchy leads: people doing what they are told without questioning become complicit in the misconduct they enable or even perform. They become alienated from their true selves and embrace their evil role within the institution—which they may even see as a worthy institution. As Goldman put it, they become "an inert mass of humanity, drilled and pounded into absolute uniformity."[27] Blindly loyal and uncritical, they engage in harms that have been approved or instigated by their higher authority. The only solution is to turn away from this reliance on authority, and to encourage individual freedom and liberty; as Goldman puts it, "Only in freedom can man grow to his full statues. Only in freedom will he learn to think and move, and give the very best in him."[28] Buffy exemplifies this insistence on her authentic self-development, as she negotiates her role of Slayer with Giles.

There's yet another problem with the Council: at their most basic, they function by getting a man (the Watcher) to watch and direct the actions of a woman (the Slayer). In this arrangement, the man represents knowledge and learning, and the woman is to be used instrumentally, as we've already discussed. The woman is placed in the subordinate position, while the man is in the dominant position.[29] This model is patriarchal in nature; it inhibits the authentic self-development of the women—the Slayers.

Thus, we can see that the Watchers Council is ultimately a patriarchal and hierarchal organization. It does not matter that it presents itself within a positive light. It does not even matter that many of its members believe that positive portrayal. The facts that the Council presents itself positively and that its leaders and members believe their own propaganda allow people to mistreat other people. They think that whatever they are doing is justified because the institution tells them it is, so they have no need to do the moral thinking themselves. But if the members and leaders of the institution are not doing moral thinking because they assume the institution is just, then no one is, and they revert to age old customs (which themselves are disrespectful and lack justification) and unexamined assumptions, which lead them to betray the very values they claim to be enacting.

The Watchers Council is not the only major institution that claims to be good, but that is, deep down, more of an agent of structural violence. When Buffy makes it to UC Sunnydale, she meets Riley Finn, who works for the Initiative. Purporting to be good guys, the Initiative, once again, symbolizes the controlling and corrupt nature of the state. Commanded by Maggie Walsh, this organization's stated purpose is to ensure the survival of the human species against the paranormal threat. Unfortunately, the motives of the Initiative are revealed to be heavily problematic as they exploit and dehumanize the beings they capture.

Further, Walsh was also experimenting on the soldiers assigned to the Initiative, without their knowledge or consent. Riley, for example, had his pain receptors rendered insensitive, so as to make him into a more effective fighter. In the process, the drugs Walsh was feeding Riley hurt his heart, causing his heartbeat to rise dangerously, which would eventually kill him. This treatment meets all the kinds of objectification we have so far discussed: instrumentality (making Riley into a fighting tool), denial of his subjectivity (not caring about Riley's feelings about the entire procedure), and denial of his autonomy (not caring about Riley's life plans for himself as a soldier and human being). But it also meets other objectification categories: ownership (treating someone as an owned item) and violability (violating someone's boundaries).[30] Thus, giving Riley drugs without his knowledge, consent, or imparting to him the possible side effects is treating Riley as if he is owned—the Initiative, who owns him, gets to make the decisions, not Riley. The act of feeding him the drugs is violating Riley's body, rendering Riley's body breached and exposed to experimentation.[31] That is the textbook definition of violability: the Initiative is committing physical assault in the name of getting a better soldier (and the assault is also mental, as it breaks Riley's trust when he finally finds out what's been going on). Part and parcel of objectification and not looking beyond their own ends, the Initiative shows itself to be corrupt, while on the surface having every appearance of doing good.

The Initiative does not encourage thinking on one's own either, which is a practice we've already identified as contrary to anarchist values. Rather, the Initiative demands following orders and not questioning authority. As such, as Jowett puts it, the Initiative demands passivity.[32] For example, when the Initiative captures Oz—who turned into a werewolf after a particularly emotional exchange with Tara Maclay—Riley tries to stand up against authority and stop the experimentation Oz is subjected to. In this scene, Oz is lying on a table with two doctors over him and many more in the background, and Riley is behind him.

> Doc 1: We gave him Haldol to keep him quiet.
> Riley: Why? He's not a threat now.
> Doc 1: I allowed you to stay as long as you let us do our work, Agent Finn. Only Colonel McNamara can place a cease order on medical testing, and he's told us to proceed ["New Moon Rising" 4.19].

Riley tries to reason with the powers in charge, but he is rebuffed and escorted out. His appeal to the doctors is ignored, and the medical experimentation continues on. Knowing how wrong this treatment is, Riley later intervenes again: he breaks Oz out. As Riley guides a weakened Oz out to freedom, the two are captured. Riley's so-called friends and fellow soldiers, Forrest and Graham, are the ones who capture him: loyalty to the cause supersedes amity. We next see Riley Finn in the brig, where the Colonel explains to him:

> Colonel: Finn, I had a look at your record and Professor Walsh's notes. Until recently, you were an exemplary soldier headed straight for the top. Then you meet this girl, this… Slayer, and suddenly you begin to exhibit signs of disloyalty. You abuse your command. But tonight… To release a lethal HST back into the population…
> Riley: Sir, the prisoner…
> Colonel: You will speak when I tell you to! Tomorrow I am going to institute a court-martial to investigate the extent of your involvement with the Slayer and her band of freaks…. *They're anarchists*, Finn … too backwards for the real world. You help us take them down, and you just might save your military career. Otherwise, you'll go to your grave labeled a traitor ["New Moon Rising" 4.19, emphasis added].

This moment captures the wrongs associated with hierarchy and authority. Colonel McNamara is intractable and does not even allow Riley to speak, where he could perhaps explain the motives behind his actions. Riley's point of view is ignored completely and he is instead threatened with punishment. This treatment epitomizes the way the state responds to dissidents: they are restrained and reprimanded. It also exemplifies how the state demands complete obedience from its soldiers.

Of course, to an anarcha-feminist like Emma Goldman, the Initiative—another Whedon analog to the state—would have looked suspicious right away. The Initiative is in the business of ignoring personal autonomy and seeking mere order-followers. According to Goldman, the soldier is a "cold-blooded, mechanical, obedient tool of his military superiors. He is ready to cut throats or scuttle a ship at the command of his ranking officer, without knowing or, perhaps, caring how, or why or wherefore."[33] A killing machine is created on the basis of unquestioning allegiance, and this instrumentalization is highly problematic for Goldman, as it is "indicative of the decay of liberty" of all involved.[34] As Goldman explains, the value of unquestioning obedience is at tension with individual liberty and self-development.[35] And in Riley's case, the scene exemplifies this tension, as Riley is told that standing up for what is right—fighting on the side of good with the Slayer and saving his friend Oz—is considered inappropriate and out of control. In fact, the Colonel says they are being *anarchists*.

Of course, the Colonel calls the Scoobies anarchists in a pejorative sense–alluding to their disorganization and to the fact that, by army standards, they are undisciplined. But for us, the Scoobies are anarcha-feminists and represent laudable values: they are organized around the tenets of collaboration, consensus building, and doing the just thing. The Scoobies are not organized around hierarchy, nor do they do things simply because they are told to do them or because they are expedient. Rather, the Scoobies' organizing principles are love and community.

The Importance of Pompons

Hierarchy though is not limited to institutional settings. We often have hierarchal relations within our one-on-one interactions. For example, the Watchers Council assigns each Slayer a Watcher. That Watcher is, for all intents and purposes, the Slayer's trainer, observer, and boss. Of course, this hierarchal relationship works better in some cases than others. While some Slayers, such as Kendra Young, embrace their subordinate roles, other Slayers, i.e., Buffy, most certainly do not.[36]

Trained by the well-respected Watcher Sam Zabuto, Kendra absorbed all of Zabuto's teachings, and was honed into a weapon. Unfortunately, as a result, she also had absolutely no sense of self-identity besides that of being a Slayer; as Goldman would argue, Kendra was pounded and kneaded out of her true self. Placed in the submissive position with her Watcher sitting comfortably in the dominant position, Kendra lived to follow orders, did not understand what friends were, and maintained a strict, formal tone in all her interactions. Consider the following scene where Kendra interrupts before Willow can join them:

> BUFFY: Back off, pink ranger! This is my friend.
> KENDRA: Friend?
> BUFFY: Yeah. As in person you hang with? Amigo?

KENDRA: I don't understand.
BUFFY [to Giles]: You try. I'm tapped.
GILES: Uh-uh, Kendra, uh, there are a-a-a few people, uh, ci-civilians, if you like, who, who know Buffy's identity. Willow is one of them, a-a- and they also, um, spend time together, uh, socially.
KENDRA: And you allow this, sir?
GILES: Well, uh…
KENDRA: But the Slayer must work in secret for security ["What's My Line, Part 2" 2.10].

Kendra is a by-the-book Slayer. Because she maintained her cover as a Slayer all of her life—which Buffy refused to do, as she actively negotiated a balance between her Slayer responsibilities and her own social development—Kendra never got to develop intimate and meaningful friendships. Kendra became so unaccustomed to thinking for herself that she lost all sense of individuality. Tellingly, she does not even know her last name ("What's My Line, Part 2" 2.10). Kendra's had her autonomy and subjectivity thwarted. When someone's autonomy and subjectivity are denied, that is once again a type of objectification. Called denial of autonomy and denial of subjectivity, this conduct is wrongful because it entails treating someone as if they lack self-determination; this treatment undermines their chance to develop as authentic, full human beings.[37]

Kendra experiences denial of autonomy and denial of subjectivity through the Watcher/Slayer model: her autonomy has been infringed upon to create a Slayer and every vestige of personality has been erased in the process.[38] Kendra is so authority oriented that she does not think for herself: in the same episode where she is introduced, she matter of factly tells Buffy that the two of them should "return to your Watcher for our orders" ("What's My Line, Part 2" 2.10). In a powerful response, Buffy answers, "I don't do orders. I do things my way" ("What's My Line, Part 2" 2.10). Buffy is autonomous; she negotiated that independence by standing up against authority and hierarchy every moment she could.

As Buffy and Kendra continue to interact, we learn of further differences between the two:

KENDRA: Your life is very different than mine.
BUFFY: You mean the part where I occasionally have one? Yeah, I guess it is.
…
KENDRA: Emotions are weakness, Buffy. You shouldn't entertain them.
BUFFY: Kendra, my emotions give me power. They're total assets! ["What's My Line, Part 2" 2.10].

Kendra's privations in life illustrate the wrong of not just objectification, but also the wrongs associated with taking one category of individuals (Slayers, who really stand-in for women in general) and arbitrarily carving out *for them* a way of life. In the real world, this sexist practice falls under the perpetuation of oppressive gender norms. As Parsons explains, these norms are antiquated and need to change. Parsons stated of these norms, "he looked upon her as a being inferior to him ... she was regarded as a sort of necessary evil as something to be used and abused to be bought and sold—as a thing fit only to cater to his pleasures and his passions—this was woman's lowly position."[39] Applicable to women and Slayers, this quote illustrates the submissive positions that both women and Slayers were relegated to, as both were instrumentalized and undervalued. In Parson's critique, this drudgery needs to stop. In fact, Parsons envisioned a new world where every woman left behind this inferior position and "she entered the arena of life's activities, to make her way in this hustling, pushing, busy world as an independent human being for the first time in the world's history."[40] That's exactly what Buffy did as a Slayer, as she broke through the Council imposed norms of being a Slayer.[41] In fashioning her own path, Buffy insisted on her autonomy and balanced her Slayer responsibilities with developing as a full human being, whatever that meant:

> BUFFY: I told you: I'm trying out for the cheerleading squad!
> GILES: You have a sacred birthright, Buffy. You were chosen to destroy vampires, not to ... wave pompoms at people. And as the Watcher I forbid it.
> BUFFY: And you'll be stopping me how?
> GILES: Well, I... By appealing to your common sense, if such a creature exists.
> BUFFY: I will still have time to fight the forces of evil, okay? I just wanna have a life, I wanna do something normal. Something safe ["Witch" 1.3].

In this scene, Buffy's autonomy is articulated through her insistence on being a cheerleader. But this persistence is not just about waving pompons, but about allowing herself to experience life fully, and having the freedom to try out roles that interest her. In other words, it is about developing authentically as a full human being and honoring her subjectivity. Furthermore, in standing up to Giles, Buffy is insisting on her independence against the patriarchy. She is stepping out of a prescribed norm and embracing her true self as she best sees fit.

While Kendra does not feel sorry for herself due to the hardships she's had in her life (through which she lacks the chance to develop her own life or develop friendships), Buffy notes that the relationships she herself is building with the Scoobies are beneficial. These connections and the emotions she experiences from them give Buffy strength and a better understanding into human and supernatural behavior; her social community allows Buffy to become a better thinker and yields insight into how to approach different situations. Buffy explains her imagination, in this sense, is an asset even in fighting. After she compliments Kendra's flawless technique, she explains why she would have won anyway:

> BUFFY: Still, I woulda kicked your butt in the end. And ya know why? No imagination.
> KENDRA: Really? You think so?
> BUFFY: Oh, I know so. You're good, but power alone isn't enough. A good fighter needs to know how to improvise, to go with the flow ["What's My Line, Part 2" 2.10].

This valuing of relationships, emotions, and imagination is inherently feminist. Under the patriarchal system we live in, emotions are usually identified as destructive or damaging, and associated with women (notice Kendra, who's been brainwashed by the patriarchy, also sees emotions as dangerous). On the other hand, cold rationality and objective thinking are seen as solely valuable, and as the domains of males. This unfair valuation is what Buffy objects to, echoing feminist thinkers who problematized this binary.[42] Instead of devaluing emotions and relationships, Buffy argues for their efficacy in slaying. Through this act, Buffy is once again standing up against the patriarchy.

Buffy's methodology of being an autonomous Slayer did not come by easily. Buffy worked against the patriarchal restraints that others attempted to impose on her. Goldman referred to this quest for autonomy as self-emancipation:

> True emancipation begins neither in the polls nor in courts. It begins in woman's soul. History tells us that every oppressed class gained true liberation from its masters through its own efforts. It is necessary that woman learns that lesson, that she realizes that her freedom will reach as far as her power to achieve her freedom reaches. It is, therefore, far more important for her to begin with inner regeneration, to cut loose from the weight of prejudices, traditions and customs.[43]

Buffy, in this sense, works as an emancipator. She insists on her own, autonomous self-development, she frees herself from the arbitrary norms imposed on her by her Watcher and the Watchers Council, and negotiates for herself what her own role should be.

However, due to the inherent hierarchy and patriarchy within the Slayer/Watcher relationship, it took Giles some time to recognize and appreciate Buffy's unique personality and to respect her self-made identity as a Slayer. Recall how in Season 1, Giles, as a stand in for the all-knowing patriarchy, would pop up from behind cemetery tombstones and offer unwanted advice to Buffy, even as she was busy turning vampires into dust:

> BUFFY: We haven't been properly introduced. I'm Buffy, and you're history! [She slays the vampire.]
> GILES: Poor technique. Prioritizing, sub-par… Execution was adequate, but a bit too bloody for my taste.
> BUFFY: Giles, don't mention it. It was my pleasure to make the world safe for humanity again.
> GILES: I'm not saying that your methods are without merit, it's, uh, y- you're

spending too much time and energy. It should simply be: plunge, and move on. Plunge and ... ["Never Kill a Boy on a First Date" 1.5].

Even as she was ridding the world of evil, Buffy was told how to perform. Analogous to the control the patriarchy imposes on women's behavior in the real world (think of how women's bodies are judged against beauty standards, or how women are judged on being decorative or not decorative enough, just to mention a few examples),[44] in the Buffyverse this unwanted advice represents a patriarchal attempt to shape Buffy into the kind of submissive Slayer that the Council wants. Note Buffy's response here: she defends herself through sarcasm and insists on respect for her way of doing things. By responding with snark or humor and by not wavering from developing her own way of doing things, Buffy thus chips away at both the patriarchy and the hierarchy that Giles represents. Eventually, Buffy forges a relationship with Giles where she does not accept a submissive role. Rather, she insists on respect and consideration, working to establish an egalitarian friendship based on mutual collaboration and acceptance. Buffy's effort at this restructuring of the patriarchy is inherently anarcha-feminist. In fact, Buffy's relationship with Giles changes so much from the Council accepted Slayer/Watcher norm, that Giles is eventually replaced as her Watcher.

Let's return to the test the Council was giving to Buffy, to test her resilience while depowered. Because Giles eventually confessed his wrongdoing to Buffy (his part in drugging her for the Cruciamentum) and because he stepped in and helped her in dealing with the out of control vampire, Kralik, who was supposed to be her challenger, the Council decrees that Giles must be replaced. The scene is a significant one, as it illustrates that Giles has stepped outside the norms of his patriarchal, authoritarian role: he is now Buffy's collaborator, not her overseer. He has also come to understand the wrongs associated with instrumentality. When a representative of the Council informs Buffy of the necessity of the test, Giles steps in and protests—a marked improvement from his earlier stance of unquestioningly supporting it—and thus shows that he is questioning authority and critiquing objectification in its various guises:

> GILES: The test is done. We're finished.
> QUENTIN [he faces Giles]: Not quite. She passed. You didn't. The Slayer is not the only one who must perform in this situation. I've recommended to the Council, and they've agreed, that you be relieved of your duties as Watcher immediately. You're fired.
> GILES: On what grounds?
> QUENTIN: Your affection for your charge has rendered you incapable of clear and impartial judgment. You have a father's love for the child, and that is useless to the cause. It would be best if you had no further contact with the Slayer ["Helpless" 3.12].

This interaction further illustrates several things. First, the Council devalues and objectifies the Slayer. Second, it also objectifies Giles, the Watcher who came to humanely interact with his charge, in the process allowing his own autonomy to flourish through respecting hers. Most importantly, this hierarchical system is shown to be inimical to true collaboration and solidarity, as it throws away a relationship based on trust and a father's love in favor of a detached and rote one. Just like the corrupt liberal state, the Council is only interested in maintaining its own way of doing things.[45]

And who do they replace Giles with? Wesley Wyndham-Pryce. An arrogant know-it-all, Wesley once again underscores the wrongs associated with the patriarchy and the hierarchy. When he first shows up in the Sunnydale Library, he's equally busy with boasting of his superior Watcher training and with unilaterally imposing his will on Buffy, as he orders her on a mission:

> WESLEY: Are you not used to being given orders?
> BUFFY: Whenever Giles sends me on a mission, he always says "please." And afterwards I get a cookie.
> WESLEY: I don't feel we're getting off on quite the right foot ["Bad Girls" 3.14].

Of course they're not on the right foot as Wesley is exhibiting an authoritarian and objectifying mindset. But Buffy is not intimidated, and, in a feminist vein, stands up to his demeaning treatment with sarcasm. She is cutting lose from the Watchers' restraints, as Goldman would put it, by not recognizing their authority. Wesley functions again and again as a tool of the Council—and an unaware one at that—exhibiting the constraints the liberal state imposes on those under its dominion.

Under the guise of helping and caring for the development of the Slayer, Wesley actually acts in a controlling manner when, time and again, he opposes Buffy's choices:

> WESLEY: I don't understand.
> BUFFY: Well, I don't think I can talk any slower, Wes. I want to leave.
> WESLEY: What? Now?
> BUFFY: No, not now. After I graduate, you know, college?
> WESLEY: But, you're a Slayer.
> BUFFY: Yeah, I'm also a person. You can't just define me by my Slayer-ness. That's … something-ism ["Choices" 3.19].

As Buffy needs to take the next step in life and attend college, Giles is congratulatory, but Wesley acts as the intractable state would against a dissident. Wesley makes it clear he is not willing to respect Buffy's autonomous development and prohibits her from leaving. He is not interested in furthering Buffy's life path. For Wesley, Buffy is simply a tool to be used, and not a human being.

Thus, we see that Buffy rejects the one-on-one hierarchal relationship that the Watchers Council attempts to force upon her. This rejection is necessary as she is the one in the cemeteries, having to draw her own judgments about whom to slay. There is no need for some man to watch her, much less to boss her around from the comfort of a safe distance. Hierarchy lurks not only within institutions, but also within personal relationships, and it is just as stymying there.

Dead but Pretty

In this chapter, we have seen that *Buffy* brings together many of the critical arguments that we saw in the other series. It can be argued that *Buffy* takes the horrors of high school and re-imagines them as supernatural horrors.[46] While we have no complaints about that re-imagining, we have simply pointed out there is an additional way to analyze the show. *Buffy* presents a critique of hierarchy in a fashion that begs for a solution. High school is itself a hierarchy, but so are vampires, the Watchers Council, the Initiative, and the individual relationships of Watchers and Slayers. Hierarchy is everywhere, and *Buffy* clearly shows us that as Buffy repeatedly stands up against it in a variety of contexts. Perhaps even more importantly, *Buffy* also suggests a direction for a solution, which we turn to next.

Six

Buffy the Vampire Slayer
The Show That Hierarchy Has Nightmares About

Fixing the Yellow Crayon

So Willow broke the yellow crayon ("Grave" 6.22). Yet, this time, it is going to be okay. Almost everything we have discussed so far has been critical. Angel could not fix Wolfram & Hart. Echo could not stop the Rossum Corporation. S.H.I.E.L.D. turned out to be Hydra. Malcolm and Jayne really need to work on releasing their libertarian angst. And Willow broke that yellow crayon in kindergarten. Anarchist theory can be a bit of a downer.

Thankfully, *Buffy the Vampire Slayer* (*Buffy* from here on) also represents a positive project, which we can again see through the anarcha-feminists: Lucy Parsons, Voltairine de Cleyre, and Emma Goldman. That positive project is that love can save us. The love that the Scoobies have for each other, time and time again, saves them from the various evils lurking in closets, alleyways, sewers, and high school classrooms and graduation ceremonies. Love can also save society. Society can be arranged according to the principles of anarchism and feminism, provided that people can learn to put aside their differences and concentrate on their shared humanity. The anarcha-feminists believe this change is not only possible, but it also would be likely if we move past our unhealthy reliance on hierarchy. The Scoobies prove it is possible as they move from separate individuals into one communal organization that brings together Buffy's physical strength, Willow's mystical strength, Giles' intellectual strength, and Xander's … well, Xander can tell jokes while they work it all out.

We Stick Together, Everything's Going to Be Fine

Under anarcha-feminism, society is organized in a fair fashion, where folks work together for the benefit of all. The idea is not to work to enrich certain individuals, as in our current wage system where, for example, workers labor for the profit of a corporation. Rather, the idea is to work harmoniously, with no emphasis on personal gain. As Goldman put it, "there can be no freedom in the large sense of the word, no harmonious development, so long as mercenary and commercial considerations play an important part in the determination of personal conduct."[1] Without working for personal profit, society would be organized "based on voluntary co-operation of productive groups, communities and societies loosely federated together" by common interests and values.[2] Greed and selfishness have no place in this organizational structure. Rather, society ought to be organized in accordance with the spirit of equality, friendship, and mutual aid (or reciprocity). As Goldman emphasized, under this new arrangement, everyone would be trained and would operate in accordance to "the spirit of mutual aid and brotherhood, their initiative and self-reliance developed, and an esprit de corps maintained whose very soul is solidarity of purpose."[3] As Parsons likewise explained, "the man and woman of loftier intellects ... think not so much of the riches to be gained by their efforts as to the good they can do for their fellow creatures."[4] Importantly, in this new society, everyone is deserving of help: not just friends, but also strangers. The Scoobies work together in just such a fashion, embodying the collaborative anarchist vision that Goldman and Parsons put forth.[5] Buffy and the Scoobies develop a sense of community that leads them to act out of love for others, even at the point of repeatedly risking their own lives to do so.

From the initial revelation in the Sunnydale library that vampires and demons are real, Willow and Xander accept Buffy's Slayer powers. Through each struggle together, whether it is to impede the Harvest, win against the Mayor, or stop Caleb in his tracks, they all grow stronger in both their friendship and their commitment to rid the world of evil. In fact, Whedon scholars Lawrence B. Rosenfeld and Scarlet L. Wynns explain that the Scoobies practiced "behaviors that provide others with the means of coping with the challenges of living everyday life or 'saving the world—a lot.'"[6] As such, they work together, they develop a routine for action, as well as an anarcha-feminist ethic.

In high school, the Scoobies organize their missions at Giles' library. Buffy and the team work together in a collaborative fashion to fight whatever big bad is wracking havoc on Sunnydale. Giles consults the books, Willow researches internet archives and eventually turns to magic, and Xander offers comic relief as a way to deal with the pressure of having to save the world. Sure, Buffy has the Slayer skills, but she doesn't act unilaterally or as the sole hero: with every patrol and every vampire or demon vanquished, the Scoobies forge egalitarian relationships, rely on one another, work together, and collectively come up with an attack strategy. They help one another as best they can, as based on their unique skills.

Consider how they all work together to handle the case of Amber catching fire in the midst of cheerleading practice:

> BUFFY: I need to get the skinny on Amber. Find out if she's had any colorful episodes before.
> WILLOW: That means hacking illegally into the school's computer system. At last, something I can do!
> XANDER: I'll ask around about her.
> BUFFY: You guys don't have to get involved.
> XANDER: What d'ya mean? We're a team! Aren't we a team?
> WILLOW: Yeah! You're the Slayer, and we're, like, the Slayerettes! ["Witch" 1.3].

Especially early on, Willow and Xander were no fighters—but one need not be a fighter to jump in the fray. Even back then, they bounced around ideas, and looked for ways to contribute. United in their mission of doing good, they are always, in fact, a team.

While in college, the Scoobies' lair might have changed to Giles' apartment, but their methodology stays the same: they still all work jointly to defeat evil. And Xander even picks up some martial arts skills in the process. Remember, when the Initiative takes Oz and they all rally together to save him? While Buffy initially only plans to take Xander, Willow suggests she should go as well, to which Buffy responds:

> BUFFY: No. Look, it's too dangerous, Will. Besides, I need you to help Giles hack into the city's electrical grid. We've gotta try to power down the Initiative.
> WILLOW: Giles can do it without me. I can give him all the instructions, I can show him exactly what to do.
> GILES: Of course.
> WILLOW: I-I can't just sit here.
> BUFFY: Okay. Okay, you can back us up ["New Moon Rising" 4.19].

They all want to contribute in the rescue; they each share responsibility and have a part to play. This motif is repeated throughout the series; their combined efforts result in success. In this case, the Scoobies successfully rescue Oz, with Riley escorting Oz out.

In this scene, we also see Riley standing up to authority and giving up his military career as he prioritizes doing the right thing over blind allegiance to authority.

COLONEL: You're a dead man, Finn.
RILEY: No, sir. I'm an anarchist. [He punches the Colonel in the face and then walks away.] ["New Moon Rising" 4.19].

Riley's self-identification as an anarchist (even if it is meant as a jokey response to the Colonel saying the Scoobies are a bunch of anarchists) underscores the values the Scoobies uphold: working for the common good and doing what's right even in the face of intimidation or personal loss. In other words, the Scoobies' ethic of action is revealed to be selfless and just. Importantly, when they repeatedly put their bodies on the line, the Scoobies also act out of love for their fellow human beings. The ultimate values of friendship and love are enshrined in the Scoobies, as they fight not only for the good of the world, but for each other, as friends and lovers. Let's discuss these themes a bit more.

While the Scoobies celebrate goodness and friendship, they are not pacifists. The Scoobies are militant insofar as they are fighting evil. Specifically, they embody the principles of militant feminism: they exemplify that women can wield violence just as capably as men; their use of aggression and violence is tempered with the realization that these tools must be responsibly employed in the fight against evil and in the fight for just, feminist ends.[7] This stance fits in with the anarcha-feminist view of violence.

Anarcha-feminist Voltairine de Cleyre viewed violence as an unfortunately necessary tool to change the world for the better. In a speech titled "Direct Action," she explained how the point of view from which aggression is employed matters in the valuation or disapprobation of such a feat; she argued against always critiquing direct action out of hand.[8] de Cleyre said, "Now every school child in the United States has had the direct action ... brought to his notice by his school history..." such as

> in the period of agitation and excitement preceding the revolution, there were all sorts and kinds of direct action from the most peaceable to the most violent ... as the inevitable growth of hostility progressed, violent direct action developed; e.g., in the matter of destroying the revenue stamps, or the action concerning the tea-ships, either by not permitting the tea to be landed, or by putting it in damp storage, or by throwing it into the harbor, as in Boston.[9]

de Cleyre continued with more examples, such as that of the Civil War or the Underground Railroad. Each example illustrated how violent means were employed for what folks upheld as the common good, be it independence from England in the Revolutionary War or fighting to free the slaves. In de Cleyre's analysis, these models of violent behavior were upheld as exemplary. She warned, "direct action has always been used, and has the historical sanction of the very people now reprobating it."[10] She further noted that because the state discouraged challenges from dissenters or because the public was taught to sympathize with bosses and not empathize with the plight of common workers, the use of aggressive methods of protest was discouraged. As such, de Cleyre warned that perspective led to illogical conclusions when it comes to violence: if endorsed by the state it was deemed acceptable, but if it was used by those without power and influence, it was deemed dangerous. Instead of allowing violence's justification depend on perspective, she felt it should depend on the permissibility of the goals: violence could be used to secure freedom, liberty, and bring an end to oppression. As such, she concluded that the use of aggressive means to negotiate justice—from gender equality to safe working conditions—was acceptable. To not fight against injustice would be wrong; otherwise, she asked, "how will the chains be broken?"[11]

Emma Goldman argued that violent acts are not born out of cruelty, but are representative of people's "supersensitiveness to the wrong and injustice surrounding them."[12] In other words, if you are truly sensitive to how much injustice exists in the world around you, then measured and effective acts of violence may seem to be an appropriate response. Goldman further argued that in such dire situations—where folks are struggling under the chains of oppression—anarchism cannot encourage submission to violent conditions since, as she explains in a rhetorical question "How can it, when it knows that all suffering, all misery, all ills, result from the evil of submission?"[13] Yet she also warns against the indiscriminate use of violence: it cannot be used for the sake of wrong, but only for just and fair ends. As such, only those individuals who are striking a blow against oppression, suffering, and injustice are right in employing it, for "otherwise despots would reign supreme, and life be unbearable."[14] The Scoobies use violence in this limited fashion. They do not embrace it fully, but carefully. Their militancy is specifically directed: they differentiate between good and bad supernatural creatures, they do not kill humans, and they do not kill innocent bystanders. They do not use violence to take revenge. Let's explore a few examples where this limited use of violence is employed.

When Riley declared himself an anarchist, he gave up his position in the Initiative because he recognized that the widespread use of violence and aggression is wrong, and that it should be curbed and only used where necessary. He connects his realization to witnessing Oz' treatment, as Riley explains: "Still... I was in a totally black and white space, people versus monsters, and it ain't like that ... especially when it comes to love" ("New Moon Rising" 4.19). Riley realizes that violence should not be used against Oz, even if he is a werewolf, because he does not constitute a threat. Riley opposes Oz's mistreatment because he realizes the indiscriminate use of force is wrong and corruptive. Further, this position suggests a wider inclusivity: instead of dividing society into the binary humans and monsters (compare to similar binaries such as men and women, white and black, cis and trans, rich and poor, etc.), we are all interconnected and can learn to move past our differences. That view is a major step forward, toward an anarchist society, especially when the differences in question are between people who turn into wolves at the full moon versus people who like to dance under the full moon. If that difference can be overcome, we can certainly overcome the fact that some of us like classical music and others like hip hop.

A further example is the Scoobies' use of violence in their fight against Adam. Adam is, after all, orchestrating a massacre between humans and supernaturals, while ultimately attempting to build up his own cyborg army. To deal with Adam, the Scoobies come together to orchestrate a plan, but they realize that a wide variety of their skills will be necessary:

> XANDER: So no problem, all we need is combo Buffy—with Slayer strength, Giles' multi-lingual know-how, and Willow's witchy power. Yeah, don't tell me. I'm just full of helpful suggestions.
> GILES: As a matter of fact, you are ["Primeval" 4.21].

Good natured banter results in the creation of an elegant solution, where, through their combined abilities, they can take down Adam: only Willow can cast the paralysis spell, only Giles can recite the incantation in Sumerian, and only Buffy can survive the necessary proximity to Adam. And it was an idea born from a half-joking Xander. Combining their talents in such a fashion results in a spell that allows Buffy's body to be infused with all of their distinct Scooby talents: Giles' wisdom, Buffy's physical prowess, Xander's loyalty, and Willow's knowledge of magic. As the physical manifestation of their collaborative spirit, this entity employs justified violence to take out Adam. This scene also literally embodies the redeeming powers of collaboration and cooperation, which are anarcha-feminist values.

As alluded to previously, the Scoobies fight not just against evil, but also for each other's emotional and psychological well-being. Even in the middle of preparing for life or death battles, they take the time to be there for one another. Consider this scene as Buffy, Willow, and Xander are discussing an estrangement caused by Spike, as they descend into a pit to infiltrate the Initiative. Buffy considers whether they have all drifted apart, to which Willow notes that it is hard to keep the gang together and Buffy responds:

> BUFFY: But I want it together. Will, I miss you. And Giles, and Xander. And it is my fault. I've been wrapped up in my own stuff, I've been a bad friend.
> WILLOW: You're the Slayer, Buffy. Your stuff is pretty crucial.
> BUFFY: I mean Riley. And… Riley, mostly.
> WILLOW: Well, I haven't been Miss Available either. I … I kept secrets. I hid things from everyone.
> BUFFY: That's not your fault. Will, you were going through something huge ["Primeval" 4.21].

As they reach the bottom of the pit, they also embrace Xander. And fully reconciled, they march into battle (which as we already know, will be successful).

When they march into battle, the Scoobies take care to not use violence indiscriminately. Unfortunately, Faith Lehane, another Slayer, does not understand that lesson. While, on one hand, Faith functions as an obvious rejection of Wesley's patriarchal and paternalistic treatment (she ignores and disdains Wesley), on the other hand, she also functions to illustrate the concept that the indiscriminate use of violence corrupts. In "Consequences" (3.15), Faith is portrayed as increasingly troubled. After all, she's done the unthinkable and killed a human, Allan Fitch. Importantly, she does not *appear* to feel remorse over it. In fact, Faith refuses to talk about the killing, and attempts to paint it as just another part of the Slayer job. Of course, deep down, this violence leaves a strong impact on Faith. Remember that even as Faith is trying to convince Buffy, at the end of "Bad Girls" (3.14), that the killing is not bothering her, she is simultaneously attempting to scrub away the blood—she is trying to wash her hands of the death she just caused, but, of course, like Pontius Pilate before her, Faith certainly cannot wash off her responsibility.

After she kills a human, Faith grows increasingly out of control. She vacillates between denying responsibility for the killing, and then excusing it as meaningless collateral damage. She even pins the murder on Buffy. As Faith acts with increasing disregard for her well-being, as well as the well-being of those around her, the Scoobies rally together to figure out how to deal with the situation. Valuing her friends' advice, Buffy first turns to Willow, and then Giles. Understanding what is at stake—a Slayer turning to the dark side—Giles indicates that some counseling could possibly help; he also discloses that the other alternative is to turn Faith over to the Council. The Scoobies all realize, however, that doing so is "the last thing Faith needs at the moment" ("Consequences" 3.15). What she really needs is to comprehend that wielding the violent power of the Slayer should be done carefully and responsibly. Only earnest support and friendly guidance has a chance to influence Faith and to get her to come to this awareness. Turning her over to the Council, a move the Scoobies oppose, would only result in Faith losing any chance of redemption. Love has a chance to work here, a stern response doesn't.

In true collaborative fashion, Angel steps in and captures Faith, just as she is about to spiral into madness even more by killing Xander. As Angel earnestly implores, "If you can trust us, Faith, this can all change. You don't have to disappear into the darkness" ("Consequences" 3.15). We are left with the idea that the Scoobies are about to attempt an intervention and save Faith from turning to the dark side. Unfortunately, we don't get a chance to see how that attempt turns out, because Wesley, in a completely authoritarian manner, storms in and captures Faith so as to turn her over to the judgment of the Council. Not only is this act misguided because it ignores the communal efforts of the Scoobies, it also results in Faith's escape (and, at least for the next few episodes, her inability to redeem herself). In this act, Wesley once again shows the inadequacies of the patriarchy and of hierarchy. He acts unilaterally, without consulting others, and is blind to the redeeming power of love and community. Thus, once again, *Buffy* illustrates that the Watchers Council is not interested in the anarcha-feminist values of collaboration and cooperation. Thankfully, Buffy and the Scoobies are.

The Power of Love

The redeeming power of love and morality is at work not just in the above exchange with Faith, but in other episodes as well. The same theme of Faith's redemption through the support and affection provided by friendship is examined when Buffy and Faith magically switch bodies through a mysterious device left for Faith by the Mayor. After Faith wakes up from her coma, the Scoobies—as well as a special operations team sent by the Council to retrieve her—are looking for her. After all, as "a sociopath, super bitch" ("This Year's Girl" 4.15), Faith needs to be dealt with and Buffy and the gang see it as their responsibility. As Faith and Buffy engage in a fight, the mystical device is activated and the two switch bodies. As Faith, now in Buffy's form, experiences the world from this altered point of view, she gets to experience the restorative power of love.

The first encounter occurs in Giles' apartment, as the gang discusses Faith's possible capture by the Council's retriever team. While Faith (embodied as Buffy) laughs at the fate that awaits the captured Buffy (who's currently embodied as Faith), she is somewhat disconcerted that the team just feels a sense of resignation at Faith's possible capture. There is no wild rejoicing in the Scoobies. Even though Willow says, "I hope they throw the book at her" ("Who Are You" 4.16), there's no sense of underlying hatred of Faith present in the Scoobies' attitudes. They see the matter as one of right and wrong, and it's almost as if they are resigned to this course of events. Instead, it is Faith (appearing as Buffy) who expresses unbridled joy: "I'm sorry.... It's just, I'm so happy. Faith is so evil, and evil is ... wrong. I'm glad she's going. To England" ("Who Are You" 4.16). For the Scoobies, Faith's capture represents the idea that justice is being served, but also that she is beyond their ability to reach and redeem. They are resigned to this outcome, but it is not a reason to celebrate. Faith doesn't really comprehend this response, as she is too busy fantasizing of ways to kill Willow.

Later that night, Faith experiences more disconcerting things. She is dancing at the Bronze (instead of being out on patrol) and meets up Willow and Tara Maclay. Willow notices that a vampire has accosted an innocent human, and she clues Faith in as to her discovery, to which Faith responds:

> FAITH [Seeing it is a vampire]: Oh yeah. Good call.
> TARA: What?
> WILLOW: Vampire.
> FAITH: He's wicked obvious... [Willow's look is clearly judging Faith's inaction.] So I better slay him then ["Who Are You" 4.16].

Faith is prompted into doing the right thing, and, to keep her cover, she does it. She follows the vampire and his date outside, where he is attacking his unsuspecting victim and biting into her neck. Breaking a pool cue apart, Faith intervenes and quickly dispatches the vampire. Then, she approaches the girl and examines her wound:

> FAITH: You'll live.
> GIRL [crying]: He attacked me ... he was so strong...
> FAITH: Well he's gone now. Put some ... medicine on that.
> DATE: Thank you. Thank you.
> FAITH: Yeah, it's cool ["Who Are You" 4.16].

This encounter continues the same theme of Faith becoming disconcerted in the presence of love. She was prompted to do the right thing, but in doing it, she found pure gratitude, and the power behind that emotion leaves Faith confused. The sincerity imbued in the thank you—just like the earlier refusal to outright celebrate her supposed capture—starts to thaw Faith's icy core. Doing good feels good; when she's not busy feeling the rush associated with aggressive action, Faith can allow herself to experience how good it feels to do good. We see the redemptive power of love and morality at work as it slowly is beginning to work a transformation within Faith's inner being.

We see this phenomenon again later that same night, as Riley and Faith (still embodied as Buffy) have sex. When Riley whispers, "I love you" ("Who Are You" 4.16), it throws Faith into a panic. Her frosty reticence and self-assuredness are shattered, as she starts to struggle and shake, almost physically fighting off the power of love. Riley only responds in a further caring manner, solicitously asking what is the matter, wrapping Faith in a blanket, and holding her. She is perplexed, not knowing how to handle things, and leaves first thing in the morning. As she is making her way out of the house, Forrest, Riley's friend, confronts her. A seemingly meaningless conversation takes place, where Forrest accuses Faith of not allowing Riley to heal and, thereby, Faith is allegedly interfering with the Initiative's mission:

> FAITH: You've got a mission? I've been fighting demons since before you could shave.

FORREST: Yeah, you're a killer.
FAITH: I'm not a killer! I'm a Slayer. You don't know the first thing about me ["Who Are You" 4.16].

This exchange is significant, as it allows Faith, in a brief moment, to set a new direction for her life through her strong response. Previously, she had killed a human but was too self-involved to see the wrong of her action (or at least deceived herself sufficiently to try to conceal the wrongness from herself); she denied, then excused the murder, and even went to work for the Mayor, thus embracing her killing nature. But now, based on her interactions with the Scoobies, Riley, and through helping an innocent, she is turning away from that dark and dangerous side of herself, and is reclaiming her role to do good, her role as a Slayer. She is coming to realize that violence should be used for just and feminist ends (as in rescuing a girl from assault) and ought not to be used indiscriminately.

Faith continues in this positive transformation as she consciously gives up her chance to evade capture so that she can instead rush to a church where vampires are holding humans hostage. She is acting selflessly in this encounter; she could have boarded her flight, but does not when she sees the special news report about the church. Faith is learning right from wrong—because she has had a chance to experience love and to feel its influence—so she rushes in, heedless to her well-being, to do the right thing and save the parishioners. Rushing to the church, she meets Riley, who tries to stop her from going in alone. Faith pushes him aside, asserting: "This is what I have to do…" ("Who Are You" 4.16). Riley may not understand the significance of Faith's words in this moment, but we do: this acceptance of responsibility symbolizes Faith's return from the dark side. While it takes her a while to deal with her self-loathing, in later episodes, after serving time in jail for her misdeed, Faith even plans on "playing social worker to the slayers. Maybe I could help walk a few bad girls from the brink" ("No Future for You" 8.2). And it is all due to the redeeming power of love.

Love, friendship, and collaboration are the cornerstones of the Scoobies. They are also the cornerstones of anarcha-feminism. Goldman and Parsons espouse the values of cooperation and mutual aid over and over again. Goldman, for example, explained that the principle of mutual aid is to be employed in all areas of life:

> And all of these Syndicalist activities are permeated with the spirit of educational work, carried on systematically by evening classes on all vital subjects treated from an unbiased, libertarian standpoint—not the adulterated "knowledge" with which the minds are stuffed in our public schools. The scope of the education is truly phenomenal, including sex hygiene, the care of women during pregnancy and confinement, the care of home and children, sanitation and general hygiene; in fact, every branch of human knowledge—science, history, art—received thorough attention.[15]

Goldman explains that all of these efforts to build one another up as informed, learned citizens are undertaken so "the people will be fully prepared to manage successfully in their affairs."[16] As such, the model presented is premised on everyone's collaboration and has the goal of everyone's enrichment, so that they all could be ready to take on whatever role they autonomously chose for themselves. Furthermore, Parsons adds to this model when she states: "Remember that we are here as one brotherhood and one sisterhood, as one humanity, with a responsibility to the downtrodden and the oppressed of all humanity."[17] This spirit of collaboration is akin to that of the Scoobies, who, through their everyday activities, work to enrich each other's lives, teach each other lessons in friendship (as they inadvertently did for Faith), and work to save the world from evil.

The confrontation between Xander and Willow at the end of Season 6 embodies the idea that the Scoobies fight for each other, as friends and lovers. Willow, distraught after Warren Mears kills Tara, turns to the powers of dark magic in an attempt to get revenge. It takes all of the Scoobies to try to contain Willow's vengeful magic, and, unfortunately, their combined powers are just not enough to defeat her. As Anya Jenkins tells Xander and Buffy, Willow's plan to destroy the world is about to be put into motion, and the only solution that could work is a love-based intervention. Let's look at the exchange:

> XANDER: First day of kindergarten. You cried because you broke the yellow crayon, and you were too afraid to tell anyone. You've come pretty far, ending the world, not a terrific notion. But the thing is? Yeah. I love you. I loved crayon-breaky Willow and I love … scary veiny Willow. So if I'm going out, it's here. If you wanna kill the world? Well, then start with me. I've earned that.
> WILLOW: You think I won't?
> XANDER: It doesn't matter. I'll still love you ["Grave" 6.22].

After Xander continues to insist that he loves Willow in spite of her protests, the scene ends with Willow crying in Xander's arms and returning to her old self, with the dark veins fading away.[18] Xander has placed himself squarely in front of Willow's potentially world-ending flow of magic. He doesn't fight Willow, but engages with her from a place of love and affection. He tries to remind her of their friendship, and proclaims himself ready to die. But at every step he proclaims his love for her. His outpouring of love quenches the fire of her hatred, and eventually Willow steps back from the brink and collapses into Xander's arms. Not having given up on her, not having turned to blind, authoritarian measures to deal with her, Xander's invocation of their camaraderie—from a broken yellow crayon in kindergarten to this present moment—is the one thing that penetrates through her rage. His tenderness is the literal balm that soothes Willow's spirit; through it, the evil literally drains out of her, making her look like her old self and not "veiny Willow" ("Grave" 6.22). It is through love that Xander saves the world.

A Slight Apocalypse

Xander's intervention is not the first time that one of the Scoobies saves the world, nor is it the last. And when it comes to Caleb and The First, it takes all of the Scoobies' skills to once again do the impossible and protect everyone. Their methodology this time, still premised in love, takes on another aspect: it is based in their respect for everyone's abilities and on their refusal to have hierarchical leadership. These anarcha-feminist values are seen in how the Scoobies realize that the only way to stop the monsters is to universalize their commitment to cooperation (through recruiting all the Potentials), and in how they replace outright authority through reliance on collaboration (as they critique the concept of single leadership and activate all of the Potentials).

We are informed that the goal of The First (an evil so great that "it pre-dates any written history and rarely shows its true face" ["Dirty Girls" 7.18]) is to eliminate all of the Slayers in the world, and thus destroy the balance between good and evil once and for all. After Buffy explains that numerous Potentials have been murdered, Giles shares the bad news with the group (including three potentials who he has brought with him), in Buffy's living room:

> GILES: We've always feared that this day would come, when there'd be an attack not just an individual Slayer, but against the whole line.
> BUFFY: The First. That's what it wants.
> GILES: Yes. To erase all the Slayers in training and their watchers, along with their methods.
> BUFFY: And then Faith. And then me. And with all the Potentials gone and no way of making another, it's the end. No more Slayer. Ever ["Bring on the Night" 7.10].

To prevent the free reign of malevolence in the world (no easy feat as The First has endless resources and "eternities to act" as Giles puts it), Buffy is told that the responsibility lies with her. She is the last shield against this evil; it is up to her to protect these remaining Potentials:

> GILES: I'm afraid it falls to you, Buffy. I'm sorry, I mean we'll do what we can, but ... you're the only one who has the strength to protect these girls ... and the world against what's coming.
> XANDER: But no pressure ["Bring on the Night" 7.10].

Responding to this serious pronouncement with fear, one of the Potentials, Kennedy, argues that they should embrace hiding. Instead of dismissing Kennedy's perspective as cowardly, Buffy interjects and explains that it is good to share emotions and critique the plan. Buffy is signaling that she is no authoritarian leader who will brook no disobedience, rather, she values the expression of different opinions and points of view. Even though in a time of fear, the group reverts to a hierarchical model with Buffy in a leadership position, Buffy still looks at the arrangement as collaborative. She embraces the power of individuals working together; as she puts it, she sees strength in unity: "We just became an army," Buffy says, and then passionately continues, "There's only one thing on this earth more powerful than evil. And that's us" ("Bring on the Night" 7.10).

The first step of the collective plan is to grow their army. Allies come in the guise of Principal Robin Wood, Faith, and Spike, whose soul has been returned to him by this point. The decision to have Spike join the army is a tough one for all the group members, except for Buffy. She trusts in his goodness and his loyalty to the Scoobies. As much as anarcha-feminists believed in the idea of individuals helping one another, Buffy trusts in Spike's ability to contribute to their cause. For example, Goldman coined the concept of a social-soul, meaning someone who worked for the benefit of improving the world and acting in harmony with it "for mutual helpfulness and social well being" with no conflict between self-interest and society because "the individual is the heart of society."[19] This social-soul was awakened through a reliance on individual autonomy as fostered through anarchism; for Buffy, Spike's soul was awakened through the power of love.[20] As Buffy tells Giles, when he suggests removing Spike:

> BUFFY: You can't beat evil by doing evil… He has a soul now. That's what gonna stop him from hurting people.
> GILES: Buffy…
> BUFFY: He can be a good man, Giles. I feel it. But he's never gonna get there if we don't give him the chance ["First Date" 7.14].

Buffy sees Spike as a much-needed ally who should be given the chance to develop his abilities to do good. And she is right in doing so, as Whedon scholar Scott McLaren notes that Spike, through Buffy's love, crosses a "moral divide" and becomes good.[21] Buffy believes in Spike's redemption; based on community and love, she further believes that the group can move forward in its fight against The First.

Unfortunately, this commitment to community is contested throughout the final season. The challenges come out of a deep sense of fear and hysteria, as folks try their best to deal with the threat that The First presents and in doing so, fall prey to blaming each other, turning against each other or thinking they know best how to handle a situation. The First is a master manipulator, and it's almost as if it is succeeding in breaking through the tight circle of the Scoobies to undermine them. First, Giles and Principal Wood unilaterally attempt to assassinate Spike, thus illustrating the dangers of one-sided, paternalistic planning. More importantly, Buffy herself is challenged as she is replaced by Faith—this occurrence provides the best analysis of the dangers associated with hierarchical leadership.

In "Bring on the Night" (7.10), Giles explains that Buffy is meant to lead everyone against The First. He sets up a model of hierarchical leadership, where Buffy is the recognized leader, and they all follow that arrangement. While all of the Scoobies work together to prepare the Potentials for battle, such as building their self-confidence, checking their weapons, offering training, and even taking care of their nutritional needs—Andrew Wells is baking after all—they nevertheless look to Buffy for guidance. Understandably, the Potentials vacillate from fear, to confidence, and then back to fear. Buffy also vacillates from being a collaborative leader to being increasingly controlling.

It is against this background that Buffy plans a raid against The First, and its agent, Caleb, at the vineyard.[22] At first, the operation seems to run smoothly, as the Potentials infiltrate the site easily, move in tight formation, and even defeat some Bringers. Unfortunately, when Caleb makes his appearance, the plan falls apart: Buffy is injured, Xander loses an eye, and a few Potentials lose their lives in the ensuing battle. Understandably, following this disaster, everyone feels fearful and let down; it is at this moment that the Scoobies and the Potentials turn against Buffy's leadership, as she tries to get them to go onto yet another mission.

> BUFFY: They're protecting something at the vineyard. I say it's their power. And I say it's time we go take it away from them.
> FAITH: Or, in the alternative, how about we ... don't. It's a neat theory, B. But I'm not going back in that place. Not without proof. And neither should you. And neither should they [the Potentials] ["Empty Places" 7.19].

Notice that Buffy opened up the discussion with a proposal she's trying to push through. But Buffy's scheme quickly got challenged. As Faith continues to criticize, Giles also steps in to disagree with Buffy:

> BUFFY: You're waiting for some kind of mystical sign to show up and tell us it's the right time, that sort of thing almost never happens, least not for us. We need to strike now.
> GILES: And I think whatever is there, if anything is there, will still be there in a few days.
> BUFFY: I don't know that. We don't know that. What if we let it go and we lose our chance? I'm not prepared to live with that ["Empty Places" 7.19].

Emotions continue to rise, and Buffy is accused of being reckless. She's is also accused of being a rigid leader:

> BUFFY: Look, I wish this could be a democracy. I really do. It would be more fair, I agree. But democracies don't win battles. It's hard truth, but there has to be a single voice. You need me to issue orders and be reckless sometimes and not take your feelings into account. You need someone to lead you ["Empty Places" 7.19].

Just like the Scoobies were speaking from a place of exhaustion and fear, so is Buffy. Leadership is being thrust onto her. In the process of working against the mighty evil of The First, they all turn toward a model where Buffy is placed in the position of boss—where she has to direct and control the Potentials. It arrives at the point where she feels that she has to act in a certain way because the stakes are so high and she is responsible for the Potentials' lives. At the same time, though, everyone else feels entitled to question her command, as they should. United and egalitarian, they would, while working together, be a challenge to The First; divided, or ruled by someone else in a hierarchical fashion, they cannot function as a cohesive shield against The First's evil.

This limitation of Buffy's ability to lead along with the right of the others to challenge her brings us back to the various organizations, such as Angel's Wolfram & Hart or Coulson's S.H.I.E.L.D., where there is a claim that hierarchy can work for good. Thus, we are reminded of the anarchist critique that hierarchy always reduces decision making to one fallible person instead of the democratic organization that Buffy merely wishes they could have. Once she is placed into that leadership position, Buffy instead thinks that the group needs a leader to be reckless and ignore the feelings of the other members. Of course, such recklessness would eventually get them all killed, and they can instead work together to ensure everyone's thoughts contribute to developing the least reckless plan.

As anarcha-feminists put it, the state presents itself as the shield against crime. In this instance in the Buffyverse, it is Buffy who is the momentary analog to the state, and she claims to be protecting them from the First through her leadership. Through its hierarchy of laws and through its method of inspiring fear when laws are broken, the state is supposed to "save" society from being overrun by crime. But as the anarcha-feminists rightly note, even in spite of the state's existence, the problem of crime still remains. As Goldman put it:

> The most absurd apology for authority and law is that they serve to diminish crime. Aside from the fact that the State is itself the greatest criminal, breaking every written and natural law, stealing in the form of taxes, killing in the form of war and capital punishment, it has come to an absolute standstill in coping with crime.[23]

Just like Buffy's plan of attacking the vineyard doesn't work—and actually harms the Scoobies and the Potentials—the existence of the State causes harms. In Goldman's view, what is needed to solve the problem of crime is to move away from "order derived through submission and maintained by terror" and to remind individuals that "true social harmony grows out of solidarity of interests."[24] Thus, the solution is a place where everyone works in accordance to what Goldman dubbed the social-soul, where all agents work together for the benefit of all. And based on all of the previous endeavors of the Scoobies, that's the model that has worked for them in the past. Furthermore, Lucy Parsons agrees to this cooperative solution:

> People have become so used to seeing the evidences of authority on every hand that most of them honestly believe that they would go utterly bad if it were not for the policeman's club or the soldier's bayonet. But the anarchist says, "Remove these evidences of brute force, and let man feel the reviving influences of self-responsibility and self-control, and see how we will respond to these better influences ... instead of the direful results predicted, we have a higher and truer standard of manhood and womanhood."[25]

Cooperation provides the solution, not an outright authority as embodied in the state. In *Buffy*, the flawed solution against The First (the equivalent of crime in our example above) was to turn to an authoritarian model with Buffy being the unequivocal leader. But the real solution lays in all of the Scoobies working together collaboratively in an egalitarian fashion.

Changing out one leader for another doesn't work, either. When Faith tries to explain her action plan—attacking the Bringers or kidnapping one—the same arguments against her plan come up. Kennedy, one of the Potentials, leads the criticism and is upset when Faith shuts her down: "I'm your leader. I didn't ask to do this. And honestly? I didn't want to. But now I'm in charge. Which means I go first and I make the rules and the rest of you follow after me, is that clear? So back the hell off, Kennedy, and let me do my job" ("Touched" 7.20). As it turns out, as this plan plays out, it leads the Potentials and Faith into danger: they are still in the same place where Buffy wanted to go (the arsenal at the vineyard), but they are now faced with a ticking time bomb, moving closer to detonation each second. Buffy's plan might have ended in the same unfortunate way. Faith's plan certainly lands them all in trouble. Either way, with this type of organization based on sole leadership, the end result is not good. Therefore, what we are supposed to glean from this outcome is obvious: authoritarian models do not work. What is needed is a return to egalitarian, communal decision-making where everyone acts in harmony for the common good.

My Power Becomes Our Power

That return to collaboration is prefaced by Buffy's reflection on her conduct—she looks inward and tells Spike, "They blame me for stuff, and honestly? I can't say they're wrong" ("Touched" 7.20)—and her subsequent rescue of the Faith-led group of Potentials. Armed with a magical Scythe, which Buffy had rightly intuited Caleb was guarding at the vineyard and which embodied the mystical essence of Slayers, Buffy joins her critics and saves them. In doing so, she signals that she is acting for the common good, not holding grudges, and she accepts that through the destruction of leadership, true community is gained. As Voltairine de Cleyre poetically puts it, "from this destruction, the flowers result."[26]

The flowers in the Buffyverse are provided by activating all of the Potentials. The act of activating them recognizes that each member of the group has something to contribute. It empowers each member, actively erasing marks of hierarchy. When Angel arrives in town to help fight against The First, he gives Buffy a magical amulet designed to imbue her with strength, but she doesn't claim it as her right. She hands it over to Spike instead, relinquishing any claim to the title of hero or leader. She sees herself as just any other person, which suddenly makes a lot more sense now that there are many Slayers.

This move foreshadows what Buffy will do with the Scythe. She won't keep it solely as her own weapon to wield into battle. Rather, she is planning to universalize the power imbued in the Scythe and to share it with all of the Potentials, so they can all fight together against The First. However, she gives the Potentials a choice: they can freely choose to embrace that power or walk away from it. Buffy gives a speech to explain the choice to the Potentials, which we quote in part here:

> BUFFY: This is about choices. I never had one. I was chosen. And I accept that. I'm not asking you to accept anything. I'm asking you to make your choice. I believe we can beat this evil—not when it comes, not after its army is ready, but now…
>
> … But I'll also need you. Every single one of you. So now you're asking yourself, "What makes this different? What makes us anything more than a bunch of girls getting picked off one by one?" It's true none of you has the power Faith and I do… Here's the part where you make a choice. What if you could have the power? Now. All of you…
>
> … I say my power should be our power. Tomorrow Willow will use the essence of this Scythe, that contains the energy and history of so many Slayers, to change our destiny… …Slayers. Every one of us. Make your choice. Are you ready to be strong? ["Chosen" 7.22].

Buffy's speech is premised on recognizing each Potential's autonomy and right to choose for herself her own life plan. Unlike her previous plan, where she wanted to convince them all to attack the vineyard, this time she gives them a choice as to whether they want to join her. She is not imposing her way of doing things on the Potentials; she allows them to freely choose. Buffy is also equalizing any power imbalance through the spell that she and Willow have devised: through sharing the power of the Scythe with all of the Potentials, they all become equally powerful, and they are all made into Slayers. They all gain vigor and potency; there's no question of one being in charge by virtue of being *the* Slayer. Through not insisting on an authoritarian mindset, Buffy is empowering all of them.

Moreover, this move functions as a strike against the patriarchy. As Buffy mentions in her speech, being a Slayer is premised on what some ancient men decided a long time ago. Their decision—that only one woman at a time should be empowered through her relationship to them—has been the only model for creating Slayers thus far. The model has been limited (only one woman can be empowered at a time) and has not been freely administered (the woman has no say in it, as power is thrust upon her). Buffy is actively breaking down this model, with support from her friends. Now, through her universalization of power, Buffy is setting up a plan where women are empowered by other women (by Willow and Buffy) and they are numerous, and thus available to help one another. These newly created Slayers can rely on one another and build each other up (returning to the collaboration motif) and, importantly, they can choose for themselves what they want to do with their newfound power. They are not forced onto a life path they would rather avoid. Hence, Buffy is enacting a plan where women are empowered far into the future; she is reimagining and reconstructing the world into a better place, filled with autonomous human beings.

This change is akin to the gender revolution that anarcha-feminists support. de Cleyre imagined a world where women would step out of the bounds prescribed for them, and embrace an autonomous journey that allowed them to dictate for themselves how their lives would unfold. Condemning how patriarchal society "has taught the inferiority of women,"[27] through its history or its customs, de Cleyre asked women to break free of their chains and "become the modern woman, who grasps her own self-hood."[28] A breaking of the chains—such as the old patriarchal formula for creating Slayers—is exactly what Buffy is enacting. Through her plan, she is unshackling other women from the constraints placed upon them and encouraging their self-development. Similarly, Goldman argued for every woman's empowerment, where "woman has learned to defy them all [patriarchal norms], to stand firmly on her own ground and to insist upon her own unrestricted freedom."[29] That is the world Buffy is attempting to create here: one where women (the Potentials) control their own lives.

In *Buffy*, this plan premised on individual choice and individual empowerment works. Each Slayer who autonomously chooses to do so takes part in the final battle. And in the end, our heroes are finally able to say:

> FAITH: Looks like the Hellmouth is officially closed for business.
> GILES: There's another one in Cleveland. Not to spoil the moment…
> XANDER: We saved the world.
> WILLOW: We *changed* the world. I can feel them, Buffy. All over. There are Slayers awakening everywhere ["Chosen" 7.22].

That happy ending was possible only through teamwork. An authoritarian model did not cut it, and in fact aided in disintegrating the unity of the Scoobies, slowing down their progress against The First. What proves effective is egalitarian collaboration and the universalization of the empowering of every Potential: Buffy takes the essence of the Scythe—imbued with the spirit of ancient Slayers before it—and shares that power with all of them. In doing so, she models a communal attitude and exemplifies anarcha-feminist principles. Thus, it is within *Buffy* that we see the solution as to how to restructure the world for the better: the way to do it is to engage in collaboration, to support one another, and to practice respect for each other's autonomy. With those tools in place, there is hope for the world—and for Cleveland.

We'll Go Be Heroes

Buffy represents the solution, and anarcha-feminism is that solution. Previously, we had spent a lot of time on the negative critique that anarchists make against hierarchy. Our analyses of *Angel, Dollhouse, Agents of S.H.I.E.L.D., Avengers,* and *Firefly* suggest that there are various and significant problems with the state, including the welfare state, capitalist corporations, do-gooding but hierarchal organizations, and anarchists that continue to embrace capitalism. *Buffy* provides many of these same critiques when it critiques the Watchers, the Initiative, and vampires, yet *Buffy* also provides a positive message: that a new system is indeed possible.

The best political theory that represents that new system is anarcha-feminism—the theory that lies at the intersection of anarchism and feminism. The critique of anarcha-feminism attacks both hierarchy and patriarchy, yet the positive message of anarcha-feminism lies in the power of love to create a new type of society. The love in question is not quite romantic love, familial love, or even love of friends. It is instead the love one has for all other humans (and maybe other animals as well), which exists independently of your relation to them.

The anarcha-feminist wishes to organize society around the central notion that we can get along if we actively collaborate and remember that we are all connected and are not enemies. Buffy and the Scoobies figure out how to work as equals. Some have more power and skills than others. Xander doesn't really have any superpowers. But they all look out for each other and act as a unit, regardless of who is more powerful. There is, as we have discussed, a tendency to fall back into the default idea that there need to be leaders and that the powerful make for good leaders. Buffy falls into this trap, as do others, yet they work their way back into the idea that they can develop a collaborative group where everyone's autonomy is respected.

Buffy then presents a picture of a different kind of society—an anarcha-feminist society. And this represents the positive message of the Whedon opus. Much of Joss Whedon's work involve criticizing society, as represented by vampires, evil corporations, evil law firms, etc., yet *Buffy* also provides a peek into another possibility. And it is this positive message that we will turn to as we wrap things up in the upcoming final chapter.

Conclusion: Internal Revolution as Solution

It is very difficult to engage in a sustained discussion of anarchism without providing a plethora of negative critiques with only minimal attention paid to positive proposals. It is likewise difficult not to notice that Joss Whedon's works are, for the most part, rather bleak, so this discussion of anarchism within the Whedonverse has, without much surprise, tended more toward analyzing problems than suggesting solutions.

This trend within anarchist analysis is not accidental. We live within hierarchy: our state, our law, our employment, our education, our culture, etc., are all organized around hierarchal principles. Someone is the top and almost everyone else is at the bottom. We are also surrounded by violence, both physical and structural. Structural violence is often harder to see, but it is even more restrictive: most of us will never be physically beaten for stepping out of line, but we also know not to step out of line. Aspects of hierarchy and violence pervade our entire lives, and the anarchist does not see this doubly limiting structure of society as coincidental: the hierarchy and violence are intimately connected, and it is up to anarchists to explain how. As it turns out, as we have argued here, we can gain insight into these analyses by watching Joss Whedon's TV shows and movies.

Yet the anarchist does not tell us much about what things would look like if we turned things around and tried out anarchism. In large part, that is because it is not up to us. We live within hierarchy and must analyze that hierarchy and figure out how to get out of it. The people who first live in anarchist society are the only ones who truly have the right to determine how anarchist society will look. It is, after all, their society and no one has any right to tell them what to do. But we can look at Joss Whedon's opus to get some ideas of what direction anarchist society might take. That is the advantage of science fiction and fantasy: they give us not only critiques of current society, but also potential directions to go from here. To examine these potential directions, we will look at a few positive themes that emerge from Whedon's works.

When we examined *Dr. Horrible* in Chapter One, we saw that Dr. Horrible provided an anarchist critique of social problems, such as homelessness. As he explained, "the 'status' is not 'quo'" (Act I). Nevertheless, Dr. Horrible merely calls for "putting power in different hands" (Act I). He has no intention to change the general structure of society—he just wants to rule it.[1] Clearly, this exchange represents the idea that lots of people believe they can fix society, but they always imagine themselves doing so by taking over the lead. They do not imagine a leaderless society fixing itself.

The answer, however, is there the whole time. Dr. Horrible seems to realize that he could fix his life if he follows love as opposed to following evil. Penny does not have the right answer herself (she is merely collecting signatures in a way that will simply treat the symptoms as opposed to curing the disease). At the same time, Penny and Dr. Horrible appear, at least initially, to have the basis for a loving and caring relationship. Of course—and as Erin Giannini points out—things do not develop in that direction, and Dr. Horrible's quest for evil recognition leads to him unintentionally killing Penny.[2] In this way, *Dr. Horrible* provides a positive message only through the opportunity that is lost due to poor choices. The first theme lies in one of the consistent positive messages that reoccurs throughout the Whedon opus: love. Love would have saved Dr. Horrible, and could save us all.

In *Angel*, we can find both thoroughly negative critiques and positive messages, but the positives are still fairly bleak. In Chapter One, we saw the former in the analysis of structural violence as present in Wolfram & Hart. Even when Angel and his team take over Wolfram & Hart, they are incapable of reversing the evil performed by the law firm. They do their best and make some limited impression, but the law firm is situated within larger social structures (the state, the law, the economy, culture, etc.) that dictate the terrain in which the law firm must act. And that terrain restricts attempts to use the law firm for good. In short, bills and taxes must be paid and evildoers tend to make for the best clients (their illegal activity causes them trouble, but also provides them money to pay for excellent representation).

Even the ending of *Angel* suggests that there is not much to be done. They can strike a blow at evil, but it is ultimately a small blow—evil shall continue. At the same time, there is also Angel's epiphany: "If there's no great glorious end to all this, if ... nothing we do matters ... then all that matters is what we do" ("Epiphany" 2.16). Even if things seem hopeless because we cannot escape hierarchy, we can still put thought and care into what we do. In fact, we have to. It is literally all that matters: we cannot escape the various problems that face us in societies plagued by structural violence, but we can act in ways that help others and make our own contributions to making life better for the people around us. And that is what Angel and his team do: try to help each other and make small differences in other people's lives on an everyday basis. Thus, our second theme is that we should do small things that make the world a bit better. The first and second themes are interconnected since love for other people motivates us to do small things for those other people.

Combining *Dr. Horrible* and *Angel*, we see that love is what matters, and we show our love for everyone by doing small things to help others. We find this same message in *Dollhouse*, as analyzed in Chapter Two. *Dollhouse*, in its negative message, points to our restraints. The hierarchal restrictions we face are not limited to the state, even broadly construed to include the law. Corporations, such as Rossum, are also, in various ways, dictating our lives. Echo and friends figure this out in a literal sense since they are programmed to be temporary slaves for the rich and powerful as part of an agreement that presents itself as a good business deal (you earn money, and all you have to give up is your freedom). Limitations to freedom come in all kinds of hierarchal forms, with some presenting themselves as "profitable."

Echo and her friends though do not simply accept these hierarchal limitations. Instead, they teach us that we have to autonomously set our lives for ourselves, regardless of how much hierarchy is trying to keep us down. Echo does not accept that Rossum gets to determine who she is. She does not even accept that she should return to being Caroline. Echo is going to figure out her life for herself, and she will follow through on what she autonomously determines is best. Thus, we have a third positive theme: instead of accepting what you are told to be from up above, you should autonomously set your life path for yourself.

Both *Agents of S.H.I.E.L.D.* and the *Avengers* films establish that the attempt to use hierarchy in a positive fashion eventually regresses and defeats itself, as we saw in Chapter Three. That is in part a furthering of the standard negative anarchist critique: hierarchy cannot work, even if we think it is being used for good. It is also, nonetheless, the start of a positive message: if hierarchy cannot work, we must move toward egalitarian, collaborative efforts to accomplish our goals. That is exactly what the Avengers are forced to do because none of them can stand out as the leader of the others. That is not to say it is easy: Iron Man, for one, sure tries to mess everything up. It is to say, though, that there is a fourth theme for a future anarchist society: we must work collaboratively with others as equals if we wish to accomplish our goals without regressing, which hierarchy necessarily does.

Chapter Four introduced two competing ideas of anarchism, from the left (anarcho-socialism) and from the right (anarcho-capitalism). *Firefly* depicts the debate between these sides in the most illuminating fashion as it has protagonists on both sides. While Mal and Jayne are closer to anarcho-capitalists, all the other protagonists are closer to the anarcho-socialist position. Both sides agree to the importance of the fundamental value of freedom, although the anarcho-capitalist believes you can be free within hierarchy along as you are free from the state's hierarchy. The anarcho-socialists, on the other hand, argue that all hierarchy is wrongfully restrictive of freedom. While Jayne is more slowly transitioning, it is much clearer that Mal is naturally inclined toward anarcho-socialism in spite of his insistence of running his boat in a hierarchal manner. Following the revelation at the end of "The Train Job" (1.2), we believe that Mal doesn't really have a choice: once he learns the details, he will see that helping others is ultimately who Mal authentically is.

The positive theme that we can take from *Firefly* is that freedom can be inherently valuable without being selfish; it is worth relinquishing selfish freedom for social freedom. Kaylee and Book cherish freedom just as much as Mal and Jayne do. They each, however, value freedom in a social way: their freedom is meaningless if it is not shared with others. Further, they both understand that their freedom consists in selflessness. Freedom can even be more fulfilling if we exercise our freedom with friends and are open to helping others around us.

Thus, the five positive themes that align the Whedonverse through a positive anarchist message are: love will save the day, our everyday actions to help others matter (regardless of whether we are saving the world), we must be allowed and encouraged to autonomously choose our own paths, we should work collaboratively together as equals, and achieving freedom does not require being selfish. Putting it all together, the anarchist goal is to put together a society where people are free (but not necessarily selfishly so), autonomous (choosing their own paths), and they work together collaboratively, as equals and with a willingness to help others in need. The one operating principle that ties it all together is love. It is neither a romantic love nor a friendship nor familial love, though those loves are all welcome and good. Instead, it is a love for others that is manifested in a willingness to help others in need.

Buffy, as seen in chapters five and six, brings it all together. We are reminded, multiple times over, throughout *Buffy*, that love is the answer. While Buffy, Willow, and others seek out romantic love, they also constantly are saved by their love for each other as friends and teammates in the fight against evil. Perhaps most importantly, it is the Scoobies' love for strangers that most consistently motivates them to save the world. Further, the Scoobies are always working collaboratively to help others. Theirs is definitely a freedom that consists in both working with friends and acting selflessly for others. The Scoobies, after all, are constantly risking their lives to do what is best for the world, and not just for themselves.

The only difficulty in *Buffy* is autonomy. Buffy does not choose her own path. It is thrust upon her. Yet autonomy requires a reaction to the world around you. Echo developed her autonomy not by returning to Caroline, but by figuring out who she wished to be given this bizarre situation that Rossum put her in by creating Echo in the first place. Buffy, similarly, cannot simply cease to be the Slayer. She can, however, decide how she wishes to be the Slayer. And that is the challenge she takes up throughout the series: it is neither the Watchers Council, nor Giles, nor any of her boyfriends, nor anyone else, that determines who Buffy is; it is Buffy herself that chooses her own path. Even though Buffy is the Slayer, she is the one who decides how she will slay.

Having shown both the negative and positive sides of anarchism through the works of Joss Whedon, it is worth concluding by testing out the applicability of the theory to the one movie that seems to only have a negative critique, so we conclude by seeking the positive message of *Cabin in the Woods*, to see if the positive anarchist message is even available there. A close look reveals that *Cabin in the Woods* is not about accepting the problems of hierarchy or institutional violence. Rather, this movie is about what happens when revolution happens on the internal level. Through a personal revolution, systematized violence and systems of oppression collapse on themselves and anarchism is able to finally solve the problems it has critiqued for so long.

Released in 2012, *Cabin in the Woods* was written by Joss Whedon and Drew Goddard. The story operates on two planes: the ordinary realm of existence where college students, Dana Polk, Holden McCrea, Marty Mikalski, Jules Louden, and Curt Vaughan, are spending the weekend at a cabin in the woods, and a deeper, underground plane, where cryptic agents such as Gary Sitterson and Steve Hadley manipulate these five individuals in the ordinary world. As the movie unfolds, we find that this underground facility is widespread and amply staffed—it has offices at least in Stockholm and Japan—and its purpose is to appease ancient gods through blood sacrifices on an annual basis so as to ensure that the "sleeping gods" do not awaken and destroy the world (*Cabin in the Woods*).

As an organization that allegedly saves the world through manipulating and murdering young people, this facility stands in for all the problems associated with hierarchy that we saw in all of the other chapters. For instance, this organization epitomizes structural violence, just like Wolfram & Hart in Chapter One. It is ubiquitous and secret, and has one sole purpose: killing innocents to purportedly save humanity (a secret organization that claims to do good, but that ultimately does not, such as when we analyzed how Hydra ran S.H.I.E.L.D. in Chapter Three). To ensure that "the giants that live in the earth, that used to rule it" stay asleep, those who run the facility manipulate young people through drugs and technology and eventually murder them for this greater cause (*Cabin in the Woods*). As the workers in the underground facility note, the system is rigged against the chosen victims; nevertheless, the facility's workers bet on the victims' fates:

> HADLEY: The Director doesn't concern himself with stuff like this. Long as everything goes smoothly upstairs and the kids do ... what they're told...
> DANIEL TRUMAN: But then it's fixed. How can you wager on this when you control the outcome?
> HADLEY: No, no. We just get 'em to the cellar, Truman. They take it from there. They have to make the choice of their own free will... [*Cabin in the Woods*].

This interaction shows several wrongs. First, the victims are manipulated and placed in a position where they are meant to be killed. Just because the victims have some input (for example, they choose the instruments of their deaths when in the cellar) does not mean that they can escape death; their fates have been predetermined and autonomy is an illusion. Secondly, the attendants running the facility objectify the victims to such a degree that the victims are merely pawns to be bet on. Sure, Truman shows some remorse and abstains from betting, but he does not do so based on the humanity of the victims, but rather on the idea that it is a fixed bet—the betting is not pure enough for him. In spite of one person's reticence, the wagering is widespread: Sitterson has a large pile of cash from everyone in the facility betting on the manner of death for the victims. These workers have been corrupted by the hierarchy that they embody. And yet they enjoy the spectacle and take bets on it; as Sitterson puts it, "Let's get this party started!" (*Cabin in the Woods*).

The facility also embodies mass coercion, for both its victims and its employees (similar to how we saw Rossum eventually wiping everyone's minds in Chapter Two). Obviously, as the victims are manipulated and placed into the cabin to die, they are being deceived and coerced. We know that even before the trip to the cabin started, Jules dyed her hair; as Wendy Lin explains, that dye was contaminated with a mind-altering drug:

> LIN: Guess how we're slowing down her cognition: the hair dye.
> SITTERSON: The dumb blonde. That's artistic.
> LIN: Works through the scalp, very gradual. The Chem Department keeps their end up [*Cabin in the Woods*].

Thus, we return to the previous idea that the system is fixed: there can be no free will if, even before going to the cabin, Jules had already been manipulated. How can the victims freely choose when their options are already limited and their wills have already been tampered with? These victims are being controlled and coerced. And while at the cabin, the same pattern continues: more mind-altering drugs are pumped into the atmosphere, to increase libido, to alter the thinking of the victims, and to put on a show for the gods. As Hadley and Sitterson explain it when Truman objects to the sexual manipulation of Jules and Curt:

> HADLEY: We're not the only ones watching, kid.
> SITTERSON: Got to keep the customer satisfied. You understand what's at stake here?
> TRUMAN: Sorry [*Cabin in the Woods*].

The victims are made to put on a sexual show, thus embodying sexual objectification (as we discussed in Chapter Five). Jules and Curt are experiencing denial of autonomy, denial of subjectivity, and instrumentality—they are made into commodities for the sexual entertainment of "the customer," presumably the gods. The voyeurism is clearly unsettling; so is the idea that Jules and Curt were orchestrated without their knowledge or consent. The sexual encounter thus takes on the dimensions of sexual assault.

But it is not just the victims that are manipulated and coerced. The workers of the facility are likewise coerced. They see themselves as agents on the side of good—they keep humanity alive—because of the great threat of the gods waking up. Hence, their choices are limited by the worry that if they do not partake in these gruesome methods, the world will end. Of course they become corrupt in the service of this death machine, but they justify their complicity to themselves. When the teens are trying to escape the cabin, the workers see it as their duty to leave the control room and actively ensure that the teens are stopped:

> HADLEY: You got family, Truman?
> TRUMAN: Yeah...
> HADLEY: Kids get through that tunnel alive, you won't anymore [*Cabin in the Woods*].

Just like Angel couldn't enact good from the underbelly of Wolfram & Hart, as we saw in Chapter One, these workers are tainted in their work through their murdering of innocents, yet they justify their activity because they feel like they are saving the world.

Further, the victims are made to fit archetypes (as we saw happen to each Doll in Chapter Two), such as the Whore, who is meant to die first. As the Director explains, there's also

> The Athlete. The Scholar. The Fool. All suffer and die, at the hands of the horror they have raised. Leaving the last, to live or die as fate decides. The Virgin.
> DANA: Me? Virgin?
> MARTY: Dude, she's a homewrecker!
> THE DIRECTOR: We work with what we have [*Cabin in the Woods*].

In an authoritarian fashion, the victims are made to fit roles that are predetermined for them, as required for the sacrifice. Their autonomy is of no concern to these manipulators; as the Director puts it, the powers that be make it work.

It is interesting to note that not only do the roles not fit—Dana was sleeping with her married professor so she does not fit the Virgin archetype—but that when individuality is allowed to manifest itself, it provides the ray of hope that allows the victims to survive. After all, Marty, who is meant to fit the role of Fool due to his drug consumption—and Jaclyn S. Parrish reminds us that "dubbing Marty the Fool is a gross misnomer"[3]—is the one who is the most aware of something not being as it should be at the cabin. For example, Marty found the camera cord. Due to his autonomy, he survives to the end, with Dana, to turn the tables on the facility. Further, his autonomous behavior (smoking weed) is what enables him to resist the mind-altering drugs. We're told that "the prep team missed one of the kid's stashes. Whatever he's been smoking has been immunizing him to all our shit" (*Cabin in the Woods*). Autonomy is thusly portrayed as a tool to resist coercion from the hidden hierarchy. The most autonomous person is the one who has the power to resist the manipulation of this death machine. It is Marty we see at the end calmly accepting the end of the world, and passing a joint to a shallow breathing Dana. The movie ends with the seeming message that these two accept the end of humanity. But is that what is really happening?

On another, deeper level *Cabin in the Woods* is portraying an internal revolution: instead of going along with the programmatic threat of accepting to die or engaging in self-sacrifice to maintain humanity, Marty is making the autonomous, free choice to not engage in that awful bargain. Thus, instead of bleak acceptance, we see instead a quiet standing up for autonomy. It is not a violent grandstanding against "the Costco of death" organization that's been manipulating them (*Cabin in the Woods*). It is a peaceful resolution that rings true for one individual. This position is best explained by anarcho-pacifist Leo Tolstoy.

Leo Tolstoy (1828–1910) was a Russian aristocrat, writer, and political thinker. He was a Christian anarchist and pacifist, who supported nonviolent resistance. He is well known for his many novels such as *War and Peace* or *Anna Karenina*, and his anarchist works, which most notably include *The Kingdom of God Is Within You*. This latter anarchist book was very influential on later leaders of non-violence, such as Mahatma Gandhi and Martin Luther King, Jr. Leo Tolstoy explains the problem that Marty is facing:

> To use violence is impossible; it would only cause reaction. To join the ranks of the Government is also impossible—one would only become its instrument. One course therefore remains—to fight the Government by means of thought, speech, actions, life, neither yielding to Government nor joining its ranks and thereby increasing its power. This alone is needed, will certainly be successful.[4]

That is exactly what Marty is doing. He is standing up against the death machine by not yielding to the command to engage in the business of death. Marty does not give in to the Director who tries to coerce him into accepting the necessity of killing Dana for the greater good. He refuses to become an agent of the government. Instead, Marty is resolute:

> THE DIRECTOR: The sun will rise in eight minutes. If you live to see it, the world will end.
> MARTY: Maybe that's the way it ought to be. Maybe it's time for a change [*Cabin in the Woods*].

Marty's stance marks him as an independent thinker who is not falling prey to the corrupt bargain. His refusal to accept self-sacrifice is his active denial of the control of hierarchy; it embodies his insistence on autonomy. As Tolstoy explains, "It is time for us to understand that our salvation lies, not in continuing along the road on which we have been moving, and not in the retention of what we have elaborated, but in the recognition that we have advanced along a false road and have entered a bog out of which we must extricate ourselves."[5] Marty is extricating himself from the situation that the Director has placed him in. His refusal is a quiet stand against systemic corruption, and a stand for respecting individual self-rule. It is a quiet revolution against the state. As Tolstoy put it, "How is this revolution to take place? Nobody knows how it will take place in humanity, but every man feels it clearly in himself. And yet in our world everybody thinks of changing humanity, and nobody thinks of changing himself."[6] Marty is feeling that revolutionary change *in himself*, and thus when he is waiting for the end of the world, he is not endorsing a bleak outlook—he is actually exemplifying anarcho-pacifism through his refusal to participate in the death work of the facility.[7] He is making his choice, just as Buffy made her choice before him— and just as she offered choices to all of the Potentials. As Tolstoy would argue, making a difficult choice in the face of oppression is revolutionary.

Significantly, *Cabin in the Woods* depicts a similar sacrifice in Japan where a group of schoolchildren are being killed for the gods. We are shown glimpses of it at the beginning of the movie, as the children run from a floating wet girl. However, this sacrifice attempt is deemed a failure. Why? Because the schoolchildren use love to stage a revolution. Hence, when we see the schoolroom scene again (toward the ends of the movie), we see no carnage. Here is the description from the script:

> The floaty girl hovers over the room, in which several Japanese schoolchildren are placing lotus flowers into a large bowl of water on the floor, all the while singing a happy song of love.
> A frog hops out the bowl. The drowny girl is consumed by light and disappears.
> Japanese schoolgirl: Now Kiko's spirit will live in the happy frog!
> They all laugh and hug [*Cabin in the Woods*].[8]

The action of the schoolchildren—moored in love and collaboration— stopped their own destruction. Love proved to be the antidote to the systemic violence of the facility. The schoolchildren sang and showed affection; their peaceful behavior allowed for the threat to disappear. Tolstoy also supports this solution. He says, "I only know that nothing evil can result from my following the higher guidance of wisdom and love, or wise love, which is implanted in me."[9] The children reacted with tenderness, and their reaction proved the undoing of the facility's plan. The outcome of this type of standing up against coercive and violent hierarchy is revolutionary, but, again, in a peaceful way. As Tolstoy explains, "And if you ask: 'What will happen?' then I reply that good will certainly happen; because, acting in the way indicated by reason and love, I am acting in accordance with the highest law known to me."[10]

The highest law—love—provides the ultimate positive message of anarchism. Tolstoy cautions that "evil cannot be abolished by evil, and that the only means of diminishing the evil of violence is abstinence from violence."[11] We even get a sense that the love-based resistance of the children in Japan broke some systems and machines designed to kill Marty and his friends: for instance, detonation mechanisms stop working. The method of love effectively dismantles the corrupt organization of the facility. Through love, the Japanese sacrifice is nullified. Through love, machines designed to murder break down. Similarly, through his insistence on dignity and autonomy, Marty is also not complicit in his own death.

Notice, also, that Marty's—and Dana's to some extent—quiet refusal to accept death is actually linked with the destruction of the old gods through an insistence on human dignity and a resistance to coercion. Yes, the last scene of the movie ends with a gigantic hand coming through the floor and smashing things—yes, that could be one of the gods coming to fulfill the threat of destroying the world. But if the gods destroy the world, they are also destroying the source for their sacrifice; they will be left without future tribute, with no one to worship them, and with no place in which to exist—the old gods will eventually cease to exist themselves. Therefore, through a refusal to embrace violence, Dana and Marty actually end the evil system.

In this fashion, we obtain the positive message of anarchism. That message is that we can do better. We can do better than selfishness. We can do better than violence. We can do better than hierarchy. And we do better by autonomously choosing to be loving, helpful, collaborative, and through acting in a team, like the Scoobies, Angel Investigations, the Serenity crew, Echo's rescued Dolls, the Avengers, and even those children in Japan. We do better by helping each other, not because we love them romantically or even as friends, but because we love them as people who need our help. And we do better by forming an anarchist society where we all—as loving, equals who respect and look out for each other—autonomously live together as a social unity.

So, all you Slayers out there, "Make your choice: Are you ready to be strong?" ("Chosen" 7.22).

Chapter Notes

Introduction

1. While mentioning racism as an important topic, it is worth noting the argument that Hélène Frohard-Dourlent makes that *Dr. Horrible*'s under-usage of co-creator and co-writer Maurissa Tancharoen's acting talent is itself potentially racist. See Hélène Frohard-Dourlent, "Someone's Asian in *Dr. Horrible*," in *Joss Whedon and Race: Critical Essays*, eds. Mary Ellen Iatropoulos and Lowery A. Woodall III (Jefferson, NC: McFarland, 2008), Chapter 15. Kindle edition.

2. That is why Amy A. Williams argues that *Dr. Horrible* is an excellent vehicle through which to study social problems. Amy A. Williams, "'All the Cash, All the Fame, and Social Change': Teaching *Dr. Horrible's Sing-Along Blog* as a Social Message Film," *Slayage: The Journal of Whedon Studies* 11.2/12.1 [38–38] (Summer 2014). Web. Moreover, Christine Jarvis refers to Whedon as a public pedagogue on social problems, educating the public through popular culture. See Christine Jarvis, "Battle of the Blockbusters: Joss Whedon as Public Pedagogue," *Slayage: The Journal of Whedon Studies* 14.1 [43] (Winter 2016). Web.

3. As Linda Jean Jencson argues, Joss Whedon is always interested in exploring power throughout his works. For more on this idea, see Linda Jean Jencson, "'Aiming to Misbehave': Role Modeling Political-Economic Conditions and Political Action in the *Serenity*verse," *Slayage: The Journal of Whedon Studies* 7.1 [25] (Winter 2008). Web. In addition, Howard Harris explains that Whedon's work is instructive in how to deal with such issues. See Howard Harris, "*Buffy the Vampire Slayer* in the Business Ethics Classroom," *Slayage: The Journal of Whedon Studies* 7.3 [27] (Winter 2009). Web. Also see Richard Greene and Wayne Yuen, "Morality on Television: The Case of *Buffy the Vampire Slayer*," in *Buffy the Vampire Slayer and Philosophy: Fear and Trembling in Sunnydale*, ed. James B. South (Chicago: Open Court, 2003), 271–281.

4. Erin Giannini points out that it is important that *Dr. Horrible*'s critique of institutional structures should be understood within the context that Joss Whedon made the miniseries during the 2008 writers' strike, and so it is also, "a critique of the corporate media structure that is nonetheless responsible for Whedon's prominence within it." See Erin Giannini, *Joss Whedon versus the Corporation: Big Business Critiqued in the Films and Television Programs* (Jefferson, NC: McFarland, 2017), 19, 80, 86.

5. Williams, "'All the Cash, All the Fame, and Social Change': Teaching *Dr. Horrible's Sing-Along Blog* as a Social Message Film." Williams calls it a "regime change." For a general discussion of this issue in Joss Whedon's works, see: Samira Nadkarni, "'I Believe in Something Greater than Myself': What Authority, Terrorism, and Resistance Have Come to Mean in the Whedonverse," *Slayage: The Journal of Whedon Studies* 13.2 [42] (Summer 2015). Web.

6. Nadkarni argues that Whedon's *Agents of S.H.I.E.L.D.* simultaneously critiques the totalitarian state while subtly reinforcing its structures. See Nadkarni, "'I Believe in Something Greater Than Myself.'"

7. Although, as we discuss shortly, no one has really used an anarchist analysis for

examining the Whedonverse, J. Michael Richardson and J. Douglass Rabb show that Whedon's work causes viewers to reflect on their attitudes toward social problems. For more on this topic, see their discussion of "issue episodes" in Whedon's work (such as homelessness): in J. Michael Richardson and J. Douglass Rabb, *The Existential Joss Whedon: Evil and Human Freedom in Buffy the Vampire Slayer, Angel, Firefly, and Serenity* (Jefferson, NC: McFarland, 2007), especially Chapters 4 and 11. Kindle edition.

8. Giannini, *Joss Whedon versus the Corporation.*

9. Sherry Ginn, *Power and Control in the Television Worlds of Joss Whedon* (Jefferson, NC: McFarland, 2012), Chapter 1. Kindle edition.

10. Linda Jean Jencson, "'Aiming to Misbehave': Role Modeling Political-Economic Conditions and Political Action in the *Serenity*verse"; Harris, "*Buffy the Vampire Slayer* in the Business Ethics Classroom." Also see Greene and Yuen, "Morality on Television: The Case of *Buffy the Vampire Slayer*," 271–281.

11. Howard Harris, "*Buffy the Vampire Slayer* in the Business Ethics Classroom"; Greene and Yuen, "Morality on Television: The Case of *Buffy the Vampire Slayer*," 271–281.

12. Robert Paul Wolff, *In Defense of Anarchism* (Berkeley: University of California Press, 1998).

13. Wolff, *Anarchism*, 14.

14. Ibid., 13.

15. Ibid., 3–12.

16. Ibid., 78–79.

17. Ibid., 18.

18. Numerous scholars have established links between these issues. For just a few examples, see Michelle Alexander, *The New Jim Crow: Mass Incarceration in the Age of Colorblindness* (New York: The New Press, 2012); David Graeber, *The Utopia of Rules: On Technology, Stupidity, and the Secret Joys of Bureaucracy* (Brooklyn: Melville House, 2015); Dorceta E. Taylor, *Toxic Communities: Environmental Racism, Industrial Pollution, and Residential Mobility* (New York: New York University Press, 2014); Tommie Shelby, *Dark Ghettos: Injustice, Dissent, and Reform* (Cambridge: Belknap, 2016); Shannon Sullivan, *Revealing Whiteness: The Unconscious Habits of Racial Privilege* (Bloomington: Indiana University Press, 2006).

19. Henry David Thoreau, "On the Duty of Civil Disobedience" (Project Gutenberg EBook, 2004[1849]), Loc. 7–10.

20. Ibid., Loc. 31–33.

21. Ibid., Loc. 48.

22. Ibid., Loc. 36.

23. Wolff, *Anarchism*, 18.

24. Ibid., 22–27.

25. Ibid., 36.

Chapter One

1. Candace Havens, *Joss Whedon: The Genius Behind Buffy* (Dallas: Benbella Books, 2003), 101–102.

2. Karen Sayer discusses the Los Angeles setting as important in that LA, a real city, lends authenticity and weight to *Angel*. Furthermore, she argues that using Los Angeles results in a "spatial script" that showcases "ambiguities around good/evil, corruption, social disintegration and disillusion." In this manner, location foreshadows the structural problems and themes that the show will pick up. See Karen Sayer, "This Was Our World and They Made It Theirs: Reading Space and Place in *Buffy the Vampire Slayer* and *Angel*," in *Reading the Vampire Slayer: The New Updated Unofficial Guide to Buffy and Angel*, ed. Roz Kaveney (London: Tauris Parke, 2007), 139, 141. Stacey Abbott also explores how *Angel*'s darkness revolves around "the series' noirish urban location." See Stacey Abbott, *Angel* (Detroit: Wayne State Press, 2009), 3, 7. Abbott also makes the same point in her chapter "Kicking Ass and Singing 'Mandy': A Vampire in LA." See Stacey Abbott, "Kicking Ass and Singing 'Mandy': A Vampire in LA," in *Reading Angel: The TV Spin-Off with a Soul*, ed. Stacey Abbott (London: I.B. Tauris, 2005), 1–2, 9. Also see Benjamin Jacob, "Los Angelus: The City of Angel," in *Reading Angel: The TV Spin-Off with a Soul*," ed. Stacey Abbott (London: I.B. Tauris, 2005), 75–77; Sarah Upstone, "'LA's Got it All': Hybridity and Otherness in *Angel*'s Postmodern City," in *Reading Angel: The TV Spin-Off with a Soul*, ed. Stacey Abbott (London: I.B. Tauris, 2005), 101–103; Daoine S. Bachran, "Mexicans in Space? Joss Whedon's *Firefly*, Reavers, and the Man They

Call Jayne," in *Joss Whedon and Race: Critical Essays*, eds. Mary Ellen Iatropolous and Lowery A. Woodall III (Jefferson, NC: McFarland, 2017), Chapter 9. Kindle edition; Rejena Saulsberry, "An Inevitable Tragedy: The Troubled Life of Charles Gunn as an Allegory for General Strain Theory," in *Joss Whedon and Race: Critical Essays*, eds. Mary Ellen Iatropolous and Lowery A. Woodall III (Jefferson, NC: McFarland, 2017), Chapter 7. Kindle edition.

3. For more on how *Angel* deals with real life problems, see: Abbott, "Kicking Ass and Singing 'Mandy': A Vampire in LA," 8; Upstone, "'LA's Got it All': Hybridity and Otherness in *Angel*'s Postmodern City," 102–103; Jacob, "Los Angelus: The City of Angel," 79; U. Melissa Anyiwo, "More Than Just A Spin-Off: The Enduring Allure of Angel," in *Buffy Conquers the Academy: Conference Papers from the 2009/2010 Popular Culture/American Culture Associations*, eds. U. Melissa Anyiwo and Karoline Szatek-Tudor (Newcastle Upon Tyne: Cambridge Scholars, 2013), 154–155; Laura Resnick, "That Angel Doesn't Live Here Anymore," in *Five Seasons of Angel: Science Fiction and Fantasy Writers Discuss Their Favorite Vampire*, ed. Glenn Yeffeth (Dallas: Benbella Books, 2004), Chapter 2. Kindle edition; Saulsberry, "An Inevitable Tragedy: The Troubled Life of Charles Gunn as an Allegory for General Strain Theory," Chapter 7; Jean Lorrah, "A World Without Love: The Failure of Family in *Angel*," in *Five Seasons of Angel: Science Fiction and Fantasy Writers Discuss Their Favorite Vampire*, ed. Glenn Yeffeth (Dallas: Benbella Books, 2004), Chapter 6. Kindle edition; Mary Ellen Iatropolous and Lowery A. Woodall III, "Introduction: The Individual, the Institutional, and the Unitentional: Exploring the Whedonverses Through Critical Race Theory," in *Joss Whedon and Race: Critical Essays*, Eds. Mary Ellen Iatropolous and Lowery A. Woodall III (Jefferson, NC: McFarland, 2017), Introductory Chapter. Kindle edition; Jennifer Stoy, "'And Her Tears Flowed Like Wine': Wesley/Lilah and the Complicated (?) Role of the Female Agent on *Angel*," in *Reading Angel: The TV Spin-Off with a Soul*, ed. Stacey Abbott (London: I.B. Tauris, 2005), 164.

4. For more on the evil of Wolfram & Hart, see: Anyiwo, "More Than Just A Spin-Off," 154–155; Abbott, *Angel*, 7; Erin Giannini, *Joss Whedon versus the Corporation: Big Business Critiqued in the Films and Television Programs* (Jefferson, NC: McFarland, 2017), 16; Iatropolous and Woodall III, "Introduction: The Individual, the Institutional, and the Unintentional: Exploring the Whedonverses Through Critical Race Theory"; Saulsberry, "An Inevitable Tragedy: The Troubled Life of Charles Gunn as an Allegory for General Strain Theory," Chapter 7; Phil Colvin, "*Angel*: Redefinition and Justification through Faith," in *Reading Angel: The TV Spin-Off with a Soul*, ed. Stacey Abbott (London: I.B. Tauris, 2005), 20, 23; Matthew Mills, "Ubi Caritas?: Music as Narrative Agent in *Angel*," in *Reading Angel: The TV Spin-Off with a Soul*, ed. Stacey Abbott (London: I.B. Tauris, 2005), 35; Roz Kaveney, "A Sense of Ending: Schrodinger's *Angel*," in *Reading Angel: The TV Spin-Off with a Soul*, ed. Stacey Abbott (London: I.B. Tauris, 2005), 57, 60, 61, 70; Jacob, "Los Angelus: The City of Angel," 85; Janine R. Harrison, "Gender Politics in *Angel*: Traditional vs. Non-Traditional Corporate Climates," in *Reading Angel: The TV Spin-Off with a Soul*, ed. Stacey Abbott (London: I.B. Tauris, 2005), 118–121; Sharon Sutherland and Sarah Swan, "The Rule of Prophecy: Source of Law in the City of Angel," in *Reading Angel: The TV Spin-Off with a Soul*, ed. Stacey Abbott (London: I.B. Tauris, 2005), 135–137.

5. Johan Galtung, "Violence, Peace, and Peace Research," *Journal of Peace Research* (Vol. 6, No. 3, 1969), 171.

6. Galtung, "Violence," 171. Emphasis in original.

7. For more on poverty as structural violence, see Kathleen Ho, "Structural Violence as a Human Rights Violation," *Essex Human Rights Review* (Vol. 4 No. 2, September 2007).

8. Giannini, *Joss Whedon versus the Corporation: Big Business Critiqued in the Films and Television Programs*, 151 (also see 23).

9. Chelsea Quin Yarbro, "Angel: An Identity Crisis," in *Five Seasons of Angel: Science Fiction and Fantasy Writers Discuss Their Favorite Vampire*, ed. Glenn Yeffeth (Dallas: Benbella Books, 2004), Chapter 8. Kindle edition.

10. Anyiwo, "More Than Just A Spin-Off," 155.

11. *Ibid.*

12. Jacqueline Lichtenberg, "Victim Triumphant," in *Five Seasons of Angel: Science Fiction and Fantasy Writers Discuss Their Favorite Vampire*, ed. Glenn Yeffeth (Dallas: Benbella Books, 2004), Chapter 14. Kindle edition.

13. Stacey Abbott, *Angel*, 29–30.

14. Besides the authors already mentioned in text, other scholars also argue that Wolfram & Hart is more likely to change Angel and friends than vice versa. See Colvin, "*Angel*: Redefinition and Justification through Faith," 23; Kaveney, "A Sense of Ending: Schrodinger's *Angel*," 58; Mills, "Ubi Caritas?: Music as Narrative Agent in *Angel*," 35; Sutherland and Swan, "The Rule of Prophecy: Source of Law in the City of Angel," 135–137; Saulsberry, "An Inevitable Tragedy: The Troubled Life of Charles Gunn as an Allegory for General Strain Theory"; Janet K. Halfyard, "The Dark Avenger: Angel and the Cinematic Superhero," in *Reading Angel: The TV Spin-Off with a Soul*, ed. Stacey Abbott (London: I.B. Tauris, 2005), 152.

15. Our view of individuals, roles, and institutions is largely based on Kwame Anthony Appiah, *The Ethics of Identity* (Princeton: Princeton University Press, 2007).

16. For more on Angel's soul, see Scott McLaren, "The Evolution of Joss Whedon's Vampire Mythology and the Ontology of the Soul," *Slayage: The Journal of Whedon Studies* 5.2 [18] (September 2005). Web. Also, Don DeBrandt refers to Angel's soul as a conscience, where he feels empathy for his victims. See Don DeBrandt, "Angelus Populi," in *Five Seasons of Angel: Science Fiction and Fantasy Writers Discuss Their Favorite Vampire*, ed. Glenn Yeffeth (Dallas: Benbella Books, 2004), Chapter 1. Kindle edition. For a similar point, see Resnick, "That Angel Doesn't Live Here Anymore." Stacey Abbott discusses Angel's soul, explaining that Angel needs to be in total control of his emotions at all time (thus also embodying male gender norms) due to his danger of losing his soul when happy. See Abbott, *Angel*, 66. Moreover, Angel's soul is exhibited through his selflessness and heroism. See Abbott, *Angel*, 68–69. Also see Kaveney, "A Sense of Ending: Schrodinger's *Angel*," 60, 71; Matt Hills and Rebecca Williams, "*Angel*'s Monstrous Mothers and Vampires with Souls: Investigating the Abject in 'Television Horror,'" in *Reading Angel: The TV Spin-Off with a Soul*, ed. Stacey Abbott (London: I.B. Tauris, 2005), 210.

17. For more on the representation of the Romani people in *Angel*, see Katia McClain, "Representations of the Roma in *Buffy* and *Angel*," in *Joss Whedon and Race*, eds. Mary Ellen Iatropoulos and Lowery A. Woodall III (Jefferson, NC: McFarland, 2008), Chapter 6. Kindle edition.

18. Upstone, "'LA's Got it All': Hybridity and Otherness in *Angel*'s Postmodern City," 110–111.

19. For others who discuss Angel being emasculated or feminized in other contexts, see Abbott, *Angel*, 66–82; Hills and Williams, "*Angel*'s Monstrous Mothers and Vampires with Souls: Investigating the Abject in 'Television Horror,'" 209–211; Lorna Jowett, *Sex and the Slayer: A Gender Studies Primer for the Buffy Fan* (Middletown: Wesleyan, 2005), 157, 205.

20. See the various scholars we listed in footnote 3 who examine how *Angel* is commendable for dealing with real world problems.

21. William Godwin, *An Enquiry Concerning Political Justice* (Oxford World's Classics: 2013[1793]), 11–12.

22. *Ibid.*, 25.
23. *Ibid.*, 26.
24. *Ibid.*, 30.
25. *Ibid.*, 29–30.
26. *Ibid.*, 30.

27. Henry David Thoreau, "On the Duty of Civil Disobedience" (Project Gutenberg EBook, 2004[1849]), Loc. 203.

28. Godwin, *Enquiry*, 31.

29. David Graeber, *The Utopia of Rules: On Technology, Stupidity, and the Secret Joys of Bureaucracy* (Melville House: 2016), 57.

30. *Ibid.*, 58.
31. *Ibid.*, 58.
32. *Ibid.*, 74.
33. *Ibid.*, 74.

34. For a gender analysis of Kate Lockley see Harrison, "Gender Politics in *Angel*: Traditional vs. Non-Traditional Corporate Climates," 123–125.

35. Graeber, *The Utopia of Rules: On Technology, Stupidity, and the Secret Joys of Bureaucracy*, 72.

36. *Ibid.*, 72.

37. *Ibid.*, 69–72.
38. Harrison, "Gender Politics in *Angel*: Traditional vs. Non-Traditional Corporate Climates," 117–125.
39. K. Stoddard Hayes, "Where Have All the Good Guys Gone?," in *Five Seasons of Angel: Science Fiction and Fantasy Writers Discuss Their Favorite Vampire*, ed. Glenn Yeffeth (Dallas: Benbella Books, 2004), Chapter 15. Kindle edition; Stacey Abbott, "Walking the Fine Line Between Angel and Angelus," *Slayage: The Journal of Whedon Studies* 3.1 [9] (August 2003). Web.
40. Harrison, "Gender Politics in *Angel*: Traditional vs. Non-Traditional Corporate Climates," 118–125; Jacob, "Los Angelus: The City of Angel," 85; Sutherland and Swan, "The Rule of Prophecy: Source of Law in the City of Angel," 134–138.
41. Godwin, *Enquiry*, 403.
42. *Ibid.*, 403.
43. *Ibid.*, 405.
44. *Ibid.*, 406.
45. *Ibid.*, 403.
46. *Ibid.*
47. *Ibid.*, 406.
48. *Ibid.*, 409.
49. For a discussion of how the legal system is problematic due to prosecutorial discretion and legal biases (through the lens of an analysis of *Buffy the Vampire Slayer* though), see Tiffany Kristin Lee, "The Justice Systems of Slayers and Vengeance Demons: Prosecutorial Discretion in *Buffy the Vampire Slayer*," *Slayage: The Journal of Whedon Studies* 10.1 [35] (Winter 2013). Web. For general critiques of the criminal justice system, see Angela J. Davis, *Arbitrary Justice: The Power of the American Prosecutor* (Oxford: Oxford University Press, 2007); Paul Butler, *Let's Get Free: A Hip-Hop Theory of Justice* (New York: The New Press, 2010); Alexandra Natapoff, *Snitching: Criminal Informants and the Erosion of American Justice* (New York: New York University Press, 2009).
50. Godwin, *Enquiry*, 406.
51. *Ibid.*, 20.
52. *Ibid.*
53. For more on Angel and friends being willing to risk everything at the end of the series, see Upstone, "'LA's Got it All': Hybridity and Otherness in *Angel*'s Postmodern City," 111; Harrison, "Gender Politics in *Angel*: Traditional vs. Non-Traditional Corporate Climates," 130.
54. Cordelia often is a communicator. For more on this theme, see Jes Battis, "Demonic Maternities, Complex Motherhoods: Cordelia, Fred, and the Puzzle of Illyria," *Slayage: The Journal of Whedon Studies* 5.2 [18] (September 2005). Web.; Jennifer Stoy, "Blood and Choice: The Theory and Practice of Family in Angel," in *Reading the Vampire Slayer: The New Updated Unofficial Guide to Buffy and Angel*, ed. Roz Kaveney (London: Tauris Parke, 2007), 226; Harrison, "Gender Politics in *Angel*: Traditional vs. Non-Traditional Corporate Climates," 126.
55. See Battis, "Demonic Maternities, Complex Motherhoods: Cordelia, Fred, and the Puzzle of Illyria." Battis explains that Cordelia does not necessarily communicate a truth that her interlocutor needs to know for their own self growth—sometimes she does that, other times she communicates about what she needs, in a self-entitled manner. But in this case, her communicating with Angel is necessary to break Angel free from the position he is in.
56. Soy, "Blood and Choice: The Theory and Practice of Family in Angel," 226.
57. Godwin, *Enquiry*, 20.
58. Thoreau, "Civil Disobedience," Loc. 153.
59. K. Stoddard Hayes explains that unwaveringly fighting against evil is what *Angel* is about. See Stoddard Hayes, "Where Have All the Good Guys Gone?" Stacey Abbott explains that the fight against evil is Angel's endless battle, especially as seen in "Reprise." See Abbott, "Walking the Fine Line Between Angel and Angelus."
60. For more on the Circle of the Black Thorn, see Abbott, "Kicking Ass and Singing 'Mandy': A Vampire in LA," 5; Iatropolous and Woodall III, "Introduction: The Individual, the Institutional, and the Unitentional: Exploring the Whedonverses Through Critical Race Theory."
61. Godwin, *Enquiry*, 108.
62. *Ibid.*
63. *Ibid.*, 109.
64. *Ibid.*, 108.
65. *Ibid.*
66. Thoreau, "Civil Disobedience," Loc. 78.

Chapter Two

1. As Whedon scholar Kate Rennebohm notes, "much of what we think in a day comes not from ourselves, but from events, individuals, and ideas in the world that encourage, train or demand that we act in certain ways." Kate Rennebohm, "The Mind Doesn't Matter, It's the Body We Want," in *Inside Joss' Dollhouse: From Alpha to Rossum*, ed. Jane Espenson (Dallas: Smart Pop, 2010), 6.
2. Noam Chomsky, *On Anarchism* (New Press, 2013). Kindle edition.
3. Chomsky, *Anarchism*, Loc. 646.
4. Heidi M. Hurd, "The Moral Magic of Consent," *Legal Theory* 2, no. 2 (1996), 121, 123–4, 137; David Archard, *Sexual Consent* (Boulder: Westview Press, 1998), 3, 5–6; Alan Wertheimer, "Consent and Sexual Relations," in *The Philosophy of Sex: Contemporary Readings*, eds. Alan Soble and Nicholas Power (New York: Rowman and Littlefield, 2008), 291; John Kleinig, "The Nature of Consent," in *The Ethics of Consent*, eds. Franklin G. Miller and Alan Wertheimer (New York: Oxford University Press, 2010), 4; Tom Dougherty, "Sex, Lies, and Consent," *Ethics* 123 (July 2013), 722; Tom Dougherty, "Yes Means Yes: Consent as Communication," *Philosophy & Public Affairs* 43.3 (2015), 226, 232–233.
5. Hurd, "The Moral Magic of Consent," 140–2; Archard, *Sexual Consent*, 46–53; Alan Wertheimer, *Consent to Sexual Relations* (Cambridge: Cambridge University Press, 2003), 215–57; Neil Manson and Onora O'Neill, *Rethinking Informed Consent* (Cambridge: Cambridge University Press, 2007); Wertheimer, "Consent and Sexual Relations," 295, 302–306; Thomas Mappes, "Sexual Morality and the Concept of Using Another Person," in *The Philosophy of Sex: Contemporary Readings*, eds. Alan Soble and Nicholas Power (New York: Rowman and Littlefield, 2008), 231–241; Kleinig, "The Nature of Consent," 13–17; Tom L. Beauchamp, "Autonomy and Consent," in *The Ethics of Consent*, eds. Franklin G. Miller and Alan Wertheimer (New York: Oxford University Press, 2010).
6. Whedon scholars usually discuss Adelle as a manipulator and strategist when it comes to the Dolls, but one who eventually takes a side by the end of the series, showing her eventual moral growth. But during the bargaining process required for consent, Adelle does not disclose information fully and purposefully manipulates those considering becoming Dolls. For instance, Peter Tupper suggests that Adelle is misleading in her claim that the Dolls voluntarily enter in this contractual agreement, noting that the agreement is "beyond the law." Peter Tupper, "Joss Whedon's *Dollhouse*: 21st Century Neo-Gothic," in *Inside Joss' Dollhouse: From Alpha to Rossum*, ed. Jane Espenson (Dallas: Smart Pop, 2010), 59. Erin Giannini also notes that "'volunteer' belongs in scare quotes" and adds that vulnerable people are targeted. See Erin Giannini, *Joss Whedon versus the Corporation: Big Business Critiqued in the Films and Television Programs* (Jefferson, NC: McFarland, 2017), 88. Also see: Tami Anderson, "Whose Story Is This, Anyway?," in *Inside Joss' Dollhouse: From Alpha to Rossum*, ed. Jane Espenson (Dallas: Smart Pop, 2010); Renee St. Louis and Miriam Riggs "A Painful, Bleeding Sleep: Sleeping Beauty in the *Dollhouse*," *Slayage: The Journal of Whedon Studies* 8.2-3 [30–31] (Summer/Fall 2010). Web.; Sharon Sutherland and Sarah Swan, "There is No Me; I'm Just a Container: Law and Loss of Personhood in *Dollhouse*," in *Reading Joss Whedon*, eds. Rhonda Wilcox, Tanya Cochran, Cynthea Masson and David Lavery (Syracuse: Syracuse University Press, 2014), 223.
7. A similar point is made by Sutherland and Swan, "There is No Me; I'm Just a Container: Law and Loss of Personhood in *Dollhouse*," 223.
8. Valerie Estelle Frankel, "All Dolled Up: Twisted Princes and Fairytale Heroines," in *Inside Joss' Dollhouse: From Alpha to Rossum*, ed. Jane Espenson (Dallas: Smart Pop, 2010), 63–64.
9. See "Joss Whedon Just Wants to be Loved," in *Joss Whedon: Conversations*, eds. David Lavery and Cynthia Burkhead (Jackson: University Press of Mississippi, 2011), 187. Also see Anderson, "Whose Story is this Anyways?," 163.
10. Sherry Ginn, *Power and Control in the Television Worlds of Joss Whedon* (Jefferson: McFarland, 2012), Chapter 1. Kindle edition.
11. See Anderson, "Whose Story is this Anyways?," 163.
12. Sutherland and Swan similarly argue

that each Doll's consent is problematic. See Sutherland and Swan, "There is No Me; I'm Just a Container: Law and Loss of Personhood in *Dollhouse*."

13. *Ibid.*, 223–225.

14. For more on the freedom requirement, see: Wertheimer, "Consent and Sexual Relations," 295, 302–4; Archard, *Sexual Consent*, 50–3; Mappes, "Sexual Morality and the Concept of Using Another Person," 231–2, 235–41.

15. Sutherland and Swan, "There is No Me; I'm Just a Container: Law and Loss of Personhood in *Dollhouse*," 224.

16. *Ibid.*

17. *Ibid.*

18. *Ibid.*, 225.

19. For more on the competency issues that compromise Victor's and November's consent, see Sutherland and Swan, "There is No Me; I'm Just a Container: Law and Loss of Personhood in *Dollhouse*," 225.

20. For more on the competence requirement, see: Mappes, "Sexual Morality," 233; Hurd, "The Moral Magic of Consent," 140–2; Wertheimer, "Consent and Sexual Relations," 295, 305–6; Archard, *Sexual Consent*, 44–6; Wertheimer, *Consent to Sexual Relations*, 215–57.

21. Anderson, "Whose Story is this Anyways?," 164. For more on how the Rossum Corporation in Dollhouse allegedly "cures" the PTSD of soldiers, or rather, just uses them for its own purposes, see Giannini, *Joss Whedon versus the Corporation: Big Business Critiqued in the Films and Television Programs*, 143–144.

22. "Joss Whedon Just Wants to be Loved," 186. Andrew Zimmerman Jones also characterizes the Dollhouse as a "gussied up prostitution ring." See Andrew Zimmerman Jones, "The Redemption of Topher Brink," in *Inside Joss' Dollhouse: From Alpha to Rossum*, ed. Jane Espenson (Dallas: Smart Pop, 2010), 82. Also see the discussion of prostitution and the Dollhouse at Sutherland and Swan, "There is No Me; I'm Just a Container: Law and Loss of Personhood in *Dollhouse*," 227–228. Erin Giannini notes the Dollhouse is illegal. Giannini also discusses the power behind the Dollhouse, Rossum, as having the goal of power and immortality, and refers to its unchecked power as leading to bad consequences such as domination and death. See Giannini, *Joss Whedon versus the Corporation: Big Business Critiqued in the Films and Television Programs*, 153, 92, 94.

23. For an analysis that shows Adelle as somewhat empathetic and not just unfeeling or manipulating, see Jonathan Mason, "Like a Boss," in *Inside Joss' Dollhouse: From Alpha to Rossum*, ed. Jane Espenson (Dallas: Smart Pop, 2010), 97. Mason argues that Adelle's use of the Dolls show not just her discipline as the boss, but also her empathy for the dolls. Another scholar, Tami Anderson, allows for the slim possibility that Adelle genuinely believes that she is helping the dolls, but Anderson then analyzes Adelle as a manipulator. See Anderson, "Whose Story is this Anyways?," 167. Erin Giannini views Adelle as possibly believing that she offers care to the Dolls, but also experiencing self-hatred for her actions. Giannini, *Joss Whedon versus the Corporation: Big Business Critiqued in the Films and Television Programs*, 135.

24. For more on the relationship between Adelle and Victor, see Sutherland and Swan, "There is No Me; I'm Just a Container: Law and Loss of Personhood in *Dollhouse*," 230. For more on prostitution and rape in the Dollhouse, see 227–230 in the same article.

25. For more on the issue of consent and rape, see Jaclyn Freidman and Jessica Valenti, eds., *Yes Means Yes: Visions of Female Sexual Power and A World Without Rape* (Berkeley: Seal Press, 2008).

26. St. Louis and Riggs "A Painful, Bleeding Sleep: Sleeping Beauty in the *Dollhouse*."

27. Sutherland and Swan "There is No Me; I'm Just a Container: Law and Loss of Personhood in *Dollhouse*," 224.

28. For more on memory and *Dollhouse* see Sherry Ginn, *Power and Control in the Television Worlds of Joss Whedon*, Chapter 6.

29. For more on the information requirement, see: Mappes, "Sexual Morality," 231–2; Wertheimer, "Consent and Sexual Relations," 295, 304–5; Archard, *Sexual Consent* (1998) 46–50; Wertheimer, *Consent to Sexual Relations*, 193–214; Manson and O'Neill, *Rethinking Informed Consent*.

30. Edward S. Herman and Noam Chomsky, *Manufacturing Consent: The Political Economy of the Mass Media* (Pantheon Books, 2002[1988]), Loc. 69.

31. *Ibid.*, Loc. 1344.

32. *Ibid.*, Loc. 7701.
33. *Ibid.*, Loc. 7669.
34. Christopher Souza, "Boyd Langton and the Fantasy of Trust," in *Inside Joss' Dollhouse: From Alpha to Rossum*, ed. Jane Espenson (Dallas: Smart Pop, 2010), 212.
35. Anderson, "Whose Story is this Anyways?," 171–172.
36. For more on how the media and advertisers manipulate our purchases or our senses of selves, see Naomi Wolf, *The Beauty Myth: How Images of Beauty Are Used Against Women* (New York: Perennial, 2002), especially the chapter titled "Culture."
37. See discussions on the various possible meanings of "autonomy," see Nomy Arpaly, *Unprincipled Virtue* (New York: Oxford University Press, 2004), 117–130; Michael McKenna, "The Relationship between Autonomous and Morally Responsible Agency," *Personal Autonomy*, James Stacey Taylor, ed. (New York: Cambridge University Press, 2005), 206–7.
38. Joseph Raz denies anyone believes in an "arbitrary self-creation doctrine," which would hold, "all value derives from choice which is itself not guided by value and is therefore free, i.e., arbitrary" (Joseph Raz, *The Morality of Freedom* (Oxford: Oxford University Press, 1986), 387–8, see also Joel Feinberg, *Harm to Self* (New York: Oxford University Press, 1986), 34; Mariana Oshana, "Autonomy and Free Agency," *Personal Autonomy*, James Stacey Taylor, ed. (New York: Cambridge University Press, 2005), 196–8; and Robert Noggle, "Autonomy and the Paradox of Self-Creation," *Personal Autonomy*, James Stacey Taylor, ed. (New York: Cambridge University Press, 2005). For a scientific discussion of these sorts of issues, see Sean Spence, *The Actor's Brain* (New York: Oxford University Press, 2009). Charles Taylor though argues against Jean-Paul Sartre's view of radical choice of motives in a vein that makes it sound like it is such a view (Charles Taylor, "Responsibility for Self," in *The Identities of Persons*, ed. Amelie Rorty (Berkeley: University of California Press, 1976), 290–4.
39. Rhonda V. Wilcox, "Echoes of Complicity: Reflexivity and Identity in Joss Whedon's Dollhouse," *Slayage: The Journal of Whedon Studies* 8.2-3 [30-31] (Summer/Fall 2010). Web.

For a similar argument that we are all basically Dolls, also see Kate Rennebohm, "'The Mind Doesn't Matter, It's the Body We Want': Identity and Body in the *Dollhouse*," 6–8.
40. James Rocha, "Autonomy within Subservient Careers," *Ethical Theory & Moral Practice* Vol. 18 (October 2011).
41. Chomsky, *Anarchism*, Loc. 479.
42. *Ibid.*, Loc. 602.
43. *Ibid.*, Loc. 653.
44. Noam Chomsky, *Necessary Illusions: Thought Control in Democratic Societies* (House of Anansi Press, 2013), Loc. 69.
45. *Ibid.*
46. *Ibid.*, Loc. 680.
47. Jones, "The Redemption of Topher Brink," 80.
48. This problem is sometimes referred to as "administrative evil." Administrative evil refers to the ways in which good people can produce seemingly non-evil labors that yet still result in evil acts. For more on administrative evil, see Guy Adams and Danny Balfour, *Unmasking Administrative Evil* (Routledge, 1998[2015]); Lisa Zanetti and Guy Adams, "In Service of the Leviathan: Democracy, Ethics and the Potential for Administrative Evil in the New Public Management," *Administrative Theory & Praxis* Vol. 22, No. 3 (2000); George Reed, "Leading questions: Leadership, Ethics, and Administrative Evil," *Leadership*, Vol. 8, No. 2 (May, 2012).
49. Anderson, "Whose Story Is This, Anyway?," 164–168.
50. Renee St. Louis and Miriam Riggs "A Painful, Bleeding Sleep: Sleeping Beauty in the *Dollhouse*"; Jones, "The Redemption of Topher Brink," 88–92. Also see Susan Quilty, "Negative Space in the 'House: How Caroline Is the Vase," in *Inside Joss' Dollhouse: From Alpha to Rossum*, ed. Jane Espenson (Dallas: Smart Pop, 2010), 141. Quilty explains that Topher supported Sierra in avenging herself by imprinting her as Priya against orders. Also see Lillian Deritter, "We're Not Men," in *Inside Joss' Dollhouse: From Alpha to Rossum*, ed. Jane Espenson (Dallas: Smart Pop, 2010), 193–194. Deritter argues that Topher realizes he is responsible for what happens to the Dolls and loses his arrogance, but notes this is "not morality per se." Giannini notes that Topher is "the embodiment of Rossum's corporate goals" but then develops a conscience. See

Giannini, *Joss Whedon versus the Corporation: Big Business Critiqued in the Films and Television Programs*, 119, 125.

51. For more on the Rossum Corporation as the villain in *Dollhouse*, see: Anderson, "Whose Story is this Anyways?," 168; Sutherland and Swan, "There is No Me; I'm Just a Container: Law and Loss of Personhood in *Dollhouse*," 223, 226–227; K. Dale Koontz, "Reflections in the Pool: Echo, Narcissus, and the Male Gaze in *Dollhouse*," in *Reading Joss Whedon*, eds. Rhonda Wilcox, Tanya Cochran, Cynthea Masson and David Lavery (Syracuse: Syracuse University Press, 2014), 209, 211; Giannini, *Joss Whedon versus the Corporation: Big Business Critiqued in the Films and Television Programs*, 92, 94.

52. Jones, "Redemption," 89.

53. Julie Hawk, "More Than the Sum of Our Imprints," in *Inside Joss' Dollhouse: From Alpha to Rossum*, ed. Jane Espenson (Dallas: Smart Pop, 2010), 251. Hawk does however remain skeptical of how thoroughly "the traces, the echoes of his thoughtpocalypse" are erased through his self-sacrifice.

54. Anderson, "Whose Story is this Anyways?," 171–172.

55. Oluwafemi Morohunfola, "What Echo's Journey to Self-Awareness Tell Us About the Human Soul," in *Inside Joss' Dollhouse: From Alpha to Rossum*, ed. Jane Espenson (Dallas: Smart Pop, 2010), 223.

56. Renee St. Louis and Miriam Riggs "A Painful, Bleeding Sleep: Sleeping Beauty in the *Dollhouse*." Wilcox makes the same point in "Echoes of Complicity: Reflexivity and Identity in Joss Whedon's Dollhouse." For a discussion of memory and how losing it could be analyzed through the Dollhouse, see Morohunfola, "What Echo's Journey to Self-Awareness Tell Us About the Human Soul," 229–230. Sherry Ginn wrote on the same theme in regards to memory and the Dollhouse. See Sherry Ginn, "Memory, Mind, and Mayhem: Neurological Tampering and Manipulation in *Dollhouse*." *Slayage: The Journal of Whedon Studies* 8.2-3 [30–31] (Summer/Fall 2010). Web.

57. Morohunfola considers Alpha to be psychopathic. See Morohunfola, "What Echo's Journey to Self-Awareness Tell Us About the Human Soul," 222, 226.

58. Renee St. Louis and Miriam Riggs "A Painful, Bleeding Sleep: Sleeping Beauty in the *Dollhouse*."

59. One of us argues that autonomy does require a moral code at Rocha, "Autonomy within Subservient Careers." For a similar position, see Susan Wolf, "Freedom within Reason," in *Personal Autonomy*, ed. James Stacey Taylor (New York: Cambridge University Press, 2005), 265–267. For the contrary position that there can be immoral versions of autonomy, see Gerald Dworkin, *The Theory and Practice of Autonomy* (New York: Cambridge University Press, 1988), 29; Marilyn Friedman, *Autonomy, Gender, Politics* (Oxford: Oxford University Press, 2003), 26–27, 42–43; Robert Noggle, "Autonomy and the Paradox of Self-Creation," in *Personal Autonomy*, ed. James Stacey Taylor (New York: Cambridge University Press, 2005), 102–104; Michael McKenna, "The Relationship between Autonomous and Morally Responsible Agency," in *Personal Autonomy*, ed. James Stacey Taylor (New York: Cambridge University Press, 2005), 223; and Alfred Mele, *Autonomous Agents* (New York: Oxford University Press), 3–4, 156–165.

60. For a similar view of Echo as a distinct person who connects her composite personalities, see: Rennebohm, "Mind," 10–11; Morohunfola, "What Echo's Journey to Self-Awareness Tell Us About the Human Soul," 222; Cynthea Masson, "Who Painted the Lion?—A Gloss on Dollhouse's 'Bella Chose,'" *Slayage* 8.2-3 [30–31], Summer/Fall 2010. Web.; Koontz, "Reflections in the Pool: Echo, Narcissus, and the Male Gaze in *Dollhouse*," 219; Sutherland and Swan, "There is No Me; I'm Just a Container: Law and Loss of Personhood in *Dollhouse*," 236; Frankel, "All Dolled Up: Twisted Princes and Fairytale Heroines," 73, 76; Ian G. Klein, "I Like My Scars: Claire Saunders and the Narrative of Flesh," in *Inside Joss' Dollhouse: From Alpha to Rossum*, ed. Jane Espenson (Dallas: Smart Pop, 2010), 117; Quilty, "Negative Space in the 'House: How Caroline Is the Vase," 138.

61. Julie Hawk, "More Than the Sum of Our Imprints," 248. Also see Julie Hawk, "Hacking the Read-Only File: Collaborative Narrative as Ontological Construction in Dollhouse." *Slayage* 8.2-3 [30–31], Summer/Fall 2010. Web; Lisa K. Perdigao, "This One's Broken: Rebuilding Whedonbots and Repro-

gramming the Whedonverse," *Slayage* 8.2–3 [30–31], Summer/Fall 2010. Web. For a view that even though Echo goes off programming, Rossum will use that act for their own purposes, see Giannini, *Joss Whedon versus the Corporation: Big Business Critiqued in the Films and Television Programs*, 105.

62. For more on Spike's choice to obtain his soul, see: Roz Kaveney, "A Sense of the Ending: Schrodinger's *Angel*," in *Reading Angel: The TV Spin-Off with a Soul*, ed. Stacey Abbott (London: I.B. Tauris, 2005), 64; Matt Hills and Rebecca Williams, "*Angel*'s Monstrous Mothers and Vampires With Souls: Investigating the Abject in 'Television Horror,'" in *Reading Angel: The TV Spin-Off with a Soul*, ed. Stacey Abbott (London: I.B. Tauris, 2005), 209.

63. Chomsky, *Illusions*, Loc. 442.
64. Chomsky, *Anarchism*, Loc. 671.
65. *Ibid.*, Loc. 675.
66. Influenced by the Marxist Theodor Adorno, Martin Shuster makes a similar point about *Dollhouse* by explaining that we are all influenced by the world, and that the world shapes how we see things. He goes on to say that we would need a different world in order to escape. See Martin Shuster, "What It Means to Mourn," in *Inside Joss' Dollhouse: From Alpha to Rossum*, ed. Jane Espenson (Dallas: Smart Pop, 2010), 238.
67. Chomsky, *Anarchism*, Loc. 680.
68. *Ibid.*, Loc. 584.

Chapter Three

1. For more on Coulson and how he represents a privileging of masculinity, see Suzanne Scott, "Modeling the Marvel Everyfan: Agent Coulson and/as Transmedia Fan Culture," *Palabra Clave* 20.4 (December 2017), 1042–1072.
2. Samira Nadkarni, "'I Believe in Something Greater than Myself': What Authority, Terrorism, and Resistance Have Come to Mean in the Whedonverse," *Slayage: The Journal of Whedon Studies* 13.2 [42] (Summer 2015). Web. Further, numerous scholars have criticized Joss Whedon for his depictions of race and for the lack of meaningful representation of people of color in his works. For instance, Ewan Kirkland notes that many of Whedon's works reflect white sensibilities and "an extremely white view of the world, of history, of the universe, and of white people's role within in." See Ewan Kirkland, "The Caucasian Persuasion of *Buffy the Vampire Slayer*," *Slayage: The Journal of Whedon Studies* 5.1 [17] (June 2005). Web. Also see Jeffrey Middents, "A Sweet Vamp: Critiquing the Treatment of Race in *Buffy* and the American Musical Once More (with Feeling)," *Slayage: The Journal of Whedon Studies* 5.1 [17] (June 2005). Web. Finally, also see the various works collected together in *Joss Whedon and Race: Critical Essays*, eds. Mary Ellen Iatropoulos and Lowery A. Woodall III (Jefferson, NC: McFarland, 2017).
3. Jennifer Beckett, "Acting with Limited Oversights: S.H.I.E.L.D. and the Role of Intelligence and Intervention in the Marvel Cinematic Universe," in *Assembling the Marvel Cinematic Universe: Essays on the Social, Cultural, and Geopolitical Domains*, eds. Julian C. Chambliss, William L. Svitavsky and Daniel Fandino (Jefferson: McFarland, 2018), Chapter 18. Kindle edition.
4. In terms of seeing Coulson as a father-figure, Whedon scholar Jason Bainbridge notes that we've also been taught that law is associated with male power, particularly the power of the male patriarch. Bainbridge explains that the "idea of the law being paternal has its roots in the Roman idea of the *pater imporiosus* who himself bears both the character of the father and the capacity of the magistrate." As such, Coulson in becoming a father figure also becomes an embodiment of law. Jason Bainbridge, "'You Were the World's First Superhero': Marvel Studio's Superheroes, Law, and the Pursuit of Justice," in *Assembling the Marvel Cinematic Universe: Essays on the Social, Cultural, and Geopolitical Domains*, eds. Julian C. Chambliss, William L. Svitavsky and Daniel Fandino (Jefferson: McFarland, 2018), Chapter 14. Kindle edition.
5. Beckett, "Acting with Limited Oversights: S.H.I.E.L.D."
6. Nadkarni, "'I Believe in Something Greater than Myself.'"
7. Peter Kropotkin, "Anarchism," from *The Encyclopedia Britannica*, in *Anarchism: A Collection of Revolutionary Writings*, ed. Roger N. Baldwin (Dover Publications, 2002[1905]), 287.
8. Peter Kropotkin, "Anarchist Commu-

nism: Its Basis and Principles," in *Anarchism: A Collection of Revolutionary Writings*, ed. Roger N. Baldwin (Dover Publications, 2002 [1887]), 46.

9. Peter Kropotkin, *The Conquest of Bread* (Dover Publications, 2013[1892]), 33, Loc. 529.

10. *Ibid.*, 31, Loc. 503.

11. *Ibid.*, 32, Loc. 508.

12. *Ibid.*, 38, Loc. 580.

13. Beckett, "Acting with Limited Oversights."

14. Kropotkin, *Conquest of Bread*, 38, Loc. 583.

15. Beckett, "Acting with Limited Oversights." Also see Samira Nadkarni, "To Be the Shield: American Imperialism and Explosive Identity Politics in Agents of S.H.I.E.L.D.," in *Assembling the Marvel Cinematic Universe: Essays on the Social, Cultural, and Geopolitical Domains*, eds. Julian C. Chambliss, William L. Svitavsky and Daniel Fandino (Jefferson: McFarland, 2018), Chapter 19. Kindle Edition.

16. Beckett, "Acting with Limited Oversights."

17. And Whedon scholars note that S.H.I.E.L.D. operations have come under increased scrutiny "just as recent events have placed the operations of the CIA and NSA and their increasing militarization under scrutiny." See Jennnifer Beckett, "Acting with Limited Oversights." Also see Samira Nadkarni, "To Be the Shield."

18. Beckett, "Acting with Limited Oversights."

19. Peter Kropotkin, *Mutual Aid; A Factor of Evolution* (A Public Domain Book, 2011 [1902]), Loc. 2924.

20. *Ibid.*, Loc. 2930.

21. For more on the dangers of corruption within an organization (and on the belief that you might be doing good while actually serving within an evil organization), see Sarah Donovan and Nick Richardson, "Shining the Light on the Dark Avengers" in *The Avengers and Philosophy: Earth's Mightiest Thinkers*, ed. Mark D. White (Wiley, 2012), 18–27. Also see Robert Powell, "The Self-Corruption of Norman Osborn: A Cautionary Tale," in *The Avengers and Philosophy: Earth's Mightiest Thinkers*, ed. Mark D. White (Wiley, 2012), 71–79.

22. A similar point is made in Beckett, "Acting with Limited Oversights."

23. Kropotkin, *Conquest of Bread*, Loc. 103.

24. Kropotkin, "Anarchist Communism," 52.

25. *Ibid.*, 52.

26. Beckett argues that the Inhumans storyline embodies critiques about the unchecked power of the military industrial complex and the problematic nature of pre-emptive measures against those deemed to be threats. See Jennifer Beckett, "Acting with Limited Oversights." Nadkarni interprets it as neo-colonialism run amok. See "'I Believe in Something Greater than Myself.'"

27. Guy Adams and Danny Balfour, *Unmasking Administrative Evil* (Routledge, 2015 [1998]); George Reed, "Leading Questions: Leadership, Ethics, and Administrative Evil," *Leadership* Vol. 8, No. 2 (May, 2012); and Lisa Zanetti and Guy Adams, "In Service of the Leviathan: Democracy, Ethics, and the Potential for Administrative Evil in the New Public Management," *Administrative Theory & Praxis* Vol. 22, No. 3 (2000).

28. For an anarchist discussion of bureaucracy, see David Graeber, *The Utopia of Rules* (Melville House, 2015).

29. Sherry Ginn, *Power and Control in the Television Worlds of Joss Whedon* (Jefferson, NC: McFarland, 2013), especially 136.

30. For more takes on the Avengers and what they represent, see Mark D. White, ed., *The Avengers and Philosophy: Earth's Mightiest Thinkers* (Wiley, 2012).

31. Kropotkin, *Mutual Aid*, Loc. 83.

32. Kropotkin, "Anarchism," 283.

33. For more on the Avengers' fellowship and drive to do what's right, see Tony Spanakos, "Gods, Beasts, and Political Animals: Why the Avengers Assemble," in *The Avengers and Philosophy: Earth's Mightiest Thinkers*, ed. Mark D. White (Wiley, 2012), 98–112.

34. Kropotkin, *Conquest of Bread*, 35, Loc. 551.

35. Sarah Zaidan, "Stark Contrasts: Reinventing Iron Man for 21st Century Cinema," in *Assembling the Marvel Cinematic Universe: Essays on the Social, Cultural, and Geopolitical Domains*, eds. Julian C. Chambliss, William L. Svitavsky and Daniel Fandino (Jefferson: McFarland, 2018), Chapter 8. Kindle edition.

36. For more on the moral instincts of Tony Stark and Captain America, see Mark D. White, "Superhuman Ethics Class with the

Avengers Prime," in *The Avengers and Philosophy: Earth's Mightiest Thinkers*, ed. Mark D. White (Wiley, 2012), 5–17.

37. Samira Nadkarni, "To Be the Shield."

38. This is an interesting parallel to the offer Dollhouse offers to those contemplating becoming Dolls.

39. For a different viewpoint, see Jason Bainbridge who argues that they are soldiers and thereby, an extension of the state. See Jason Bainbridge, "'You Were the World's First Superhero.'"

40. Nadkarni, "'I Believe in Something Greater than Myself.'"

41. Kropotkin, *Conquest of Bread*, 32, Loc. 516.

42. Antony Mullen reflects on the use of violence against non–American bodies. He explains that the loss of American lives or bodies are presented as pivotal and traumatic, while the loss of others is seen as acceptable in the grand narrative of good vs. evil. See Antony Mullen, "Bodies That Shatter: Violence and Spectacle in The Avengers," in *Assembling the Marvel Cinematic Universe: Essays on the Social, Cultural, and Geopolitical Domains*, eds. Julian C. Chambliss, William L. Svitavsky, and Daniel Fandino (Jefferson: McFarland, 2018), Chapter 12. Kindle edition.

43. Kropotkin, *Conquest of Bread*, 37, Loc. 568.

44. *Ibid.*, 34, Loc. 537.

45. Kropotkin, *Mutual Aid*, Loc. 76.

46. *Ibid.*, Loc. 19.

Chapter Four

1. An earlier version of this chapter first appeared in *Slayage: The Journal of Whedon Studies*. We thank them for providing permission to turn that article into a chapter here. For the earlier version, please see James Rocha, "The Black Reaching Out: An Anarchist Analysis of *Firefly*," *Slayage: The Journal of Whedon Studies*, 14.2 [44] (Summer 2016): 1–23. Web.

2. Sara T. Hinson, "Freedom and Firefly—Mal Reynolds, Libertarian," *America's Future Foundation* (America's Future Foundation); Julian Sanchez, "Out to the Black," *Reason.com* (Reason Foundation, 2005); P. Gardner Goldsmith, "Freedom in an Unfree World," in *Serenity Found: More Unauthorized Essays on Joss Whedon's Firefly Universe*, edited by Jane Espenson (Dallas: BenBella Books, 2007); Amy H. Sturgis, "'Just Get Us a Little Further': Liberty and the Frontier in *Firefly* and *Serenity*," in *The Philosophy of Joss Whedon*, edited by Dean A. Kowalski and S. Evan Kreider (Lexington: University of Kentucky Press, 2011).

3. "Right libertarianism" is a bit misleading since right libertarians would share social and cultural views with both left libertarians and standard liberals. The directional distinction mainly refers to economic perspectives.

4. In agreement with our eventual interpretation, J. Douglas Rabb and J. Michael Richardson argue that "Jayne is really a parody of Rand's egoistic heroes" (199). See J. Douglas Rabb and J. Michael Richardson, *Joss Whedon as Shakespearean Moralist: Narrative Ethics of the Bard and the Buffyverse* (Jefferson, NC: McFarland, 2014).

5. For progressive, and clearly not libertarian, interpretations of *Buffy* see: Daniel A. Clark and P. Andrew Miller, "Buffy, the Scooby Gang, and Monstrous Authority: *BtVS* and the Subversion of Authority," *Slayage: The Online International Journal of Buffy Studies* 1.3 [3] (June 2001). Web; Bruce McClelland, "By Whose Authority? The Magical Tradition, Violence, and the Legitimation of the Vampire Slayer," *Slayage: The Online International Journal of Buffy Studies* 1.1 [1] (January 2001). Web. For a Marxist, and incredibly not libertarian, interpretation of *Dollhouse*, see Tom Connelly and Shelley S. Rees, "Alienation and the Dialectics of History in Joss Whedon's *Dollhouse*," *Fantasy Is Not Their Purpose: Joss Whedon's Dollhouse*, eds. Cynthea Masson and Rhonda V. Wilcox for *Slayage: The Online International Journal of the Whedon Studies Association* 8.2 & 8.3 [30–31] (Summer/Fall 2010). Web. For a progressive, and again not libertarian, interpretation of *Dr. Horrible*, see Alyson Buckman, "'Go Ahead! Run Away! Say It Was Horrible!': *Dr. Horrible's Sing-Along Blog* as Resistant Text," *Slayage: The Online International Journal of Buffy Studies* 8.1 [29] (Spring 2010). Web.

6. For more progressive, and not libertarian, interpretations of *Firefly*, see: Mercedes Lackey, "*Serenity* and Bobby McGee: Freedom and the Illusion of Freedom in Joss Whedon's *Firefly*," in *Finding Serenity: Anti-Heroes, Lost*

Shepherds, and Space Hookers in Joss Whedon's Firefly, edited by Jane Espenson (Dallas: BenBella Books, 2004); Linda Jean Jencson, "'Aiming to Misbehave': Role Modeling Political-Economic Conditions and Political Action in the *Serenityverse*," *Slayage: The Online International Journal of Buffy Studies*, special issue edited by Tanya R. Cochran and Rhonda V. Wilcox 7.1 [25] (Winter 2008). Web.

7. David D. Friedman, *The Machinery of Freedom: Guide to a Radical Capitalism* (Chu Hartley LLC, 2014), Loc. 206. Also see Loc. 287–289. Kindle edition.

8. Also see: Jan Narveson, *The Libertarian Idea* (Ontario: Broadview Press, 2001), 66–68.

9. F. A. Hayek, *The Constitution of Liberty* (Chicago: U of Chicago Press, 1960), 207–209; Robert Nozick, *Anarchy, State, and Utopia* (New York: Basic Books, 1974), 171–182; Friedman, *Machinery*, Loc. 300.

10. Nozick, *Anarchy*, 171.

11. *Ibid.*, 58.

12. Narveson, *Libertarian*, 110–184, esp. 165.

13. Friedman, *Machinery*, Loc. 213.

14. *Ibid.*, Loc. 290.

15. *Ibid.*, Loc. 2253.

16. Nozick, *Anarchy*, xix–xx, see also: 16, 119.

17. Friedman, *Machinery*, Loc. 2270–2399.

18. Ricardo Flores Magón, "To the Soldiers of Carranza," in *Dreams of Freedom*, eds. Chaz Bufe and Mitchell Cowen Verter (Oakland: AK Press, 2005[1915]), 169.

19. Ricardo Flores Magón, "Letter from L.A. County Jail," in *Dreams of Freedom*, eds. Chaz Bufe and Mitchell Cowen Verter (Oakland: AK Press, 2005[1908]), 114.

20. Ricardo Flores Magón, "Class Struggle," in *Dreams of Freedom*, eds. Chaz Bufe and Mitchell Cowen Verter (Oakland: AK Press, 2005[1911]), 188.

21. Peter Marshall, *Demanding the Impossible: A History of Anarchism* (Oakland: PM Press, 2010), 6–11.

22. For a fascinating fictional account of how a society without property could work, see Ursula Le Guin's *The Dispossessed* (New York: Harper Collins, 1974).

23. Friedman, *Machinery*, Loc. 346–353.

24. Ricardo Flores Magón, "The Right to Property," in *Dreams of Freedom*, eds. Chaz Bufe and Mitchell Cowen Verter (Oakland: AK Press, 2005[1911]), 275.

25. *Ibid.*, 275.

26. Ricardo Flores Magón, "Solidarity," in *Dreams of Freedom*, eds. Chaz Bufe and Mitchell Cowen Verter (Oakland: AK Press, 2005[1910]), 278.

27. *Ibid.*, 278.

28. For more on these distinctions, see: Ian Carter, "Positive and Negative Liberty," *Stanford Encyclopedia of Philosophy* (2003).

29. Narveson, *Libertarian*, 22–31.

30. Marshall, *Demanding the Impossible*, 36.

31. Errico Malatesta, *Errico Malatesta: His Life and Ideas*, ed. Vernon Richards (London: Freedom Press, 1965), 24.

32. Magón, "Solidarity."

33. Sanchez, "Out to the Black."

34. Joss Whedon, Brett Matthews, Will Conrad (Art), Laura Martin (Colors), Michael Heisler (Letters), and Adam Hughes (Cover Art), *Serenity: Those Left Behind* (Milwaukee: Dark Horse Books, Serenity Series, Book 1, 2nd Edition, 2012), Loc. 1302. Kindle edition.

35. Goldsmith, "Freedom," 59.

36. *Ibid.*, 60.

37. *Ibid.*, 59–60.

38. In the comic, *Those Left Behind*, Mal admits this point to himself (Whedon et al., Loc. 102).

39. In regards to an earlier draft of a version of this essay, I want to thank an anonymous reviewer from *Slayage: The Online International Journal of Buffy Studies* for pointing out the importance of responding to the sexism in the show (as well as other bigotries). Anarcho-socialists, in being committed to equality, must take strong stances against bigotry of any form. Of course, this theoretical entailment does not mean that an anarcho-socialist show would have only egalitarian characters, or that the writers and producers would not fall prey to their own biases (as many historically important and contemporary anarcho-socialists do as well). For example, though Inara has a female client in "War Stories" (1.10), there is no sustained attempt to deal with LGBTQ issues in *Firefly*. Racial issues in *Firefly* are much more complex and require a more serious treatment than can be given here.

40. Joss Whedon, Zack Whedon, Chris

Samnee (Art), Dave Stewart (Colors), Michael Heisler (Letters), and Steve Morris (Cover Art), *Serenity: The Shepherd's Tale* (Milwaukee: Dark Horse Books, Serenity Series, Book 3, 2010). Kindle edition.
  41. Whedon et al., *Shepherd's Tale*, Loc. 51–55.
  42. *Ibid.*, Loc. 56.
  43. *Ibid.*, Loc. 56.
  44. *Ibid.*, 28–42.
  45. *Ibid.*, 28–42.
  46. *Ibid.*, Loc. 29.
  47. *Ibid.*, Loc. 24–26.
  48. *Ibid.*, Loc. 26.
  49. *Ibid.*, Loc. 26.
  50. Sturgis, "Liberty and Frontier," 24–25.
  51. *Ibid.*, 25.
  52. Ricardo Flores Magón, "The Chains of 'The Free,'" in *Dreams of Freedom*, eds. Chaz Bufe and Mitchell Cowen Verter (Oakland: AK Press, 2005[1910]), 182.
  53. Ricardo Flores Magón, "Outlaws," in *Dreams of Freedom*, eds. Chaz Bufe and Mitchell Cowen Verter (Oakland: AK Press, 2005[1910]), 241.
  54. Magón, "Chains," 183.

Chapter Five

  1. For more on feminism and the various goals of feminism groups, see Nancy MacLean, *The American Women's Movement, 1945–2000* (Bedford, 2009); Ruth Rosen, *The World Split Open: How the Modern Women's Movement Changed America* (New York: Penguin, 2006); Leslie Tanner, ed., *Voices From Women's Liberation* (Signet, 1970); Jessica Valenti, *Full Frontal Feminism: A Young Woman's Guide to Why Feminism Matters* (Berkeley: Seal Press, 2014).
  2. Lucy Parsons, "The Principles of Anarchism," in *Lucy Parsons: Freedom, Equality, and Solidarity, Writings and Speeches, 1878–1937*, eds. Gale Ahrens and Roxanne Dunbar Ortiz (Chicago: Charles H. Kerr, 2004), 30.
  3. For more on the integration of gender and the "sex question" into American anarchism, see Brigitte Koenig, "American Anarchism: The Politics of Gender, Culture, and Community from Haymarket to the First World War" (PhD Dissertation, University of California, Berkeley, 2000). For various perspectives on sex and sexuality in the Whedonverse, see Lorna Jowett, *Sex and the Slayer: A Gender Studies Primer for the Buffy Fan* (Middletown: Wesleyan, 2005); Erin B. Waggoner, ed., *Sexual Rhetoric in the Works of Joss Whedon: New Essays* (Jefferson, NC: McFarland, 2010).
  4. Jes Battis, "Demonic Maternities, Complex Motherhoods: Cordelia, Fred, and the Puzzle of Illyria," *Slayage: The Journal of Whedon Studies* 5.2 [18] (September 2005). Web.
  5. *Ibid.* Cordelia shows growth throughout the series, and also while on *Angel*.
  6. Rachel Simmons, *The Hidden Culture of Aggression in Girls* (Mariner Books: New York, 2002). Sherry Ginn also discusses relational aggression in regards to Xander and Buffy. See Sherry Ginn, *Power and Control in the Television Worlds of Joss Whedon* (Jefferson, NC: McFarland, 2012), Chapter 3. Kindle edition.
  7. Emma Goldman, "The Individual, Society, and the State," in *Red Emma Speaks: An Emma Goldman Reader*, ed. Alix Kates Shulman (New York: Humanity Books, 1996), 109.
  8. *Ibid.*, 114–115.
  9. *Ibid.*, 116.
  10. Voltairine de Cleyre, "Sex Slavery," in *Exquisite Rebel: The Essays of Voltairine de Cleyre: Anarchist, Feminist, Genius*, eds. Sharon Presley and Crispin Sartwell (Albany: State University of New York Press, 2005), 234.
  11. *Ibid.*, 235.
  12. Rhonda V. Wilcox, "There Will Never Be a 'Very Special *Buffy*': *Buffy* and the Monsters of Teen Life," *Slayage: The Journal of Whedon Studies* 1.2 [2] (March 2001). Web.
  13. For more on Cordelia's moral development throughout *Buffy* and going into *Angel*, see Karin Beeler, *Seers, Witches and Psychics on Screen: An Analysis of Women Visionary Characters in Recent Television and Film* (Jefferson, NC: McFarland, 2008), especially the chapter titled "Cheerleader/Seer: The Hybrid Visions of Cordelia Chase in *Buffy the Vampire Slayer* and *Angel*."
  14. Wilcox, "There Will Never Be a 'Very Special *Buffy*.'"
  15. For more scholarly essays on vampires in *Buffy*, see Jowett, *Sex and the Slayer*; Jeffrey L. Pasley, "Old Familiar Vampires: The Politics of the Buffyverse," in *Buffy The Vampire Slayer and Philosophy*, ed. James B. South (Chicago: Open Court, 2003), 254–267.

16. Lucy Parsons, "The Principles of Anarchism," 30.

17. *Ibid.*, 30.

18. Stacey Abbott also discusses how some of the vampires in the Buffyverse have a sense of religious ritual, which boosts this sense of hierarchy. She also makes the same point about the Watchers Council. See Stacey Abbott, "A Little Less Ritual and a Little More Fun: The Modern Vampire in Buffy the Vampire Slayer," *Slayage: The Journal of Whedon Studies* 1.3 [3] (June 2001). Web.

19. For more on Angel, see Stacey Abbott, *Angel* (Detroit: Wayne State University Press, 2009).

20. Voltairine de Cleyre, "Why I Am an Anarchist," in *Exquisite Rebel: The Essays of Voltairine de Cleyre: Anarchist, Feminist, Genius*, eds. Sharon Presley and Crispin Sartwell (Albany: State University of New York Press, 2005), 55.

21. *Ibid.*, 33.

22. Emma Goldman, "Anarchism: What It Really Stands For," in *Red Emma Speaks: An Emma Goldman Reader*, ed. Alix Kates Shulman (New York: Humanity Books, 1996), 69.

23. *Ibid.*

24. Lucy Parsons, "The Principles of Anarchism," 33.

25. Emma Goldman, "The Social Importance of the Modern School," in *Red Emma Speaks: An Emma Goldman Reader*, ed. Alix Kates Shulman (New York: Humanity Books, 1996), 140.

26. Martha Nussbaum, "Objectification," *Philosophy and Public Affairs*, 24(4): 249–291.

27. Emma Goldman, "The Social Importance of the Modern School," 143.

28. Emma Goldman, "Anarchism: What It Really Stands For," 72.

29. For a similar point, see Jowett, *Sex and the Slayer*, 26.

30. Nussbaum, "Objectification."

31. For more on Riley and the general sense of experimentation within the Initiative, see Sherry Ginn, *Power and Control in The Television Worlds of Joss Whedon*, especially the section titled "Manipulating the Brain as a Method of Control."

32. Jowett, *Sex and the Slayer*, 104.

33. Emma Goldman, "What I Believe," in *Red Emma Speaks: An Emma Goldman Reader*, ed. Alix Kates Shulman (New York: Humanity Books, 1996), 52.

34. *Ibid.*, 54.

35. *Ibid.*, 53.

36. For more on Kendra, see Lynne Edwards, "'The black chick always gets it first': Black Slayers in Sunnydale," in *Joss Whedon and Race: Critical Essays*, eds. Mary Ellen Iatropoulos and Lowery A. Woodall III (Jefferson, NC: McFarland, 2017). Kindle edition.

37. Nussbaum, "Objectification."

38. For more on Kendra, see Jessica Prata Miller, "The I in Team: Buffy and Feminist Ethics," in *Buffy The Vampire Slayer and Philosophy*, ed. James B. South (Chicago: Open Court, 2003), 35–48.

39. Lucy Parsons, "Woman: Her Evolutionary Development," in *Lucy Parsons: Freedom, Equality, and Solidarity, Writings and Speeches, 1878–1937*, eds. Gale Ahrens and Roxanne Dunbar Ortiz (Chicago: Charles H. Kerr, 2004), 93.

40. *Ibid.*

41. For more on Buffy's insistence on carving out an autonomous life path, see Mona Rocha, "A Layered Message of Resistance: Buffy, Violence, and the Double Bind," in *Buffy Conquers the Academy: Conference Papers from the 2009/2010 Popular Culture/American Culture Associations*, ed. U. Melissa Anyiwo and Karoline Szatek-Tudor (Newcastle Upon Tyne: Cambridge Scholars, 2013), 32–47.

42. For some feminist thinkers who make these points, see Alison Jaggar, "Love and Knowledge: Emotion in Feminist Epistemology," *Inquiry* 32(2): 151–176. Also see Carol Gillian, *In a Different Voice* (Cambridge: Harvard University Press, 1982).

43. Emma Goldman, "The Tragedy of Woman's Emancipation," in *Red Emma Speaks: An Emma Goldman Reader*, ed. Alix Kates Shulman (New York: Humanity Books, 1996), 167.

44. For more on these themes, see Deborah L. Rhode, *The Beauty Bias: The Injustice of Appearance in Life and Law* (Oxford: Oxford University Press, 2011); Roxanne Gay, *Hunger: A Memoir of My Body* (New York: Harper, 2017); Naomi Wolf, *The Beauty Myth: How Images of Beauty Are Used Against Women* (New York: Harper Perennial, 2002).

45. For more on The Council, see Nagine

Farghaly, "Patriarchy Strikes Back: Power and Perception in Buffy the Vampire Slayer," in *Buffy Conquers the Academy: Conference Papers From the 2009/2010 Popular Culture/ American Culture Associations*, ed. U. Melissa Anyiwo and Karoline Szatek-Tudor (Newcastle Upon Tyne: Cambridge Scholars, 2013), 19–31.

46. For more on the theme of high school as metaphor, see Tracy Little, "High School is Hell: Metaphor Made Literal in *Buffy the Vampire Slayer*," in *Buffy the Vampire Slayer and Philosophy*, ed. James B. South (Chicago: Open Court, 2003), 282–293. Also see Candace Havens, *Joss Whedon: The Genius Behind Buffy* (Dallas: Benbella Books, 2003), 33. Havens quotes Whedon on the subject.

Chapter Six

1. Emma Goldman, "What I Believe," in *Red Emma Speaks: An Emma Goldman Reader*, ed. Alix Kates Shulman (New York: Humanity Books, 1996), 52, 50.

2. *Ibid.*

3. Emma Goldman, "Syndicalism: Its Theory and Practice," in *Red Emma Speaks: An Emma Goldman Reader*, ed. Alix Kates Shulman (New York: Humanity Books, 1996), 96.

4. Lucy Parsons, "The Principles of Anarchism," in *Lucy Parsons: Freedom, Equality, and Solidarity, Writings and Speeches, 1878–1937*, eds. Gale Ahrens and Roxanne Dunbar Ortiz (Chicago: Charles H. Kerr, 2004), 34.

5. Lawrence B. Rosenfeld and Scarlet L. Wynns note that *Buffy the Vampire Slayer* illustrates and models for the viewing audience several values, such as emotional support, personal assistance support, and task challenge support, among others. See Lawrence B. Rosenfeld and Scarlet L. Wynns, "Perceived Values and Social Support in Buffy the Vampire Slayer," *Slayage: The Journal of Whedon Studies* 3.2 [10] (November 2003). Web.

6. *Ibid.*

7. For more on militant feminism, see Mona Rocha and James Rocha, "No Women Up In the Game," in David Bzdak, Joanna Crosby, and Seth Vannatta, eds, *The Wire and Philosophy* (Chicago: Open Court, 2013). For an interesting parallel to another TV show, consider how former Whedon writer Marti Noxon's new AMC show, *Dietland*, also embodies a militant response to the problems of misogyny, sexism, etc., through its depictions of the Jennifers. See Marti Noxon, creator. *Dietland*. Skydance Television and AMC Studios, 2018.

8. It is important to point out that the media during this time period usually took the term direct action to mean the use of violence, even the use of assassination. For more on this concept, see Crispin Sartwell, "Introduction," in *Exquisite Rebel: The Essays of Voltairine de Cleyre: Anarchist, Feminist, Genius*, eds. Sharon Presley and Crispin Sartwell (Albany: State University of New York Press, 2005), 269.

9. Voltairine de Cleyre, "Direct Action," in *Exquisite Rebel: The Essays of Voltairine de Cleyre: Anarchist, Feminist, Genius*, eds. Sharon Presley and Crispin Sartwell (Albany: State University of New York Press, 2005), 275–276.

10. *Ibid.*, 276.

11. *Ibid.*, 284.

12. Emma Goldman, "The Psychology of Political Violence," in *Red Emma Speaks: An Emma Goldman Reader*, ed. Alix Kates Shulman (New York: Humanity Books, 1996), 257

13. Goldman, "The Psychology of Political Violence," 279.

14. Emma Goldman, "An Open Letter," *Emma Goldman: Made for America, 1890–1901*, ed. Candace Falk (Urbana: University of Illinois Press, 2008), 435.

15. Goldman, "Syndicalism: It's Theory and Practice," 98.

16. *Ibid.*, 99.

17. Lucy Parsons, "Speeches at the Founding Convention of the Industrial Workers of the World," in *Lucy Parsons: Freedom, Equality, and Solidarity, Writings and Speeches, 1878–1937*, eds. Gale Ahrens and Roxanne Dunbar Ortiz (Chicago: Charles H. Kerr, 2004), 78.

18. For more on Willow and her use of magic, and the idea that dark magic turns Willow veiny, see Caroline Ruddell, "'I am the Law' 'I am the Magics': Speech, Power and the Split Identity of Willow in *Buffy the Vampire Slayer*," *Slayage: The Journal of Whedon Studies* 5.4 [20] (May 2006). Web.

19. Emma Goldman, "Anarchism: What It Really Stands For," in *Red Emma Speaks: An*

Emma Goldman Reader, ed. Alix Kates Shulman (New York: Humanity Books, 1996), 64–65.

20. For more on Spike's soul and growth, see K. Dale Koontz, *Faith and Choice in the Works of Joss Whedon* (Jefferson, NC: McFarland, 2008), especially the chapter titled "Growing After Death: Angel, Spike, and the Evolution of the Soul."

21. Scott McLaren, "The Evolution of Joss Whedon's Vampire Mythology and the Ontology of the Soul," *Slayage: The Journal of Whedon Studies* 5.2 [18] (September 2005). Web. McLaren also notes that Spike's determination also allowed for his change to good.

22. For Kevin Durand, Caleb represents hegemonic masculinity. See Kevin K. Durand, "'Are You Ready to Finish This?': The Battle Against the Patriarchal Forces of Darkness," *Slayage: The Journal of Whedon Studies* 7.4 [28] (Summer 2009). Web.

23. Goldman, "Anarchism: What It Really Stands For," 71.

24. *Ibid.*, 70–71.

25. Parsons, "The Principles of Anarchism," 33–34.

26. Voltairine de Cleyre, "Anarchism," in *Exquisite Rebel: The Essays of Voltairine de Cleyre: Anarchist, Feminist, Genius*, eds. Sharon Presley and Crispin Sartwell (Albany: State University of New York Press, 2005), 82.

27. Voltairine de Cleyre, "Sex Slavery," in *Exquisite Rebel: The Essays of Voltairine de Cleyre: Anarchist, Feminist, Genius*, eds. Sharon Presley and Crispin Sartwell (Albany: State University of New York Press, 2005), 231, 235.

28. Voltairine de Cleyre, "The Case of Woman Versus Orthodoxy," in *Exquisite Rebel: The Essays of Voltairine de Cleyre: Anarchist, Feminist, Genius*, eds. Sharon Presley and Crispin Sartwell (Albany: State University of New York Press, 2005), 218.

29. Emma Goldman, "The Tragedy of Woman's Emancipation," in *Red Emma Speaks: An Emma Goldman Reader*, ed. Alix Kates Shulman (New York: Humanity Books, 1996), 165.

Conclusion

1. Amy A. Williams, "'All the Cash, All the Fame, and Social Change': Teaching *Dr. Horrible's Sing-Along Blog* as a Social Message Film." *Slayage: The Journal of Whedon Studies* 11.2/12.1 [38–38] (Summer 2014). Web. She calls it a "regime change."

2. Erin Giannini, *Joss Whedon Versus the Corporation: Big Business Critiqued in the Films and Television Programs* (Jefferson, NC: McFarland, 2017), Chapter 4. Kindle edition.

3. Jaclyn S. Parrish, "People vs. Humanity: Utilitarianism and Genre Critique in the *Cabin in the Woods*," *Slayage: The Journal of Whedon Studies* 15.1 [45] (Winter/Spring 2017). Web.

4. Leo Tolstoy, "On Anarchy," 1900, available at An Online Research Center on the History and Theory of Anarchism, http://dwardmac.pitzer.edu/Anarchist_Archives/bright/tolstoy/onanarchy.html (accessed 8 February 2018).

5. Leo Tolstoy, "The End of the Age: An Essay on the Approaching Revolution," 1905, available at An Online Research Center on the History and Theory of Anarchism, http://dwardmac.pitzer.edu/Anarchist_Archives/bright/tolstoy/onanarchy.html (accessed 8 February 2018).

6. Leo Tolstoy, "On Anarchy."

7. For an opposite view that does not find any agency at work in this refusal, see Michael J. Blouin, "Research Cluster—'A Growing Global Darkness': Dialectics of Culture in Goddards' *The Cabin in the Woods*," *Horror Studies* 6.1 (2015): 83–99. Parrish discusses Marty and Dana as showing agency and as vindicated in refusing to conform to utilitarian outcomes. See Parrish, "People vs. Humanity: Utilitarianism and Genre Critique in the *Cabin in the Woods*."

8. Joss Whedon and Drew Goddard, *The Cabin in the Woods* script, 2012, p. 73.

9. Leo Tolstoy, "On Anarchy."

10. *Ibid.*

11. Leo Tolstoy, "The End of the Age: An Essay on the Approaching Revolution."

Bibliography

Abbott, Stacey. *Angel*. Detroit: Wayne State Press, 2009.
_____. "Kicking Ass and Singing 'Mandy': A Vampire in LA." In *Reading Angel: The TV Spin-Off with a Soul*, ed. Stacey Abbott, 1–13. London: I.B. Tauris, 2005.
_____. "A Little Less Ritual and a Little More Fun: The Modern Vampire in Buffy the Vampire Slayer." *Slayage: The Journal of Whedon Studies* 1.3 [3] (June 2001). Web.
_____. "Walking the Fine Line Between Angel and Angelus." *Slayage: The Journal of Whedon Studies* 3.1 [9] (August 2003). Web.
Adams, Guy, and Danny Balfour. *Unmasking Administrative Evil*. Routledge, 1998[2015].
Alexander, Michelle. *The New Jim Crow: Mass Incarceration in the Age of Colorblindness*. New York: The New Press, 2012.
Anderson, Tami. "Whose Story Is This, Anyway?." In *Inside Joss' Dollhouse: From Alpha to Rossum*, ed. Jane Espenson, 161–173. Dallas: Smart Pop, 2010.
Anyiwo, U. Melissa. "More Than Just A Spin-Off: The Enduring Allure of Angel." In *Buffy Conquers the Academy: Conference Papers from the 2009/2010 Popular Culture/American Culture Associations*, eds. U. Melissa Anyiwo and Karoline Szatek-Tudor, 149–161. Newcastle Upon Tyne: Cambridge, 2013.
Appiah, Kwame Anthony. *The Ethics of Identity*. Princeton: Princeton University Press, 2007.
Archard, David. *Sexual Consent*. Boulder: Westview Press, 1998.
Arpaly, Nomy. *Unprincipled Virtue*. New York: Oxford University Press, 2004.
Bachran, Daoine S. "Mexicans in Space? Joss Whedon's *Firefly*, Reavers, and the Man They Call Jayne." In *Joss Whedon and Race: Critical Essays*, eds. Mary Ellen Iatropolous and Lowery A. Woodall III, Chapter 9. Jefferson NC: McFarland, 2017. Kindle edition.
Bainbridge, Jason. "'You Were the World's First Superhero': Marvel Studio's Superheroes, Law, and the Pursuit of Justice." In *Assembling the Marvel Cinematic Universe: Essays on the Social, Cultural, and Geopolitical Domains*, eds. Julian C. Chambliss, William L. Svitavsky and Daniel Fandino, Chapter 14. Jefferson NC: McFarland, 2018. Kindle edition.
Battis, Jes. "Demonic Maternities, Complex Motherhoods: Cordelia, Fred, and the Puzzle of Illyria." *Slayage: The Journal of Whedon Studies* 5.2 [18] (September 2005). Web.
Beauchamp, Tom. "Autonomy and Consent." In *The Ethics of Consent*, eds. Franklin G. Miller and Alan Wertheimer, 55–78. New York: Oxford University Press, 2010.
Beckett, Jennifer. "Acting with Limited Oversights: S.H.I.E.L.D. and the Role of Intelligence and Intervention in the Marvel Cinematic Universe." In *Assembling the Marvel Cinematic Universe: Essays on the Social, Cultural, and Geopolitical Domains*, eds. Julian

C. Chambliss, William L. Svitavsky and Daniel Fandino, Chapter 18. Jefferson, NC: McFarland, 2018. Kindle edition.
Beeler, Karin. *Seers, Witches and Psychics on Screen: An Analysis of Women Visionary Characters in Recent Television and Film*. Jefferson NC: McFarland, 2008.
Blouin, Michael J. "Research Cluster—'A Growing Global Darkness': Dialectics of Culture in Goddards' *The Cabin in the Woods*." *Horror Studies* 6.1 (2015): 83–99.
Buckman, Alyson. "'Go ahead! Run away! Say it was Horrible!': *Dr. Horrible's Sing-Along Blog* as Resistant Text." *Slayage: The Journal of Whedon Studies* 8.1 [29] (2010). Web.
Butler, Paul. *Let's Get Free: A Hip-Hop Theory of Justice*. New York: The New Press, 2010.
Carter, Ian. "Positive and Negative Liberty." *Stanford Encyclopedia of Philosophy* (2003). Stanford Encyclopedia of Philosophy. Spring 2016. Web.
Chomsky, Noam. *Necessary Illusions: Thought Control in Democratic Societies*. House of Anansi Press, 2013. Kindle edition.
_____. *On Anarchism*. New Press, 2013. Kindle edition.
Clark, Daniel A., and P. Andrew Miller. "Buffy, the Scooby Gang, and Monstrous Authority: *BtVS* and the Subversion of Authority." *Slayage: The Journal of Whedon Studies* 1.3 [3] (2001). Web.
Colvin, Phil. "*Angel*: Redefinition and Justification through Faith." In *Reading Angel: The TV Spin-Off with a Soul*, ed. Stacey Abbott, 17–30. London: I.B. Tauris, 2005.
Connelly, Tom, and Shelly S. Rees. "Alienation and the Dialectics of History in Joss Whedon's *Dollhouse*." *Slayage: The Journal of Whedon Studies* 8.2 & 3 [30–31] (2010). Web.
Davis, Angela J. *Arbitrary Justice: The Power of the American Prosecutor*. Oxford: Oxford University Press, 2007.
de Cleyre, Voltairine. "Anarchism." In *Exquisite Rebel: The Essays of Voltairine de Cleyre: Anarchist, Feminist, Genius*, eds. Sharon Presley and Crispin Sartwell, 69–82. Albany: State University of New York Press, 2005.
_____. "The Case of Woman Versus Orthodoxy." In *Exquisite Rebel: The Essays of Voltairine de Cleyre: Anarchist, Feminist, Genius*, eds. Sharon Presley and Crispin Sartwell, 207–219. Albany: State University of New York Press, 2005.
_____. "Direct Action." In *Exquisite Rebel: The Essays of Voltairine de Cleyre: Anarchist, Feminist, Genius*, eds. Sharon Presley and Crispin Sartwell, 271–286. Albany: State University of New York Press, 2005.
_____. "Sex Slavery." In *Exquisite Rebel: The Essays of Voltairine de Cleyre: Anarchist, Feminist, Genius*, eds. Sharon Presley and Crispin Sartwell, 225–237. Albany: State University of New York Press, 2005.
_____. "Why I Am an Anarchist." In *Exquisite Rebel: The Essays of Voltairine de Cleyre: Anarchist, Feminist, Genius*, eds. Sharon Presley and Crispin Sartwell, 53–65. Albany: State University of New York Press, 2005.
DeBrandt, Don. "Angelus Populi." In *Five Seasons of Angel: Science Fiction and Fantasy Writers Discuss Their Favorite Vampire*, ed. Glenn Yeffeth, Chapter 1. Dallas: Benbella Books, 2004. Kindle edition.
Deritter, Lillian. "We're Not Men." In *Inside Joss' Dollhouse: From Alpha to Rossum*, ed. Jane Espenson, 189–203. Dallas: Smart Pop, 2010.
Donovan, Sarah, and Nick Richardson. "Shining the Light on the Dark Avengers." In *The Avengers and Philosophy: Earth's Mightiest Thinkers*, ed. Mark D. White, 18–27. Wiley, 2012.
Dorceta E. Taylor, *Toxic Communities: Environmental Racism, Industrial Pollution, and Residential Mobility*. New York: New York University Press, 2014.
Dougherty, Tom. "Sex, Lies, and Consent." *Ethics* 123 (July 2013): 717–744.
Durand, Kevin K. "'Are You Ready to Finish This?': The Battle Against the Patriarchal

Forces of Darkness." *Slayage: The Journal of Whedon Studies* 7.4 [28] (Summer 2009). Web.
Dworkin, Gerald. *The Theory and Practice of Autonomy*. New York: Cambridge University Press, 1988.
Edwards, Lynne. "'The black chick always gets it first': Black Slayers in Sunnydale." In *Joss Whedon and Race: Critical Essays,* eds. Mary Ellen Iatropoulos and Lowery A. Woodall III, Chapter 1. Jefferson NC: McFarland, 2017. Kindle edition.
Farghaly, Nagine. "Patriarchy Strikes Back: Power and Perception in Buffy the Vampire Slayer." In *Buffy Conquers the Academy: Conference Papers From the 2009/2010 Popular Culture/American Culture Associations,* eds. U. Melissa Anyiwo and Karoline Szatek-Tudor, 19–31. Newcastle Upon Tyne: Cambridge Scholars, 2013.
Feinberg, Joel. *Harm to Self.* New York: Oxford University Press, 1986.
Frankel, Valerie Estelle. "All Dolled Up: Twisted Princes and Fairytale Heroines." In *Inside Joss' Dollhouse: From Alpha to Rossum,* ed. Jane Espenson, 63–77. Dallas: Smart Pop, 2010.
Freidman, David. *The Machinery of Freedom: Guide to Radical Capitalism.* La Salle, Illinois: Open Court, 1995.
Freidman, Jaclyn, and Jessica Valenti, eds. *Yes Means Yes: Visions of Female Sexual Power and a World Without Rape.* Berkeley: Seal Press, 2008.
Friedman, Marilyn. *Autonomy, Gender, Politics.* Oxford: Oxford University Press, 2003.
Frohard-Dourlent, Hélène. "Someone's Asian in *Dr. Horrible.*" In *Joss Whedon and Race: Critical Essays,* eds. Mary Ellen Iatropoulos and Lowery A. Woodall III, Chapter 15. Jefferson NC: McFarland, 2008. Kindle edition.
Galtung, Johan. "Violence, Peace, and Peace Research." *Journal of Peace Research* Vol. 6, no. 3 (1969): 167–191.
Gay, Roxanne. *Hunger: A Memoir of My Body.* New York: Harper, 2017.
Giannini, Erin. *Joss Whedon versus the Corporation: Big Business Critiqued in the Films and Television Programs.* Jefferson NC: McFarland, 2017.
Gillian, Carol. *In a Different Voice.* Cambridge: Harvard University Press, 1982.
Ginn, Sherry. "Memory, Mind, and Mayhem: Neurological Tampering and Manipulation in *Dollhouse.*" *Slayage: The Journal of Whedon Studies* 8.2-3 [30–31] (Summer/Fall 2010). Web.
_____. *Power and Control in the Television Worlds of Joss Whedon.* Jefferson NC: McFarland, 2012. Kindle edition.
Godwin, William. *An Enquiry Concerning Political Justice.* 1793. Oxford World's Classics: 2013.
Goldman, Emma. "Anarchism: What It Really Stands For." In *Red Emma Speaks: An Emma Goldman Reader,* ed. Alix Kates Shulman, 61–77. New York: Humanity Books, 1996.
_____. "The Individual, Society, and the State." In *Red Emma Speaks: An Emma Goldman Reader,* ed. Alix Kates Shulman, 109–123. New York: Humanity Books, 1996.
_____. "An Open Letter." In *Emma Goldman: Made for America, 1890–1901,* ed. Candace Falk, 434–437. Urbana: University of Illinois Press, 2008.
_____. "The Psychology of Political Violence." In *Red Emma Speaks: An Emma Goldman Reader,* ed. Alix Kates Shulman, 256–279. New York: Humanity Books, 1996.
_____. "The Social Importance of the Modern School." In *Red Emma Speaks: An Emma Goldman Reader,* ed. Alix Kates Shulman, 140–149. New York: Humanity Books, 1996.
_____. "Syndicalism: Its Theory and Practice." In *Red Emma Speaks: An Emma Goldman Reader,* ed. Alix Kates Shulman, 87–100. New York: Humanity Books, 1996.
_____. "The Tragedy of Woman's Emancipation." In *Red Emma Speaks: An Emma Goldman Reader,* ed. Alix Kates Shulman, 158–167. New York: Humanity Books, 1996.

_____. "What I Believe." In *Red Emma Speaks: An Emma Goldman Reader*, ed. Alix Kates Shulman, 48–60. New York: Humanity Books, 1996.
Goldsmith, P. Gardner. "Freedom in an Unfree World." In *Serenity Found: More Unauthorized Essays on Joss Whedon's Firefly Universe*, ed. Jane Espenson, 55–65. Dallas: BenBella Books, 2007.
Graeber, David. *The Utopia of Rules: On Technology, Stupidity, and the Secret Joys of Bureaucracy*. Brooklyn: Melville House, 2015.
Greene, Richard, and Wayne Yuen. "Morality on Television: The Case of *Buffy the Vampire Slayer*." In *Buffy the Vampire Slayer and Philosophy: Fear and Trembling in Sunnydale*, ed. James B. South, 271–281. Chicago: Open Court, 2003.
Halfyard, Janet K. "The Dark Avenger: Angel and the Cinematic Superhero." In *Reading Angel: The TV Spin-Off with a Soul*, ed. Stacey Abbott, 149–162. London: I.B. Tauris, 2005.
Harris, Howard. "*Buffy the Vampire Slayer* in the Business Ethics Classroom." *Slayage: The Journal of Whedon Studies* 7.3 [27] (Winter 2009). Web.
Harrison, Janine R. "Gender Politics in *Angel*: Traditional vs. Non-Traditional Corporate Climates." In *Reading Angel: The TV Spin-Off with a Soul*, ed. Stacey Abbott, 117–131. London: I.B. Tauris, 2005.
Havens, Candace. *Joss Whedon: The Genius Behind Buffy*. Dallas: Benbella Books, 2003.
Hawk, Julie. "Hacking the Read-Only File: Collaborative Narrative as Ontological Construction in Dollhouse." *Slayage: The Journal of Whedon Studies* 8.2–3 [30–31], Summer/Fall 2010. Web.
_____. "More Than the Sum of Our Imprints." In *Inside Joss' Dollhouse: From Alpha to Rossum*, ed. Jane Espenson, 247–257. Dallas: Smart Pop, 2010.
Hayek, F.A. *The Constitution of Liberty*. Chicago: University of Chicago Press, 1960.
Hayes, K. Stoddard. "Where Have All the Good Guys Gone?." In *Five Seasons of Angel: Science Fiction and Fantasy Writers Discuss Their Favorite Vampire*, ed. Glenn Yeffeth, Chapter 15. Dallas: Benbella Books, 2004. Kindle edition.
Herman, Edward S., and Noam Chomsky. *Manufacturing Consent: The Political Economy of the Mass Media*. Pantheon Books, 2002[1988]. Kindle edition.
Hills, Matt, and Rebecca Williams. "*Angel*'s Monstrous Mothers and Vampires with Souls: Investigating the Abject in 'Television Horror.'" In *Reading Angel: The TV Spin-Off with a Soul*, ed. Stacey Abbott, 203–217. London: I.B. Tauris, 2005.
Hinson, Sara T. "Freedom and Firefly—Mal Reynolds, Libertarian." *America's Future Foundation*. America's Future Foundation, n.d. Web.
Ho, Kathleen. "Structural Violence as a Human Rights Violation." *Essex Human Rights Review* Vol. 4, no. 2 (September 2007): 1–17.
Hurd, Heidi M. "The Moral Magic of Consent." *Legal Theory* 2, no. 2 (1996): 121–146.
Iatropolous, Mary Ellen, and Lowery A. Woodall III. "Introduction: The Individual, the Institutional, and the Unitentional: Exploring the Whedonverses Through Critical Race Theory." In *Joss Whedon and Race: Critical Essays*, eds. Mary Ellen Iatropolous and Lowery A. Woodall III, Introductory Chapter. Jefferson NC: McFarland, 2017. Kindle edition.
_____. *Joss Whedon and Race: Critical Essays*. Jefferson NC: McFarland, 2017. Kindle edition.
Jacob, Benjamin. "Los Angelus: The City of Angel." In *Reading Angel: The TV Spin-Off with a Soul*, ed. Stacey Abbott, 75–87. London: I.B. Tauris, 2005.
Jaggar, Alison. "Love and Knowledge: Emotion in Feminist Epistemology." *Inquiry* 32(2): 151–176.
Jarvis, Christine. "Battle of the Blockbusters: Joss Whedon as Public Pedagogue." *Slayage: The Journal of Whedon Studies* 14.1 [43] (Winter 2016). Web.

Jencson, Linda Jean. "'Aiming to Misbehave': Role Modeling Political-Economic Conditions and Political Action in the *Serenity*verse." *Slayage: The Journal of Whedon Studies* 7.1 [25] (Winter 2008). Web.
"Joss Whedon Just Wants to be Loved." In *Joss Whedon: Conversations*, eds. David Lavery and Cynthia Burkhead, 184–190. Jackson: University Press of Mississippi, 2011.
Jowett, Lorna. *Sex and the Slayer: A Gender Studies Primer for the Buffy Fan*. Middletown: Wesleyan, 2005.
Kaveney, Roz. "A Sense of Ending: Schrodinger's *Angel*." In *Reading Angel: The TV Spin-Off with a Soul*, ed. Stacey Abbott, 57–72. London: I.B. Tauris, 2005.
Kirlkand, Ewan. "The Caucasian Persuasion of *Buffy the Vampire Slayer*." *Slayage: The Journal of Whedon Studies* 5.1 [17] (June 2005). Web.
Klein, Ian G. "I Like My Scars: Claire Saunders and the Narrative of Flesh." In *Inside Joss' Dollhouse: From Alpha to Rossum*, ed. Jane Espenson, 117–131. Dallas: Smart Pop, 2010).
Kleinig, John. "The Nature of Consent." In *The Ethics of Consent*, eds. Franklin G. Miller and Alan Wertheimer, 3–24. New York: Oxford University Press, 2010.
Koenig, Brigitte. "American Anarchism: The Politics of Gender, Culture, and Community from Haymarket to the First World War." PhD Dissertation, University of California, Berkeley, 2000.
Koontz, K. Dale. *Faith and Choice in the Works of Joss Whedon*. Jefferson NC: McFarland, 2008.
_____. "Reflections in the Pool: Echo, Narcissus, and the Male Gaze in *Dollhouse*." In *Reading Joss Whedon*, eds. Rhonda Wilcox, Tanya Cochran, Cynthea Masson and David Lavery, 205–220. Syracuse: Syracuse University Press, 2014.
Kropotkin, Peter. "Anarchism." Originally in *The Encyclopedia Britannica*. In *Anarchism: A Collection of Revolutionary Writings*, ed. Roger N. Baldwin, 283–299. Dover Publications, 2002[1905].
_____. "Anarchist Communism: Its Basis and Principles." In *Anarchism: A Collection of Revolutionary Writings*, ed. Roger N. Baldwin, 44–78. Dover Publications, 2002[1887].
_____. *The Conquest of Bread*. 1892. Dover Publications, 2013.
_____. *Mutual Aid; A Factor of Evolution*. 1902. A Public Domain Book, 2011.
Lackey, Mercedes. "*Serenity* and Bobby McGee: Freedom and the Illusion of Freedom in Joss Whedon's *Firefly*." In *Finding Serenity*, ed. Jane Espenson, 63–73. Dallas: BenBella Books, 2004.
le Guin, Ursula. *Dispossessed*. New York: HarperCollins, 1974.
Lee, Tiffany Kristin. "The Justice Systems of Slayers and Vengeance Demons: Prosecutorial Discretion in *Buffy the Vampire Slayer*." *Slayage: The Journal of Whedon Studies* 10.1 [35] (Winter 2013). Web.
Lichtenberg, Jacqueline. "Victim Triumphant." In *Five Seasons of Angel: Science Fiction and Fantasy Writers Discuss Their Favorite Vampire*, ed. Glenn Yeffeth, Chapter 14. Dallas: Benbella Books, 2004. Kindle edition.
Little, Tracy. "High School is Hell: Metaphor Made Literal in *Buffy the Vampire Slayer*." In *Buffy the Vampire Slayer and Philosophy*, ed. James B. South, 282–293. Chicago: Open Court, 2003.
Lorrah, Jean. "A World Without Love: The Failure of Family in *Angel*." In *Five Seasons of Angel: Science Fiction and Fantasy Writers Discuss Their Favorite Vampire*, ed. Glenn Yeffeth, Chapter 6. Dallas: Benbella Books, 2004. Kindle edition.
MacLean, Nancy. *The American Women's Movement, 1945–2000*. Bedford, 2009.
Magón, Ricardo Flores. "The Chains of 'The Free.'" 1910. In *Dreams of Freedom*, eds. Chaz Bufe and Mitchell Cowen Verter, 182–185. Oakland: AK Press, 2005.

_____. "Class Struggle." 1911. In *Dreams of Freedom,* eds. Chaz Bufe and Mitchell Cowen Verter, 187–195. Oakland: AK Press, 2005.
_____. "Letter from L.A. County Jail." 1908. In *Dreams of Freedom,* eds. Chaz Bufe and Mitchell Cowen Verter, 111–116. Oakland: AK Press, 2005.
_____. "Outlaws." 1910. In *Dreams of Freedom,* eds. Chaz Bufe and Mitchell Cowen Verter, 241–242. Oakland: AK Press, 2005.
_____. "The Right to Property." 1911. In *Dreams of Freedom,* eds. Chaz Bufe and Mitchell Cowen Verter, 275–277. Oakland: AK Press, 2005.
_____. "Solidarity." 1910. In *Dreams of Freedom,* eds. Chaz Bufe and Mitchell Cowen Verter, 278–280. Oakland: AK Press, 2005.
_____. "To the Soldiers of Carranza." 1915. In *Dreams of Freedom,* eds. Chaz Bufe and Mitchell Cowen Verter, 166–169. Oakland: AK Press, 2005.
Malatesta, Errico. *Errico Malatesta: His Life and Ideas,* ed.Vernon Richards. Freedom Press, 1965.
Manson, Neil, and Onora O'Neill. *Rethinking Informed Consent in Bioethics.* Cambridge: Cambridge University Press, 2007.
Mappes, Thomas A. "Sexual Morality and the Concept of Using Another Person." In *The Philosophy of Sex: Contemporary Readings,* ed. Alan Soble and Nicholas Power, 229–249. New York: Rowman and Littlefield, 2008.
Marshall, Peter. *Demanding the Impossible: A History of Anarchism.* Oakland: PM Press, 2010.
Mason, Jonathan. "Like a Boss." In *Inside Joss' Dollhouse: From Alpha to Rossum,* ed. Jane Espenson, 95–103. Dallas: Smart Pop, 2010.
Masson, Cynthea. "Who Painted the Lion?—A Gloss on Dollhouse's 'Bella Chose.'" *Slayage: The Journal of Whedon Studies* 8.2-3 [30–31], Summer/Fall 2010. Web.
McClain, Katia. "Representations of the Roma in *Buffy* and *Angel.*" In *Joss Whedon and Race,* eds. Mary Ellen Iatropoulos and Lowery A. Woodall III, Chapter 6. Jefferson NC: McFarland, 2008. Kindle edition.
McClelland, Bruce. "By Whose Authority? The Magical Tradition, Violence and the Legitimation of the Vampire Slayer." *Slayage: The Journal of Whedon Studies* 1.1 [1] (2001). Web.
McKenna, Michael. "The Relationship between Autonomous and Morally Responsible Agency." In *Personal Autonomy,* James Stacey Taylor, ed., 205–234. New York: Cambridge University Press, 2005.
McLaren, Scott. "The Evolution of Joss Whedon's Vampire Mythology and the Ontology of the Soul." *Slayage: The Journal of Whedon Studies* 5.2 [18] (September 2005). Web.
Mele, Alfred. *Autonomous Agents.* New York: Oxford University Press, 2001.
Middents, Jeffrey. "A Sweet Vamp: Critiquing the Treatment of Race in *Buffy* and the American Musical Once More (with Feeling)." *Slayage: The Journal of Whedon Studies* 5/1 [17] (June 2005). Web.
Miller, Jessica Prata. "The I in Team: Buffy and Feminist Ethics." In *Buffy The Vampire Slayer and Philosophy,* ed. James B. South, 35–48. Chicago: Open Court, 2003.
Mills, Matthew. "Ubi Caritas?: Music as Narrative Agent in *Angel.*" In *Reading Angel: The TV Spin-Off with a Soul,* ed. Stacey Abbott, 31–43. London: I.B. Tauris, 2005.
Morohunfola, Oluwafemi. "What Echo's Journey to Self-Awareness Tell Us About the Human Soul." In *Inside Joss' Dollhouse: From Alpha to Rossum,* ed. Jane Espenson, 219–231. Dallas: Smart Pop, 2010.
Mullen, Antony. "Bodies That Shatter: Violence and Spectacle in The Avengers." In *Assembling the Marvel Cinematic Universe: Essays on the Social, Cultural, and Geopolitical Domains,* eds. Julian C. Chambliss, William L. Svitavsky, and Daniel Fandino, Chapter 12. Jefferson: McFarland, 2018. Kindle edition.

Nadkarni, Samira. "'I Believe in Something Greater than Myself': What Authority, Terrorism, and Resistance Have Come to Mean in the Whedonverse." *Slayage: The Journal of Whedon Studies* 13.2 [42] (Summer 2015). Web.

_____. "To Be the Shield: American Imperialism and Explosive Identity Politics in Agents of S.H.I.E.L.D." In *Assembling the Marvel Cinematic Universe: Essays on the Social, Cultural, and Geopolitical Domains*, eds. Julian C. Chambliss, William L. Svitavsky and Daniel Fandino, Chapter 19. Jefferson: McFarland, 2018. Kindle Edition.

Narveson, Jan. *The Libertarian Idea*. Ontario: Broadview Press, 2001.

Natapoff, Alexandra. *Snitching: Criminal Informants and the Erosion of American Justice*. New York: New York University Press, 2009.

Noggle, Robert. "Autonomy and the Paradox of Self-Creation." In *Personal Autonomy*, ed. James Stacey Taylor, 87–108. New York: Cambridge University Press, 2005.

Noxon, Marti. Creator. *Dietland*. Skydance Television and AMC Studios, 2018.

Nozick, Robert. *Anarchy, State, and Utopia*. New York: Basic Books, 1974.

Nussbaum, Martha. "Objectification." *Philosophy and Public Affairs* 24(4): 249–291.

Oshana, Mariana. "Autonomy and Free Agency." In *Personal Autonomy*, ed. James Stacey Taylor, 183–204. New York: Cambridge University Press, 2005.

Parrish, Jaclyn S. "People vs. Humanity: Utilitarianism and Genre Critique in the *Cabin in the Woods*." *Slayage: The Journal of Whedon Studies* 15.1 [45] (Winter/Spring 2017). Web.

Parsons, Lucy. "The Principles of Anarchism." In *Lucy Parsons: Freedom, Equality, and Solidarity, Writings and Speeches, 1878–1937*, eds. Gale Ahrens and Roxanne Dunbar Ortiz, 29–38. Chicago: Charles H. Kerr, 2004.

_____. "Speeches at the Founding Convention of the Industrial Workers of the World." In *Lucy Parsons: Freedom, Equality, and Solidarity, Writings and Speeches, 1878–1937*, eds. Gale Ahrens and Roxanne Dunbar Ortiz, 77–85. Chicago: Charles H. Kerr, 2004.

_____. "Woman: Her Evolutionary Development." In *Lucy Parsons: Freedom, Equality, and Solidarity, Writings and Speeches, 1878–1937*, eds. Gale Ahrens and Roxanne Dunbar Ortiz, 92–93. Chicago: Charles H. Kerr, 2004.

Pasley, Jeffrey L. "Old Familiar Vampires: The Politics of the Buffyverse." In *Buffy The Vampire Slayer and Philosophy*, ed. James B. South, 254–267. Chicago: Open Court, 2003.

Perdigao, Lisa K. "This One's Broken: Rebuilding Whedonbots and Reprogramming the Whedonverse." *Slayage: The Journal of Whedon Studies* 8.2-3 [30–31] (Summer/Fall 2010). Web.

Powell, Robert. "The Self-Corruption of Norman Osborn: A Cautionary Tale." In *The Avengers and Philosophy: Earth's Mightiest Thinkers*, ed. Mark D. White, 71–82. Wiley, 2012.

Quilty, Susan. "Negative Space in the 'House: How Caroline Is the Vase." In *Inside Joss' Dollhouse: From Alpha to Rossum*, ed. Jane Espenson, 133–144. Dallas: Smart Pop, 2010.

Rabb, J. Douglas, and J. Michael Richardson. *Joss Whedon as Shakespearean Moralist: Narrative Ethics of the Bard and the Buffyverse*. Jefferson NC: McFarland, 2014.

Raz, Joseph. *Morality of Freedom*. Oxford: Oxford University Press, 1988.

Reed, George. "Leading questions: Leadership, Ethics, and Administrative Evil," *Leadership*, Vol. 8, no. 2 (May, 2012).

Rennebohm, Kate. "The Mind Doesn't Matter, It's the Body We Want." In *Inside Joss' Dollhouse: From Alpha to Rossum*, ed. Jane Espenson, 5–19. Dallas: Smart Pop, 2010.

Resnick, Laura. "That Angel Doesn't Live Here Anymore." In *Five Seasons of Angel: Science Fiction and Fantasy Writers Discuss Their Favorite Vampire*, ed. Glenn Yeffeth, Chapter 2. Dallas: Benbella Books, 2004. Kindle edition.

Rhode, Deborah L. *The Beauty Bias: The Injustice of Appearance in Life and Law.* Oxford: Oxford University Press, 2011.

Richardson, J. Michael, and J. Douglass Rabb. *The Existential Joss Whedon: Evil and Human Freedom in Buffy the Vampire Slayer, Angel, Firefly, and Serenity.* Jefferson NC: McFarland, 2007. Kindle edition.

Rocha, James. "Autonomy within Subservient Careers," *Ethical Theory & Moral Practice* Vol. 18 (October 2011): 313–328.

_____. "The Black Reaching Out: An Anarchist Analysis of *Firefly.*" *Slayage: The Journal of Whedon Studies.* 14.2 [44]. Summer 2016: 1–23.

Rocha, Mona. "A Layered Message of Resistance: Buffy, Violence, and the Double Bind." In *Buffy Conquers the Academy: Conference Papers From the 2009/2010 Popular Culture/American Culture Associations,* eds. U. Melissa Anyiwo and Karoline Szatek-Tudor, 32–47. Newcastle Upon Tyne: Cambridge Scholars, 2013.

Rocha, Mona, and James Rocha. "No Women Up In the Game." In *The Wire and Philosophy,* eds. David Bzdak, Joanna Crosby, and Seth Vannatta, 153–163. Chicago: Open Court, 2013.

Rosen, Ruth. *The World Split Open: How the Modern Women's Movement Changed America.* New York: Penguin, 2006.

Rosenfeld, Lawrence B., and Scarlet L. Wynns. "Perceived Values and Social Support in Buffy the Vampire Slayer." *Slayage: The Journal of Whedon Studies* 3.2 [10] (November 2003). Web.

Ruddell, Caroline. "'I am the Law' 'I am the Magics': Speech, Power and the Split Identity of Willow in *Buffy the Vampire Slayer.*" *Slayage: The Journal of Whedon Studies* 5.4 [20] (May 2006). Web.

St. Louis, Renee, and Miriam Riggs. "A Painful, Bleeding Sleep: Sleeping Beauty in the *Dollhouse.*" *Slayage: The Journal of Whedon Studies* 8.2–3 [30–31] (Summer/Fall 2010). Web.

Sanchez, Julian. "Out to the Black." *Reason.com.* Reason Foundation, 30 September 2005. Web.

Sartwell, Crispin. "Introduction." In *Exquisite Rebel: The Essays of Voltairine de Cleyre: Anarchist, Feminist, Genius,* eds. Sharon Presley and Crispin Sartwell, 269–270. Albany: State University of New York Press, 2005.

Saulsberry, Rejena. "An Inevitable Tragedy: The Troubled Life of Charles Gunn as an Allegory for General Strain Theory." In *Joss Whedon and Race: Critical Essays,* eds. Mary Ellen Iatropolous and Lowery A. Woodall III, Chapter 7. Jefferson NC: McFarland, 2017. Kindle edition.

Sayer, Karen. "This Was Our World and They Made It Theirs: Reading Space and Place in *Buffy the Vampire Slayer* and *Angel.*" In *Reading the Vampire Slayer: The New Updated Unofficial Guide to Buffy and Angel,* ed. Roz Kaveney, 132–155. London: Tauris Parke, 2007.

Scott, Suzanne. "Modeling the Marvel Everyfan: Agent Coulson and/as Transmedia Fan Culture." *Palabra Clave* 20.4 (December 2017): 1042–1072.

Shelby, Tommie. *Dark Ghettos: Injustice, Dissent, and Reform.* Cambridge: Belknap, 2016.

Shuster, Martin. "What It Means to Mourn." In *Inside Joss' Dollhouse: From Alpha to Rossum,* ed. Jane Espenson, 233–245. Dallas: Smart Pop, 2010.

Simmons, Rachel. *The Hidden Culture of Aggression in Girls.* Mariner Books: New York, 2002.

Souza, Christopher. "Boyd Langton and the Fantasy of Trust." In *Inside Joss' Dollhouse: From Alpha to Rossum,* ed. Jane Espenson, 205–217. Dallas: Smart Pop, 2010.

Spanakos, Tony. "Gods, Beasts, and Political Animals: Why the Avengers Assemble." In

The Avengers and Philosophy: Earth's Mightiest Thinkers, ed. Mark D. White, 98–112. Wiley, 2012.

Spence, Sean. *The Actor's Brain.* New York: Oxford University Press, 2009.

Stoy, Jennifer. "'And Her Tears Flowed Like Wine': Wesley/Lilah and the Complicated (?) Role of the Female Agent on *Angel.*" In *Reading Angel: The TV Spin-Off with a Soul,* ed. Stacey Abbott, 163–175. London: I.B. Tauris, 2005.

_____. "Blood and Choice: The Theory and Practice of Family in *Angel.*" In *Reading the Vampire Slayer: The New Updated Unofficial Guide to Buffy and Angel,* ed. Roz Kaveney, 220–232. London: Tauris Parke, 2007.

Sturgis, Amy H. "'Just Get Us a Little Further': Liberty and the Frontier in *Firefly and Serenity.*" In *The Philosophy of Joss Whedon,* eds. Dean A. Kowalski and S. Evan Kreider, 24–38. Lexington: University of Kentucky Press, 2011.

Sullivan, Shannon. *Revealing Whiteness: The Unconscious Habits of Racial Privilege.* Bloomington: Indiana University Press, 2006.

Sutherland, Sharon, and Sarah Swan. "The Rule of Prophecy: Source of Law in the City of Angel." In *Reading Angel: The TV Spin-Off with a Soul,* ed. Stacey Abbott, 132–145. London: I.B. Tauris, 2005.

_____. "There is No Me; I'm Just a Container: Law and Loss of Personhood in *Dollhouse.*" In *Reading Joss Whedon,* eds. Rhonda Wilcox, Tanya Cochran, Cynthea Masson and David Lavery, 221–236. Syracuse: Syracuse University Press, 2014.

Tanner, Leslie, ed. *Voices From Women's Liberation.* Signet, 1970.

Taylor, Charles. "Responsibility for Self." In *The Identities of Persons,* ed. Amelie Rorty, 281–300. Berkeley: University of California Press, 1976.

Thoreau, Henry David. "On the Duty of Civil Disobedience." 1849. Project Gutenberg EBook, 2004.

Tolstoy, Leo. "The End of the Age: An Essay on the Approaching Revolution." 1905. Available at An Online Research Center on the History and Theory of Anarchism, http://dwardmac.pitzer.edu/Anarchist_Archives/bright/tolstoy/onanarchy.html. Accessed 8 February 2018.

_____. "On Anarchy." 1900. Available at An Online Research Center on the History and Theory of Anarchism, http://dwardmac.pitzer.edu/Anarchist_Archives/bright/tolstoy/onanarchy.html. Accessed 8 February 2018.

Tupper, Peter. "Joss Whedon's *Dollhouse*: 21st Century Neo-Gothic." In *Inside Joss' Dollhouse: From Alpha to Rossum,* ed. Jane Espenson, 47–61. Dallas: Smart Pop, 2010.

Upstone, Sarah. "'LA's Got it All': Hybridity and Otherness in *Angel*'s Postmodern City." In *Reading Angel: The TV Spin-Off with a Soul,* ed. Stacey Abbott, 101–113. London: I.B. Tauris, 2005.

Valenti, Jessica. *Full Frontal Feminism: A Young Woman's Guild to Why Feminism Matters.* Berkeley: Seal Press, 2014.

Waggoner, Erin B., ed. *Sexual Rhetoric in the Works of Joss Whedon: New Essays.* Jefferson NC: McFarland, 2010.

Wertheimer, Alan. "Consent and Sexual Relations." In *The Philosophy of Sex: Contemporary Readings,* ed. Alan Soble and Nicholas Power, 289–317. New York: Rowman and Littlefield, 2008.

_____. *Consent to Sexual Relations.* Cambridge: Cambridge University Press, 2003.

Whedon, Joss, and Drew Goddard. *The Cabin in the Woods* script. 2012.

Whedon, Joss, Brett Matthews, Will Conrad (Art), Laura Martin (Colors), Michael Heisler (Letters), and Adam Hughes (Cover Art). *Serenity: Those Left Behind.* Milwaukee: Dark Horse Books, Serenity Series, Book 1, 2nd Edition, 2012. Kindle edition.

Whedon, Joss, Zack Whedon, Chris Samnee (Art), Dave Stewart (Colors), Michael Heisler

(Letters), and Steve Morris (Cover Art). *Serenity: The Shepherd's Tale.* Milwaukee: Dark Horse Books, Serenity Series, Book 3, 2010. Kindle edition.

White, Mark D., ed. *The Avengers and Philosophy: Earth's Mightiest Thinkers.* Wiley, 2012.

_____. "Superhuman Ethics Class with the Avengers Prime." In *The Avengers and Philosophy: Earth's Mightiest Thinkers,* ed. Mark D. White, 5–17. Wiley, 2012.

Wilcox, Rhonda V. "Echoes of Complicity: Reflexivity and Identity in Joss Whedon's Dollhouse." *Slayage: The Journal of Whedon Studies* 8.2-3 [30–31] (Summer/Fall 2010). Web.

_____ "There Will Never Be a 'Very Special *Buffy*': *Buffy* and the Monsters of Teen Life." *Slayage: The Journal of Whedon Studies* 1.2 [2] (March 2001). Web.

Williams, Amy A. "'All the Cash, All the Fame, and Social Change': Teaching *Dr. Horrible's Sing-Along Blog* as a Social Message Film." *Slayage: The Journal of Whedon Studies* 11.2/12.1 [38–38] (Summer 2014). Web.

Wolf, Naomi. *The Beauty Myth: How Images of Beauty Are Used Against Women.* New York: Perennial, 2002.

Wolf, Susan. "Freedom within Reason." In *Personal Autonomy,* ed. James Stacey Taylor, 258–276. New York: Cambridge University Press, 2005.

Wolff, Robert Paul. *In Defense of Anarchism.* Berkeley: University of California Press, 1998.

Yarbro, Chelsea Quin. "Angel: An Identity Crisis." In *Five Seasons of Angel: Science Fiction and Fantasy Writers Discuss Their Favorite Vampire,* ed. Glenn Yeffeth, Chapter 8. Dallas: Benbella Books, 2004. Kindle edition.

Zaidan, Sarah. "Stark Contrasts: Reinventing Iron Man for 21st Century Cinema." In *Assembling the Marvel Cinematic Universe: Essays on the Social, Cultural, and Geopolitical Domains,* eds. Julian C. Chambliss, William L. Svitavsky and Daniel Fandino, Chapter 8. Jefferson: McFarland, 2018. Kindle edition.

Zanetti, Lisa, and Guy Adams. "In Service of the Leviathan: Democracy, Ethics and the Potential for Administrative Evil in the New Public Management." *Administrative Theory & Praxis* Vol. 22, No. 3 (2000): 534–554.

Zimmerman Jones, Andrew. "The Redemption of Topher Brink." In *Inside Joss' Dollhouse: From Alpha to Rossum,* ed. Jane Espenson, 79–92. Dallas: Smart Pop, 2010.

Index

Adam 159
administrative evil *see* evil
"Agents of Hydra" 92
Agents of S.H.I.E.L.D. see *Marvel Agents of S.H.I.E.L.D.*
Aida "Ophelia" 95–96
The Alarm 136
The Alliance 17, 20, 108, 115–117, 119–121, 127–130, 132
Alpha 55, 61, 71–72, 74
anarcha-feminism 3, 18, 112, 133–139, 151, 154–155, 157, 159, 161, 163, 165–166, 168, 171–173
"Anarchist Communism: Its Basis and Principles" 91
anarcho-capitalism 9, 17, 106, 107–108, 110–112, 114–115, 117–118, 123–126, 132, 139, 177; *see also* capitalism; libertarianism
anarcho-collectivism 112
anarcho-communism 83–85, 91, 97, 101, 112
anarcho-pacifism 181–182
anarcho-socialism 17, 77, 83, 106, 107, 109, 112–116, 120–123, 125, 130, 132–133, 136, 139, 176–177, 197n39
anarcho-syndicalism 112, 163
Angel (TV series) 1, 7, 15, 17, 19–20, 22, 23–24, 43, 49–50, 60, 72–73, 79, 80–81, 87, 107–108, 134, 142, 172, 175–176
Angel (vampire) 1, 18, 19–20, 23–27, 28–31, 33–34, 36, 38, 41–46, 80, 100, 107–108, 128–129, 137, 142, 154, 160, 168, 170, 175, 180, 188n16; *see also* Angelus
Angel Investigations 3, 24, 29, 36–37, 80, 183
Angelus 25–26, 140; *see also* Angel
Archduke Sebassis 44
Archduke Sebassis' slave 44
"Ariel" (*Firefly* 1.9) 117
The Attic 66, 72
authority 10–11, 138–139, 141–142, 144–146, 148, 151–152, 156, 165, 168–169, 171–172, 180
autonomy 9–11, 16–18, 48, 50–51, 62–78, 83, 89–90, 93, 96, 108, 134, 136, 138–146, 148, 150, 152, 163–164, 166, 170–172, 176–183

Avengers 3, 16, 82–83, 85, 96–97, 101–107, 176, 183
Avengers (film) 7, 16, 78, 83, 85–86, 101–103, 105, 109, 172, 176
Avengers: Age of Ultron 16, 78, 82–83, 101–102, 104, 105, 109, 172

"Bad Girls" (*Buffy* 3.14) 160
Badger 110
Ballard, Paul 72, 74
Banner, Bruce *see* The Hulk
Barton, Clint *see* Hawkeye
Barton, Laura 102
belief 44, 60, 117, 127–129
Bell, Jeffrey 80
belly of the beast 28–29
Bester 131
big bad 2, 20, 102, 108, 134, 155
Black Thorn *see* Circle of the Black Thorn
Black Widow 100, 104
Book, Derrial "Shepherd" 80, 110, 119–120, 124–125, 127–130, 177
brain-pocalypse *see* thought-pocalypse
"A Brief History of the Universe" 117
"Bring on the Night" (*Buffy* 7.10) 167
Brink, Topher 50–51, 55, 58, 62, 65–71, 78, 192–193n50
The Bronze 162
Browncoats 117
Buffy, the Vampire Slayer 1, 3, 15, 17–18, 20, 48, 72–73, 109, 133–134, 137, 139, 142, 153–154, 161, 169, 171–173, 177
Buffyverse 140, 151, 168, 170,
bureaucracy 29, 92–95
Burgess, Rance 124, 126
Burkle, Winifred "Fred" 27, 41–42
"Bushwhacked" (*Firefly* 1.3) 127

Cabin in the Woods 18, 20, 178–183
Caleb 155, 165, 167, 169
Campbell, Lincoln 89–90
Canton 123–124
capitalism 24–25, 33–34, 49, 59–61, 63–64,

67, 70–71, 84, 88, 90–91, 99, 106, 108, 112, 114–115, 123–124, 126, 132, 135–136, 155, 172, 175–176; *see also* anarcho-capitalism; libertarianism
Captain America 98, 100–101, 104
Captain America: The Winter Soldier 86
"The Cautionary Tale of Numero Cinco" (*Angel* 5.6) 29–30
Ceccoli, Anthony *see* Victor
Chase, Cordelia 1, 42–44, 80, 109, 137–139, 144, 189n55
Chitauri 85, 101, 103
Chomsky, Noam 51, 59–61, 63–65, 67, 75–78, 106
Circle of the Black Thorn 45–46
Clairvoyant *see* Garrett, John
Cleveland 171–172
Cobb, Jayne 17, 108–110, 117–118, 120, 122–125, 127, 154, 176–177
coercion 9, 11, 13, 31, 35, 41, 48, 52, 64, 76–77, 91, 114, 123, 136, 138, 140, 179–183
competency 55
composite personality 71–77
Connor 44
The Conquest of Bread 84, 90, 112
consent 16, 48, 50–55, 57–61, 75, 77–78, 108–111, 114, 118–122, 124–125, 130–131, 134, 140–143, 145, 180
"Consequences" (*Buffy* 3.15) 160
"Conversations with Dead People: A Buffy & Angel Podcast" 4
corporation 14, 16, 23, 38, 60, 66, 75, 78, 88, 93, 100, 109, 155, 172–173, 176
the Costco of death 181
Costley, Madeline *see* November
Coulson, Phil 79–83, 85, 87–90, 92–96, 100, 106, 168, 194n4
Craft, Carl William *see* Alpha
Cruciamentum 144, 151

Darla 140–141
death 6, 11, 16, 19, 22, 49, 66, 74–75, 100, 126, 128–130, 140, 145, 160, 164, 175, 179–183
death machine 181
de Cleyre, Voltairine 136, 138, 154, 157–158, 170–171
democracy 11, 14, 24, 167–168
DeWitt, Adele 51–52, 54–56, 61, 66–70, 190n6, 191n23
direct action 157–158, 200n8
The Director 179–182
Dobson, Lawrence 117–119, 130
Dr. Horrible 6–7, 11–14, 20, 36, 175
Dr. Horrible's Sing-Along Blog 6–7, 20, 80, 175–176, 185n1–185n4
The Dollhouse 49, 53–59, 61, 68, 74, 196n38
Dollhouse (TV series) 1, 15–16, 20, 48–51, 54, 59–61, 67, 78, 79–81, 87, 107–109, 134, 142, 145, 172, 176
Drake, Lucien 37–38
Drusilla 140–141

Early, Jubal 127
Echo 16, 50–55, 61, 62, 64, 66, 68, 71–77, 109, 154, 176, 178, 183
egalitarianism 91, 134–135, 139, 151, 155–156, 158, 168–172, 176–177
An Enquiry Concerning Political Justice 31–32
epiphany 47–48, 129, 175
"Epiphany" (*Angel* 2.16) 47–48
"Epitaph Two: Return" (*Dollhouse* 2.13) 51, 72
Eve 23, 25, 40
evil 19–23, 25–30, 39, 41–42, 44–48, 66, 69, 71–73, 80, 82, 87–88, 90, 93–95, 98, 103, 106, 126, 129, 135, 139, 141–144, 149, 151, 154–159, 161, 164–166, 168, 170, 173, 175, 183; administrative evil 93, 192n48
Evil League of Evil 20

the facility 18, 20, 178, 179, 181–183
Farrell, Caroline *see* Echo
feminism 2, 37, 109, 125, 135–137, 150, 152, 154, 157, 163, 172; militant feminism 157
Finn, Riley 145–147, 156–158, 162–163
Firefly 1, 15, 17, 20, 21, 80, 106, 107–109, 114–115, 126–127, 129, 131–134, 172, 176–177
The First 165–170, 172
Fitch, Allan 160
Fitz, Leopold 95, 106
floaty girl 182
The Framework 95–96
freedom 2, 48, 49–53, 55, 57, 63–64, 77, 79, 82, 84–85, 90–91, 97, 99–100, 102, 104, 110, 112, 114–117, 119, 121, 131–133, 136, 141, 143–144, 147, 149–150, 155, 158, 170–171, 176–177, 179, 181; economic 91, 112, 114, 117; political 91, 112, 141; social 53, 112, 177
Friedman, David 110–111, 113
friendship 50–51, 63–64, 70, 75, 93, 137–139, 143, 146–149, 151, 155, 157, 159–164, 172, 177
Fries, Corbin 40–41
Frye, Kaylee 109, 117, 120, 127, 129–131, 177
Fury, Nicholas "Nick" 86, 92, 99–102, 104

Galtung, Johan 21–22
Gandhi, Mahatma 181
Garrett, John "Clairvoyant" 87, 89
gender norms 135–138, 144, 149, 151, 180–181
gender revolution 171
Ghost Rider 92
Giles, Rupert 143–144, 148–152, 154–156, 159–161, 165–167, 171, 178
global warming 66
Godwin, William 31–33, 39–42, 44, 46–48, 106
Goldman, Emma 136, 138, 141, 144, 146–147, 150, 152, 154–155, 158, 163–164, 166, 168, 171
government 1–3, 7–9, 13, 20, 22, 24, 31–34, 47, 59, 70, 75, 78, 82, 84, 88, 91, 93–94, 97, 104, 112, 115–117, 123, 131–132, 139, 181–182
Graeber, David 34–37, 106
grief 55, 58, 74–76
Gunn, Charles 27, 29–30, 37–39, 40–41, 80

Hadley, Steve 178–180
Hammer, Captain 12
Hand, Victoria 85, 88–89
Harris, Xander 135, 154–156, 159–160, 164–165, 167, 171–172
Hawkeye 100, 102
"Heart of Gold" (*Firefly* 1.13) 124–127
Hellmouth 137, 171
Herman, Edward S. 59–61, 65
"Hero of Canton: The Ballad of Jayne Cobb" 123–124
Hessiah Stitch *see* Stitch
hierarchy 2, 7–9, 12, 14, 16–18, 21, 31, 35, 48–51, 64, 67–68, 71, 78, 79–88, 90, 92–93, 95–97, 99–102, 105–106, 107–109, 112, 114, 117, 132–137, 139–142, 144, 146–147, 150, 152–154, 161, 165–168, 170, 172, 174–179, 181–183
Higgins, Boss 123–124
high school 1, 134, 137–139, 143, 153–155
Hill, Maria 101
history professor/teacher 83
Hive 90, 92
homelessness 10, 12, 15, 19, 31, 35, 77, 175
hope 12, 18, 30, 42–43, 62, 70–71, 78, 104, 131, 172, 181
hubris 102–104, 106
Hulk 97–99, 102–104
Hydra 16, 82, 87–90, 92, 94–96, 106, 154, 178

indoctrination 76–77, 135
Industrial Workers of the World 4, 112, 136
Inhumans 81, 91–92, 195n26
Initiative 134, 142, 145–146, 153, 158–159, 162, 172
instrumentality 142–145, 147, 149, 151–152, 180–181
internal revolution 178, 181–182
Iron Man 98–102, 104, 106, 176
Ivy 72

Jarvis 98, 104; *see also* Vision
"Jaynestown" (*Firefly* 1.7) 123–124, 126
Jenkins, Anya 164
Johnson, Daisy *see* Skye

Kendall, Harmony 138
Kennedy 165, 169
King, Martin Luther, Jr. 181
The Kingdom of God Is Within You 181
Kinnard, Nolan 55, 68
Koenig, Eric 89
Krevlornswath of the Deathwok Clan *see* Lorne
Kropotkin, Peter 82–87, 90–92, 97, 101, 104–106, 112

Langton, Boyd 55, 66, 68
law 13–14, 20–22, 23, 25–28, 32–42, 87, 133, 141, 168, 173–176
Lehane, Faith 160–167, 169–171
libertarianism 107–126, 128–132, 134, 154, 196n3; *see also* anarcho-capitalism; capitalism
liberty *see* freedom
Lin, Wendy 179
Living My Life 136
Lockley, Kate 36, 47
Loki 85, 98–101, 103
Lorne 25, 40–41
Los Angeles 19, 22, 23, 31, 51, 186n2
Louden, Jules 178–180
love 3, 18, 72–76, 79, 105, 115, 117, 122, 125–126, 147, 152, 154–155, 157–158, 160–166, 172, 175–177, 182–183
"A Love Supreme" (*Dollhouse* 2.8) 74–75

Mace, Jeffrey 81, 92–95
MacKenzie, Alphonso "Mack" 79, 106
Madame Hydra Ophelia *see* Aida "Ophelia"
Magón, Ricardo Flores 112–113, 115, 132–133
Malatesta, Errico 115, 122, 129
"Man on the Street" (*Dollhouse* 1.6) 74
Manners, Holland 19–20
marketing 34, 49, 60–61
martyrdom 46–47, 70
Marvel Agents of S.H.I.E.L.D. 16, 20, 78, 79–85, 92, 95–96, 102, 105–107, 134, 142, 176, 185n6
Marxism 2, 90
The Master 140–141
Maximoff, Wanda *see* Scarlet Witch
May, Melinda 79, 92–94, 106
the Mayor 155, 161, 163
McClay, Tara 146, 162, 164
McCrea, Holden 178
McDonald, Lindsey 46
media 59–61, 63–65, 67, 70–71, 75–78, 79, 82, 142
medical ethics 118
"Meet the New Boss" (*Marvel Agents of S.H.I.E.L.D.* 4.2) 93–94
"The Message" (*Firefly* 1.12) 130–131
Mikalski, Marty 178, 180–183
mind stone 104
morality 8, 10, 11, 13–14, 23–24, 27–29, 31–34, 37–38, 40–41, 43–44, 46–48, 50, 52–55, 57, 64–73, 76–77, 83–84, 86–87, 89, 96–99, 101, 103–105, 108–131, 137, 139, 142–145, 147, 156–158, 160–166, 172, 175, 179–180, 183
Morgan, Lilah 27–28, 37
Mother Earth 136
Mouse, Mickey 100
mudders 21, 108, 123–124
mutual aid 48, 105–106, 113, 115, 155, 163
"Mutual Aid & Mutual Support" 105
Mynor, Joel 74–75
Mynor, Rebecca 74–75

Nandi 125–126
narcissism 65–70
Nazis 95–96
negative duties 114–115, 121

negative liberty 114–115, 129
Newscorp 22
Niska, Adelai 120–121
November 55, 58, 61
Nozick, Robert 110–111

objectification 140, 142–145, 148, 152, 179–180
"On the Duty of Civil Disobedience" 12–13
oppression 32–34, 36–37, 41, 81, 125, 135, 137, 139, 141, 149–150, 152, 158, 164, 178, 182, 197n39
Order of Aurelius 141
Osbourne, Daniel "Oz" 146–147, 156, 158
outlaw 132–133

Parsons, Albert 136
Parsons, Lucy 136, 139, 141, 149, 154–155, 163–164, 169
paternalism 115, 132, 160, 166
patriarchy 37, 125, 134–136, 138, 142, 144, 149–152, 160–161, 171–172; *see also* sexism
Penny 175
Pescaline D 120–122
philosophy professor 27, 83
Polk, Dana 178, 180–183
positive duties 111, 114–122, 124, 126–129, 131
positive liberty 114–116, 122, 124–126, 131–132
positive obligation 108
positive right 133
Potentials 165, 167–172, 182
poverty 12, 22, 108, 111, 126, 128
power 2, 6–7, 9–12, 20–24, 32, 41, 49, 61, 65, 69, 75–77, 79, 81–82, 84–87, 90–91, 94, 97, 100, 112–114, 126, 136–137, 139–141, 146, 148, 150, 158, 160–162, 164, 166–167, 170–172, 176, 180–181, 185n3
propaganda 51, 59–60, 65, 95, 141–142, 145
property 17, 31, 34–35, 57, 83, 91, 110–113, 115, 121, 135; common property 112–113, 115, 123
prostitution 40, 56, 124–127
public relations 93–94
The Purge 3

Quake *see* Skye

race theory 2, 185n1, 194n2
rape 44, 55, 68
reavers 127
relational aggression 137–138
"Reprise" (*Angel* 2.15) 19–20, 47
Reynolds, Malcolm "Mal" 7, 17, 80, 108–110, 116–122, 124–125, 127–128, 130–133, 154, 176–177
Rodriguez, Elena "Yo-Yo" 79, 106
Rogers, Steve *see* Captain America
Romanoff, Natasha *see* Black Widow
Rosenberg, Willow 137–139, 147, 154–156, 159–162, 164, 170–171
Ross, Marcie 137
Rossum Corporation 1, 3, 14, 16, 20, 54, 60, 64, 66, 69–70, 76, 78, 108, 154, 176, 178–179

"Safe" (*Firefly* 1.5) 118
Saffron 133
sarcasm 99, 135, 151–152
saving the world 3, 16, 90, 99, 102–104, 142, 150, 155–156, 164–165, 171–172, 177–178, 180–182
Scarlet Witch 103
Scoobies 3, 7, 18, 134–135, 137, 139, 147, 149, 154–161, 163–169, 172, 183
secrecy 1, 85–95, 98, 102, 148, 159, 178
self-aware 71–72, 147, 162–163
self-ownership 108, 110–111, 114–117, 121–122, 126
self-sacrifice 97, 117–118, 123–125, 128, 131, 163, 181–182
Serenity (film) 17, 116–118, 127
"Serenity" (*Firefly* 1.1) 118, 130
Serenity (ship) 17, 116–117, 126, 131, 183
Serra, Inara 80, 109, 125, 132
sex 56–57, 62, 68, 125, 131, 136, 162–163, 180; sex question 136
sexism 37, 125–126, 134, 142, 144, 149; *see also* patriarchy
The Shepherd's Tale 128
S.H.I.E.L.D. 3, 16, 20, 80–96, 98, 100–103, 105–106, 154, 168, 178
Sierra 55, 67–69
Simmons, Jemma 92, 94–95, 106
siring 139–142
Sitterson, Gary 178–180
Skye 79, 81, 89, 92–93, 106
slavery 44, 55, 57, 132, 157, 176; voluntary slavery 49; wage slavery 132
The Slayer 134–135, 142–144, 147–149, 151–152, 155–156, 159–160, 163, 165, 169–172, 178, 183
Smith, Tracey 130–131
social structure 19–21, 23–25, 28–32, 34, 37–39, 41–43, 45–46, 60, 75, 87, 140, 175
Sokovia Accords 94
solidarity 48, 105, 113–115, 131, 133, 152, 155, 164, 168
soul 24, 25, 27, 72–73, 141, 166, 188n16; social soul 166, 168–169
Spectrum of Security 92–93
Spike 46, 72–73, 140–141, 159, 166, 169–170
Stark, Tony *see* Iron Man
state 2, 7–11, 17, 20–21, 41, 95, 100–101, 103, 107–109, 111–112, 115–116, 123, 131–132, 134–136, 139–141, 145–146, 152, 157–158, 168, 172, 174–177; *see also* welfare state
statism 7, 49, 67, 71, 82, 86, 103, 111, 117; minimal statism 107–108, 110–111, 115, 117
stereotypes 26, 135
Stitch 123–124
structural violence 12, 15, 16, 18, 19–25, 29–37, 39, 41–43, 45–47, 100, 108, 123–124, 129, 134, 145, 174–175, 178, 182–183
stupidity 34–35
subjectivity 145, 148–149, 180
Summers, Buffy 7, 18, 72–73, 109, 134–135,

137–139, 143–145, 147–156, 159–162, 165–172, 177–178, 182
Sunnydale High School 137–138, 152

tabula rasa 71, 73, 76
Tam, River 110, 116–120, 127, 128
Tam, Simon 109, 116–120, 127, 128, 130–131
Tancharoen, Maurissa 80
"The Target" (*Dollhouse* 1.2) 62
Tesseract 98–99, 101
Thanos 102
Thor 98–99, 101, 103–104
Thoreau, Henry David 12–14, 33, 45, 48, 106
Those Left Behind 117
thought-pocalypse 69–70
Thurman, Owen 137, 143
Tolstoy, Leo 181–183
"The Train Job" (*Firefly* 1.2) 120–122, 126–127, 177
Truman, Daniel 179–180
Tsetsang, Priya *see* Sierra
"Turn, Turn, Turn" (*Marvel Agents of S.H.I.E.L.D.* 1.17) 88–89

Ultron 102–105
Unification War 117
United Nations 94

vampire 25–27, 42, 72–73, 134–135, 139–142, 144, 149–150, 153, 155–156, 162–163, 172–173
Vaughan, Curt 178–180
Victor 55–58, 61
vineyard 167–170
violability 145
violence 3, 15–16, 21–22, 31, 34–36, 39–40, 45–49, 71, 89, 99–101, 103, 113, 139, 143, 145, 157–160, 163, 174, 181, 183, 196n42
Vision 104; *see also* Jarvis

Walsh, Maggie 145
war 10–11, 55, 117, 168
"War Stories" (*Firefly* 1.10) 127
Ward, Grant 81, 85, 89
Washburne, Hoban "Wash" 117, 122
Washburne, Zoe 116, 124
Watcher 134–135, 144, 147–148, 150–152, 165, 172
Watchers Council 20, 134, 142–145, 147, 149–153, 160–161, 178
Weaver, Anne 85–86
welfare state 111–112, 142, 172; *see also* state
Wells, Andrew 167
Weyland Yutani 22
Whedon, Jed 80
Whedon, Joss 1–4, 6–9, 14, 18, 19, 48, 52, 56, 78, 79–80, 94, 105, 107–109, 114, 116–117, 127, 133–134, 173–174, 178
Whiskey 55
white male savior 80–81
Wolff, Robert Paul 9–11, 14, 19, 106
Wolfram & Hart 1–3, 7, 15, 19–25, 27–30, 32–47, 80, 100, 142, 154, 168, 175, 178, 180
Wood, Robin 166
world peace 15, 22, 99
World Security Council 86, 101
Wyndam-Pryce, Wesley 23, 37–38, 42, 80, 152, 160–161

yellow crayon 154, 164
Young, Kendra 147–150
"You're Welcome" (*Angel* 5.12) 43–44
Yoyodyne 22

Zabuto, Sam 147

www.ingramcontent.com/pod-product-compliance
Ingram Content Group UK Ltd.
Pitfield, Milton Keynes, MK11 3LW, UK
UKHW041955140426
52171PUK00015B/803